Democracy
Past
and
Future

Columbia Studies in
Political Thought /
Political History
Dick Howard, General Editor

Columbia Studies in Political Thought /
Political History
Dick Howard, General Editor

Columbia Studies in Political Thought / Political History is a series
dedicated to exploring the possibilities for democratic initiative and the
revitalization of politics in the wake of the exhaustion of twentieth-
century ideological "isms." By taking a historical approach to the politics
of ideas about power, governance, and the just society—and by
interpreting historical and contemporary events—this series seeks to
foster and illuminate new political spaces for human action and choice.

PIERRE ROSANVALLON

Democracy
Past
and
Future

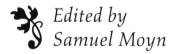 *Edited by*
Samuel Moyn

COLUMBIA UNIVERSITY PRESS   NEW YORK

9-27-2006
ww
₽ 38

Columbia University Press
Publishers Since 1893
New York, Chichester, West Sussex
Copyright © 2006 Columbia University Press
All rights Reserved

Library of Congress Cataloging-in-Publication Data
Rosanvallon, Pierre, 1948–

　　Democracy past and future / Pierre Rosanvallon ; edited by Samuel Moyn.
　　　p. cm.
　　A collection of essays from different works including the author's inaugural lecture at the Collège de France.
　　Includes bibliographical references and index.
　　ISBN 0–231–13740–0 (cloth : alk. paper)
　　　1. Democracy. 2. Liberalism. 3. Civil society. I. Moyn, Samuel. II. Title.

JC423.R6169 2006
321.8—dc22

2005051944

Columbia University Press books are printed on permanent
and durable acid-free paper
Printed in the United States of America

c 10 9 8 7 6 5 4 3 2 1

Contents

Acknowledgments and Permissions

Chapter 1 was originally published as *Leçon inaugurale faite jeudi le 21 mars 2002* (Paris, 2002), and reprinted as *Pour une histoire conceptuelle du politique* (Paris, 2003). © Éditions du Seuil, reprinted by permission.

Chapter 2 was originally published as "Towards a Philosophical History of the Political," in Dario Castiglione and Iain Hampsher-Monk, eds., *The History of Political Thought in National Context* (Cambridge, 2002), after a manuscript original and in a translation substantially revised here. © Cambridge University Press, reprinted by permission.

Chapter 3 was originally published as *Le peuple introuvable: Histoire de la représentation démocratique en France* (Paris, 1998, 2000), 35–55, along with a section on the Terror from *La démocratie inachevée: Histoire de la souveraineté du peuple en France* (Paris, 2000, 2003), 84–89. © Gallimard, reprinted by permission.

Chapter 4 was originally published in this form as "La république du suffrage universel," in François Furet et Mona Ozouf, eds., *Le Siècle de l'avènement républicain* (Paris, 1993), translated by Laura Mason as "The Republic of Universal Suffrage," in Biancamaria Fontana, ed., *The Invention of Modern Republic* (Cambridge, 1994), 192–205. © Cambridge University Press, reprinted by permission. It also essentially coincides with

Rosanvallon, *Le sacre du citoyen: Histoire du suffrage universel en France* (Paris, 1992, 2001), 342–47, 364–66, 372–87.

Chapter 5 was originally published as the editorial matter to François Guizot, *Histoire de la civilisation en Europe*, ed. Rosanvallon (Paris, 1985). Different parts of the editorial matter—one section of it, entitled "Préface: Le Gramsci de la bourgeoisie," introduced the book, while another presented a previously unpublished essay by Guizot on sovereignty—have been combined and interwoven in this selection.

Chapter 6 was originally published as "Rationalisme politique et démocratie en France (XVIIIe–XIXe siècles)," *Zinbun, Annals of the Institute of Research in Humanities* 29 (1994): 17–32, translated anonymously into English as "Political Rationalism and Democracy in France in the 18th and 19th Centuries," *Philosophy and Social Criticism* 28, 6 (November 2002): 687–702, heavily revised here. © Sage Publications, reprinted by permission.

Chapter 7 was originally published as "Culture politique libérale et réformisme," *Esprit* 251 (March 1999): 161–70, and is reprinted by permission of the journal. The text also appeared under the title "Le marché et les trois utopies libérales" as the preface to the new edition of Pierre Rosanvallon, *Le capitalisme utopique: Histoire de l'idée de marché* (Paris, 1999).

Chapter 8 was originally published as "Marx et la société civile," *Commentaire* 4 (Winter 1978–79): 468–77, reprinted as Rosanvallon, *Le capitalisme utopique: Critique de l'idéologie économique* (Paris, 1979), chap. 9, "Marx et le retournement du libéralisme." © Éditions du Seuil, reprinted by permission. This book has since been republished, most recently as *Le capitalisme utopique: Histoire de l'idée de marché* (Paris, 1999).

Chapter 9 was originally published as *La démocratie inachevée: Histoire de la souveraineté du peuple en France* (Paris, 2000, 2003), 413–50 (the last section of chap. 11 and all of the conclusion). © Gallimard, reprinted by permission.

Chapter 10 was originally published as "Le déficit démocratique européen," *Esprit* 288 (October 2002): 87–100, from remarks originally delivered in 2001 at the Cini Foundation in Venice, and is reprinted by permission of the journal. The text conserves the lecture format; the translation is based, if distantly, on Karsten Sand Iversen's earlier English-language rendering. The Postscript is an original text.

Democracy
Past
and
Future

Antitotalitarianism and After

Samuel Moyn

Democracy and Disarray

It was not long after democracy triumphed as a regime, in the post–cold war era, that the theory and practice of democracy fell into disarray. In the United States, as in the rest of the world, democracy has never been more prestigious, among intellectuals and policymakers, even as its practical implications for foreign policy have become disquieting and its institutional content at home has undergone massive shifts. The unanimity—left, right, and center—about the value and importance of democracy is remarkable, to be sure. But it occurs at the same time that it is hollowed out or even perverted, made—as many think—into a cunning apology for imperial advancement. Yet the disarray that garners most attention and inspires most debate in the field of foreign policy is far more general, and it is above all internal and theoretical.

The situation is especially serious for the left, liberal and progressive, on the defensive and out of power in the United States and throughout much of the rest of the world. But the loss of practical energy, which might have prompted theoretical introspection, has instead led to the embrace of superannuated approaches. For the moment, the effect of September 11, one confirmed rather than unsettled by the more recent electoral victory of conservative politicians, has been a revival of an old ideological couple. An antiterroristic or "antitotalitarian" liberalism has become the favored approach of many political elites in Western democracies, and in America not least, while hostility to liberalism in the name of radical democracy wins more and more converts everyday in the ranks of intellectuals and activists.

Among the numerous connections between the antitotalitarian liberalism and the dominant, populist alternative to it that present themselves today, one is their shared source in the practical and intellectual experience of a particular nation: France. The antitotalitarian perspective, of course, resonates in obvious ways with the historical anticommunism of a certain strand of American liberalism. But in the form in which it has recently been renovated for the post–September 11 world, most prominently but far from exclusively in Paul Berman's war pamphlet *Terror and Liberalism*, the "fighting faith" of antitotalitarian liberalism is both negatively and positively inspired by French intellectual politics.[1] Berman, for instance, offers a narrative that paints contemporary "Muslim totalitarianism" against which the new liberalism is supposed to direct itself as the outcome of the disastrous and delusional politics of French modernism, one drunk on the fantasy of redemptive politics, that stretched from Saint-Just to Saddam Hussein, and from Charles Baudelaire to Osama bin Laden. But the remedy he offered likewise claimed inspiration from a rival tradition of French "antitotalitarianism," emblematically associated with Albert Camus and, in the generational biography of the left, with the anti-Marxist insights of the "new philosophy" of the 1970s and since, a school of which Berman is the most influential American follower.[2]

The post–September 11 atmosphere makes antitotalitarian liberalism define itself above all, like rival doctrines, as a foreign policy doctrine. And it is there that it attracts most criticism. As the external campaign against enemies continues, as antitotalitarians make common cause with imperialists, the internal politics that might have distinguished them remains neither the focus of attention nor the subject of revision. In the meantime, the American invasion of Iraq—justified and supported in the breach in liberal antitotalitarianism's rhetoric and with the support of many of its partisans—has increasingly looked to much of the world like an apology for the advancement of imperial power. Few observers have failed to notice this, and the implausibility of the antitotalitarian response to the real challenges of unilateral American action abroad and the effects of globalization everywhere have invited a response.

The frailties of the revival of the antitotalitarian vision when it has outlived its era explain why it makes little or no headway outside liberal elites, notably in the antiglobalization movement or in the academic world. Alas, the most popular alternative to it is a project even more archaic—and equally bound up with French history and thought—as the one it resists. Home of the true revolution, even if Karl Marx became its theorist, France's quest for a fulfilled democracy that would overcome the limits of liberalism and capitalism in the name of all men and women still nourishes the dream of bringing the old regime of evil oppression crashing down. In fact, it is a surprise that historians will have some day to explain that after September 11, 2001, a confused mélange of revolutionary Marxism, academic postmodernism, and nationalist third-worldism came to dominate the hearts and minds of so many in the academy as the most plausible response to the blind spots of contemporary antitotalitarianism. In particular, Marxism—updated by more recent theories of total "biopolitical" control, under conditions in which the exception has become the norm—came to enjoy a second life.

For all its local critical insights, one thing unites this radical democratic and anti-imperial alternative with the antitotalitarian liberalism it abhors: a programmatic aphasia on the question of what it means to constitute and regulate a modern democracy. Both approaches, that is, are above all negative. The proposal of theorists advancing the synthesis of Marxism and postmodernism, lacking any plausible institutional program, has been to pray for a "multitude" to arise. What that entity would do, if it came on the scene, remains more hazy. In the academic world, however, the call has been heeded, *faute de mieux*. Prophesying resistance against an unlocalizable empire, with a programmatically empty appeal in the tradition of St. Francis to the poor and beset masses, "French theory" updated itself with a new political edge so that old fashions could continue their campus appeal. But St. Francis, even made into a democratic activist before his time, unfortunately had no institutional program.[3]

Though the contrast between the rival perspectives is superficially one of external politics, then, one should not fail to miss the internal programmatic emptiness of both dominant schools of thought. For antitotalitarianism, it is as if the main problem for liberal democracy were its enemies, conservatives at home and totalitarians abroad, as if the programmatic and institutional alternative to rival forces were simply obvious—as if, then, the contemporary disarray of democracy were not the sign of deep theoretical and practical perplexity about its content, as if there were no need to ponder the historical variations and untried possibilities of democracy. Externalizing the disarray to focus on democracy's enemies, at times by fueling their creation, involves the concealment, rather than the consideration, of the problem. As for Marxism-postmodernism, it is as if the main barrier to instituting democracy were simply the evil reign of the imperial opposition. And so the approaches conspire in propagating the false belief that the problem of democracy was primarily one of identifying the proper enemy.

Beyond their historical origins, critical limitations, and programmatic hesitations, the two options, supposedly poles apart, are complicit, finally, in mutually maintaining a space of debate in which both can thrive: they strengthen one another, the existence of each making the other seem plausible in a way that neither would on its own. The triumph of antitotalitarian liberalism fuels the triumph of neo-Marxist populism, and vice versa. Rarely have defective positions more fully deserved one another. But though a catastrophe for the progressive cause, practical disempowerment and theoretical inadequacy define the most important challenge for political thought and life in the present day.

The work of Pierre Rosanvallon, which this volume introduces, suggests that it is no trivialization to take this apparently wholly contemporary and post–September 11 alternative as the point of departure for responding to the challenge, because the alternative, seemingly new and up-to-date, is in fact very old.

Rosanvallon, a professor at the Collège de France, represents a perspective dispiritingly little known in the United States compared to the antitotalitarian new philosophy of the moment and the Marxist-postmodernist resistance in response—a perspective that allows one to see the contemporary debate as another act of a pathological rivalry that extends very far back in modernity, and is even constitutive of it. The alternatives are not simply to be dismissed as passing fancies or poor options, since they are consequences of a modernity in which everyone now shares. Rosanvallon's proposal, indeed, is that only by rooting such recurrent dilemmas in their long history, and recognizing the duration of their compulsive repetition, can a potential way beyond them come into view.

Yet another French theorist, one finally worthy of prostration after the twilight of the old idols? It is true that Rosanvallon is in the first rank of contemporary European intellectuals and, in his own country, in a position at the institutional apex of intellectual life—as Claude Lévi-Strauss, Michel Foucault, and Pierre Bourdieu once were. The range of his work, written over a period of more than three decades, might justify such an attitude, too. And one might add that Rosanvallon offers an approach with the scope and depth of theories of democracy from comparatively better-known figures like Jürgen Habermas and John Rawls (both of whom Rosanvallon criticizes for having excessively normative approaches to democracy that do not sufficiently respect its historicity). But searching for premises for a new discussion rather than another humbling master is the point or the purpose of the selection of texts that follow. Rosanvallon's work, indeed, is notable for its lack of hermetic obscurity and for a modesty often absent in theorists who invite discipleship rather than debate. Most of all, it presents an effort of thought that takes seriously the importance of the antitotalitarian perspective today—Rosanvallon's career emerged out of that school—even as it suggests the need for a next step. It outlines, by considering the vicissitudes of democracy past, a way to begin thinking about democracy future.

An Itinerary in Theory and Practice

Born in 1948, Rosanvallon is a member of the 1968 generation, and his democratic theory is tethered, from beginning to end, to the hopes for democratic revitalization—with democracy redefined not as a matter of party control of the state but reinvention of everyday life—of which his generation became the historical bearer. But unlike much of his generation, the brand of left-wing militancy in which he engaged committed him both to a highly continuous, and highly reflective, itinerary. Never a Trotskyist or a Maoist—the two most significant of the welter of allegiances for young leftists in the brief but spectacular period of *gauchisme* in the years after France's May events—Rosanvallon joined a trade union called the Confédération Française Démocratique du Travail (CFDT) as a house intellectual and spent his early career advancing and rethinking its particular brand of radicalism within the turbulent and fascinating battle for a plausible left-wing vision of the period.[4]

The CFDT had evolved from Christian syndicalism of the interwar years and became secular, noncommunist, and reformist in the postwar period (unlike its major competitor, the dominant and staunchly communist Confédération Générale du Travail). Thanks to its enterprising general secretary after 1968, Edmond Maire, the CFDT affiliated itself quite rapidly with one of the principal ideals of the student revolt, that of *autogestion*, or self-management. In its origins, the coinage referred to the autonomous organization of enterprise, but it quickly became a generalized term for what life in all sectors would look like after the refusal of hierarchy symbolized by the May 1968 events. The

CFDT became the principal vehicle for the spread of the *autoges-tionnaire* ideal in French politics of the period, and Rosanvallon, in turn, became its principal theorist. He published his first book under his own name in 1976, in which he celebrated and attempted to refine it.[5] Self-management meant the liberation of the forces and freedoms of civil society outside and against the state, though some of its partisans took their enthusiasm for it so far as to think that it portended the withering away of politics altogether. It stood for the condemnation of the bureaucratic state—whether Western or Eastern, capitalist or communist in its lineage—in the name of a revived civil society. (In fact, the celebrated concept of "civil society" returned in France in this socialist current that came to be called, retrospectively, the "second" or "other" left, shortly before East European dissidence would spread the concept globally.)

Though overly simple and institutionally vague, the self-management concept offered a partial programmatic translation of the aspirations of May 1968, placing traditional leftist egalitarian concerns within a much broader, and much more libertarian, framework. It augured a new definition for progressive politics that helped break the left's historical ties to the communist Soviet Union and its conceptual basis in an outmoded vision of politics as state capture and control (through electoral means or not). The concept had to make its way, however, in a complicated struggle for what vision should claim the hearts and minds of French socialists, and it was together with a number of other intellectuals that Rosanvallon agitated in the Parti Socialiste for a cleavage between "two cultures of the left," statism and self-organization, whose existence their standard-bearer Michel Rocard proclaimed in a famous speech, co-written by Rosanvallon, at the party's July 1977 Nantes congress.[6] Rocard, however, lost out to François Mitterrand as party leader. It was around this time that Rosanvallon turned his energies to scholarship, without ever losing his interest in day-to-day politics.

Following on the heels of the collapse of *gauchisme* and the decline of hopes for imminent social transformation, the critique of totalitarianism counted as the decisive intellectual event of the French 1970s. It is well known, of course, that the publication of Alexandr Solzhenitsyn's *The Gulag Archipelago* in the early 1970s set off, in France far more spectacularly than in any other land, a fundamental rethinking of the nature of the Soviet Union and of the validity of any revolutionary enterprise. The versions of and sequels to the antitotalitarian moment have been various. But it stood above all for the lasting proposition that the left had to be reinvented in light of its twentieth-century failures. It demanded a left meaningfully chastened by the Soviet Union's perversion of the quest for freedom into repressive tragedy. It put many intellectuals on guard against the persistent return of an archaic vision of progressive politics that has occurred, once again, today.

Along with François Furet, Claude Lefort—the central thinker of the antitotalitarian moment—became Rosanvallon's major teacher and influence. (Both taught at the École des Hautes Études en Sciences Sociales, where Rosanvallon did his graduate work, and later became a professor.) Lefort's philosophy, though difficult, is nonetheless the key theoretical basis and precedent for Rosanvallon's work, and beyond much doubt the most lasting monument of the antitotalitarian era. According to Lefort, no societies are characterized by factual unity, but the source of division and conflict that characterizes all societies is not just of a factual or sociological nature. For there is also a necessary gap or difference between a society and its self-representation. And since the latter is a necessary part of the former (no society is possible without a self-representation split away from it), what Lefort called "symbolic division" is constitutive of society. The sources of this theory in French intellectual history are complex; but Lefort mobilized it to create a fascinating—and in the Anglo-American world undeservedly obscure—new classification for political regimes and their historical relation to one other, running from primitive societies without a state, through the democratic emancipation of civil society, and culminating in totalitarian statism.[7]

Democracy and totalitarianism are, according to Lefort, the key couplet of modern ideological history. Democracy, Lefort argued, is a disincorporated political form in multiple senses. It is organized around individuals rather than corporations, and it loses the monarchical, personally embodied, and partly exterior symbol of power that clearly organized society. Finally—and again in corporal terms—by dispensing with the king's body, and thus by making the central site of power "empty," in Lefort's celebrated phrase, democracy also invited the temptation that society might finally dispense the exteriority that makes all polities possible, allowing it to become one with itself. The violence of totalitarianism, according to Lefort, flows from its attempt to make society in democracy forcibly coincide with its representation of itself as a collection of free and equal individuals—to transcend "formal democracy" in the name of a putative real democracy. In this sense, in Lefort's conception, totalitarianism is possible only on the basis of, and as a kind of perverted attempt to realize, democratic aspirations. But Lefort's refusal of this totalitarian aspiration did not mean falling back on some existing institutional repertory or on a conservative return to some prior defense of representative government. It did not, in other words, mean taking the opposition to totalitarianism as an end in itself, as occurred in the so-called "new philosophy" of the time and since. Instead, it meant the pursuit of democratic emancipation in better awareness of its potential ruin. "Democracy? It is a dream to suppose that we already know what it is, whether out of satisfaction with our present state or to attack its misery," Lefort wrote in the 1970s. "It is simply a play of open possibilities, inaugurated in a past still close to us, and we have barely begun to explore it."[8]

It was Furet's *Interpreting the French Revolution* that extended Lefort's theory and provided one culmination of the antitotalitarian moment in French politics by rethinking the history of their nation in precisely such a spirit.[9] For Furet, French history afforded the most illuminating materials for understanding the dynamics Lefort described. In an account owing much to Lefort, Furet painted the French revolution as giving rise to a voluntaristic drive to unify society according to Jean-Jacques Rousseau's theory of the general will, to incarnate it institutionally, and to purify it of its sociological differences and its internal antitheses, in a bloody purgative ritual of terror that also bequeathed a highly problematic—indeed potentially criminal—legacy to the modern political imaginary. That such a campaign is unfulfillable did not make the fantasy of its completion any less alluring in its appeal to revolutionaries, or less disastrous in its political consequences. And not simply at the time: it made it the permanent temptation of progressive thought and action to achieve "real" democracy, unity at the price of pluralism, in a withering away of politics in the violent name of its realization. The idea of a politics that would begin by putting terror at the center of its concern—internalized in the French Revolution, externalized for the antitotalitarians of today—is given classic form in Furet's work.

The philosophy of Lefort and the history of Furet laid the intellectual and professional foundations for their follower's career as a student of democracy, encouraging Rosanvallon to face up to the task of envisioning the emergence and history of the sovereign people—including its perverted and pathological forms, beginning with the revolution. It was Furet too, among other things a great intellectual impresario, who initially conscripted Rosanvallon into a small coalition of senior intellectuals like Lefort and Cornelius Castoriadis and younger thinkers like Marcel Gauchet, Pierre Manent, and Bernard Manin, and later founded the Institut Raymond Aron, which has served as the institutional focus of "new French thought," and whose successor center at the École des Hautes Études Rosanvallon has directed in recent years. (Furet and Rosanvallon also collaborated on the

Fondation Saint-Simon, an important and influential think-tank of the 1980s and 1990s.)

Far from a homogeneous group of thinkers, however, this coterie, though united by an opposition to the totalitarian potential they saw in modern politics and an interest in the history of political thought and experience, lived through and applied the antitotalitarian moment in diverse ways. Above all, it is a mistake to interpret the antitotalitarian moment as a "liberal" moment in French intellectual history, even if some of the group's members championed liberalism and all of them interested themselves in liberalism's classical texts.[10] Indeed, as the following selections rather graphically show, for Rosanvallon liberalism is also a central source of a dangerous utopianism in modern life that could also climax in totalitarianism. And yet it is undeniable that Rosanvallon came to be highly influenced by the new style of thinking about modern politics and French history that flowed out of the antitotalitarian moment. Among the earliest to join in and attempt to update it, Rosanvallon has spent most of his scholarly time since the 1970s engaged in a vast reconstruction of the history of democracy, of which this volume provides a basic and introductory overview.

In 2001, Rosanvallon received his appointment to the Collège de France, which marked a turning point in his career at the same time as more global ideological shifts were showing the limits of the antitotalitarian perspective which generated many of the lasting efforts that this volume showcases. For this reason alone, one would be making an enormous mistake to consider Rosanvallon's work as simply another exercise in antitotalitarian history or philosophy, much less a stalwart and lucid defense of antitotalitarian liberalism deemed so relevant by many, in the United States not least, today. It is true that very little about his project is intelligible (even or especially when his writings venture into historically distant periods) if it is not kept in mind that the horizon of the inquiry remained for a long time how the ingredients of totalitarianism were assembled in modern history.

But Rosanvallon's work now stands for the proposition that antitotalitarianism, too, has limits, and is not the sole basis for theorizing and practicing democracy today, for conducting a foreign policy, or for conceptualizing one's own society. This volume, accordingly, does not simply illustrate antitotalitarianism in its historical applications, but also intimates what plausibly might come after, or at least supplement, that commitment.

The History of Politics and the Politics of History

This selection begins with Rosanvallon's reflections on methodology, texts of independent interest to theorists and historians in an era of fecund controversy about approaching political thought and its past chapters. In particular, the collection opens with Rosanvallon's inaugural *leçon* at the Collège de France—his contribution to a now centuries' old genre, bearing the marks of the oral ritual of induction that it performs, including its references to biographical influences and institutional predecessors. The usefully condensed and summary introduction to Rosanvallon's approach provided there is balanced by a second and more detailed and formal set of methodological reflections in the following chapter.

Rosanvallon practices what he calls "the history of the political," a venture that draws on the existing historical disciplines of political, social, and intellectual history, but with a new object that exhausts their methodologies as they have been developed over time. The political, as Rosanvallon defines it in Lefort's footsteps, is in effect the foundation of society and the sole point of view from which its basic coherence comes into view. It is, very precisely, an approach in which the material reality (in the guise of the economy) that Marxist theory made the foundation of society is dislodged from that position. In the following writings, Rosanvallon explains his conception of the relationship between the study of this object and the inherited practices of political, social, and intellectual history. Its criticism of materialist and social history does not imply that the history of the political restores idealism to a long-lost but always deserved status of primacy. Nevertheless, and in spite of Rosanvallon's criticism of intellectual history for artificially separating texts from society and insulating them in a canonical series, the history of the political requires a strong philosophical turn. As a result, the country from which the rival materialist approaches of the *Annales* school and Marxist historiography once flowed is now the source of a reinvigorated defense of the importance of philosophical interpretation and even of great texts as apertures on the political constitution of their ages. Rosanvallon's methodological essays offer a useful point of entry into this recent development.

But the history of the political as Rosanvallon defends it goes beyond strict historiographical debate and demands more than a simple redefinition of the historical object. It likewise insists on the avowed search for contemporary relevance. Rosanvallon's distinctive insistence on the overlap—indeed, identity—between political theory and historical study not only makes his work uniquely relevant to historians of the modern democratic experience, suggesting to them the price they pay for antipathy to philosophy. It also suggests the limitations of political theories that do not find a way between the equally unsatisfactory, if popular, methodologies represented by an antiquarianism that attempts to free the study of past theories from the pressure of contemporary questions and a presentism that dispenses with the burden of history in framing its inquiries. Both alternatives, Rosanvallon says, are objectionable.

The obvious comparative point of reference, in this regard, is the methodology of the Cambridge School, as epitomized in the theory and practice of Quentin Skinner. In his most famous methodological piece, now more than three decades old, Skinner recommended a kind of enforced antiquarianism to keep presentist commitments from interfering with the intelligibility of texts, gained by restoring them to their place and time.[11] For

Skinner, the alternative seemed to be a supracontextual belief in a set of immemorial concepts, as pioneered in the "history of ideas" of Arthur Lovejoy, or else the antihistoricist premise of a continuity of fundamental human problems that Leo Strauss vigorously defended. Rosanvallon thinks Skinner's concern about the autonomy of the past is justified, but that an antiquarian reaction in its name simply goes to the opposite, and equally implausible, extreme. If it is false to think that the true and deep questions are immune to change (*philosophia perennis*), then it is equally misleading to believe that their lability makes their study over the long term impossible.

None of the essays that follow, by themselves, fully illustrates the unique combination of political theory and historical study that Rosanvallon has attempted in his full-length works. The translation of one of those, however, roughly coincides with the publication of this collection, which has a different intent: to introduce through a proper selection of texts the main lines of Rosanvallon's overall interpretation of modernity.[12] Rosanvallon's methodology, then, is wholly independent of the work that he has made it perform, but it is to the latter that the core of the volume turns. Modernity, Rosanvallon says, is unified enough to chart long debates over "relatively constant" questions, even if historical experience leads them to shift in their details; and, above all, it is run through by the same decisive quandaries for it to give rise to sets of interrelated pathologies to which moderns are typically and continuously prone (76). The main thrust of Rosanvallon's work has been in their identification.

Voluntarism, Rationalism, Liberalism

The first of these pathologies is voluntarism, to which the second part of this collection is dedicated, and the analysis and condemnation of which Rosanvallon inherited from his teachers and has extended in his own studies. Its most evident theoretical source, of course, is Jean-Jacques Rousseau's political thought, and its founding practical institutionalization is the French Revolution and its legacy in modern history. The first of the selections in this section presents an example of Rosanvallon's writing on the French revolutionary moment, and the essay that follows illustrates the resumption of the Jacobin drive for voluntaristic fusion and unity that the revolution sparked in the history of universal suffrage. If the reader keeps in mind that these selections are not simply historical vignettes but just as much critiques of archaic visions of revolutionary unity that continue to inspire the progressive imagination, then their theoretical interest is redoubled.

The second selection in this section is an extract from Rosanvallon's longest and one of his most prominent academic studies, *Le Sacre du citoyen* (1992), a monumental history of universal suffrage. Comparison of its premises with more conventional histories of suffrage, however historically rich, suggests what makes the history of the political distinctive in practice.[13] For Rosanvallon, universal suffrage is not a simple aim to be interpreted as merely a victory to be won against reactionary obstacles over time. Instead, the question is what rival functions its conquest played in the political imaginary. Universal suffrage in France, for a long time and notably in the spring of 1848, did not function, he says, to institutionalize a pluralistic and divided society and was not intended to work as a mechanism for managing its differences; instead, it resumed the Jacobin tradition, reviving its dream of popular fusion. The object of Rosanvallon's study is itself striking in French intellectual history—in Rosanvallon's youth Jean-Paul Sartre could dismiss elections as *"pièges à cons"* (roughly, for suckers)—but the key in Rosanvallon's interpretation of the French history of suffrage is how long the vote figured in the political imaginary as the mechanism for the fusion of the people, so that formal democracy would simply make possible "real" democracy without responding to the challenge of representation. Such a fantasy, in Rosanvallon's view, continued to nourish the potential for the revolutionary abrogation of the existing state of things.

Understanding Rosanvallon's portrait of revolutionary voluntarism—the attempt to remake society into the unified and homogeneous whole that "we the people" are thought to be already—is all-important for grasping the intent of the balance of the collection. In the succeeding essays, Rosanvallon introduces his more proprietary concept of rationalism that has been, in his view, the chief ideological response to voluntaristic democracy in modern French history. Rationalism, as Rosanvallon portrays it, has deep taproots in the Enlightenment (notably in the physiocratic movement), but it was the postrevolutionary figure of François Guizot, above all, who revived it against the voluntaristic tradition that climaxed in the Terror and haunted modernity thereafter. Rosanvallon's essay on Guizot serves to introduce some of main themes of his outstanding book on the subject, *Le Moment Guizot* (1985).

As Rosanvallon defines it, rationalism is the dream of an impersonal science of politics, available to an elite, that would preempt conflict, usually by transfer of authority to experts in management of the nation in its name. Guizot's genius, according to Rosanvallon, was to renovate the rationalism he inherited in order to make it the philosophy of a new and democratic age. Rationalism, seen from the inside, is not simply a vitiation of democracy, always haunted by the specter of the real thing, but an *interpretation* of it responding to its frequent voluntarist entanglements. In particular, rationalism, which often empowers elites, is based on a theory of representation, highly controversial but philosophically serious in its articulation. It understands suffrage rights, for example, not according to the impulse of popular fusion but as the winnowing of transcendent reason from incarnated passion.

By contrast to voluntarism, then, rationalism offered a program to represent the people, avoiding the violence of the attempt to do so by means of voluntarism and unity. That virtue, of course, came linked to equally constitutive vices, like the empowerment of elites and the acceptance of hierarchy. For all the plausibility of his attempt to find a theory and practice of democracy that would avoid its terroristic potential, Guizot also ended up illustrating an equal and opposite pathology: liberalism against democracy. Rosanvallon places Guizot in his longer historical genealogy in the second essay in this section of the volume, and argues, in the best available summation of overall conception of French modernity, that voluntarism and rationalism are in effect the theories between which French history permanently has oscillated, its constitutive rival pathologies, their competition the sign of a failure to master the aporias of modern emancipation.[14] Is it a mistake to see in the confrontation of radical democracy and antiterroristic liberalism a new version—except that it is no longer simply history—of an old and constant dilemma in modern political experience?

This is the place to acknowledge that, notably in his study of voluntarism and rationalism, Rosanvallon's work is centered on France and French history and politics. Those interested or professionally concerned with French culture and history will find a novel reading of their materials in these chapters, but those with no particular connection to or expertise in events in France should not mistake the point of the focus. In the writings from the stage of his career just reviewed, the implicit and often explicit comparative reference is England (and the Anglo-American world more generally) (see esp. 111, 119–20, and chap. 6, *passim*). The implication to draw from this fact is not, however, that the study of national specificities implies the availability of a healthy model *somewhere else*, as if there were a healthy, normative modernity simply to contrast to a pathological, deviant one. It is not that France, born in terror or captive of rationalism, is to be compared negatively with other nations, havens of redeemed and realized democracy. Furet sometimes suggested as much; and one dimension of antitotalitarianism, indeed, is that it occasionally fell prey to a vice of thought indicting deviation from a usually imagined norm, reviving Alexis de Tocqueville's suggestion to look abroad for the remedies to French maladies.[15]

There is no denying national particularity, either in history or Rosanvallon's historiography. But taking voluntarism and rationalism—those pathologies covered so far—as wholly French diseases ignores the obvious fact that all of the pathologies Rosanvallon emphasizes are deeply bound up with modern American (and modern world) history, too, even if they have appeared in different forms and were mastered—if they were mastered at all—in different ways. Beneath the superficial continuity of its regime, American democracy, for example, is in the end not *fundamentally* different than French democracy, and indeed one could reconstruct its history along somewhat similar lines. Fusion of "the people" is no more foreign to American history or to its political imaginary than the rationalistic fantasy of a rule of wisdom or expertise is.[16] As another product and laboratory of modernity, America is also the home of a drive for popular sovereignty as well as a country where various "mysterious sciences" to master it could exert serious appeal. If the history of French democracy thus presents a relative specificity (all historical formations are specific), the implication is not that some other history presents a safe harbor for democratic modernity adrift. And so it is much more interesting to regard these pathologies as the common fate of moderns.

In fact, it is Rosanvallon's true and considered view that modernity as such—anywhere and everywhere—is the problem, and that study of France is, in certain respects, a privileged occasion for facing up to it. (More recently, other countries have served a similar purpose: he could write on the American presidential campaign of 2004, which he had an opportunity to witness up close, in the same diagnostic spirit.)[17] So if it is undeniable that Rosanvallon's investigations into the history of democracy are focused on France's exceptional history, with its wild swings between will and reason, it is not because it illustrates a modernity to which there is an available existing alternative but because it illustrates modern options so vividly. The point is not that France is incomparable but that the study of its democratic experience is incomparably illuminating for those who care about democracy anywhere. "The problem now is not that of a 'French exception,' relative or absolute, that has to be mastered," Rosanvallon remarks in his most recent book. "The problem *everywhere* is that of a crisis of politics and a debate on democracy."[18]

For Anglo-American readers, then, the comparative singularity of focus even in the early essays is best understood as one that helps explain and advance beyond the dilemmas of their history, too, distant and recent, as well as the contemporary ideological situation, local and global, that pits a radical populism against a constrictive liberalism. Such a point is made forcefully if implicitly in the following section of this collection, which broadens Rosanvallon's study of modern pathology beyond rationalism to liberalism more generally—an ideology evidently, in its various forms, quite central to the Anglo-American historical experience and contemporary world politics.

The section should come as a particular surprise to those who refer summarily to "contemporary French liberalism," a category as intellectually bland as it is falsely homogeneous, for in these essays one finds a searching critique of economic liberalism, understood as the fantasy of an emancipated civil society that would harmonize interests or men. Of course, some diehard Marxists are unwilling to grant that the critique of liberalism might not automatically entail their doctrine, and they will see the search for alternatives to both only as a cunning or craven betrayal of the democratic impulse.[19] But one of the most startling, in fact shocking, filiations Rosanvallon offers in this section involves Adam Smith and Karl Marx. They were far more similar than their votaries themselves have ever acknowledged, for both were theorists of (in Rosanvallon's phrase) "the withering away of politics." In the chapter on the market, Smith is interpreted, quite powerfully, as theorizing commercial interactions above all out of his reflection that the social contract model of mastering political conflict was failing so that some other agent of social integration had to be found. But, just as in the voluntaristic fusion Rousseau hoped the social contract would accomplish, Smith's harmonizing market equally suppresses democratic conflict and is a promised alternative to it.

The implication, if Rosanvallon is right, is that the totalitarian extinction of politics has many sources, some of them still very much alive. Radicalizing Smith's aspiration for a harmonious civil society unto itself, Marx purified and updated Smith's conception, Rosanvallon contends in perhaps the most virtuoso chapter in the book, by transferring the ideal of harmonization from interests to men. The upsetting conclusion of this argument is that Marx's thought, as an extension of liberalism, casts light on the imperatives that have driven it (and continue to do so). To the extent radical democracy today is driven by the dream of a wholly realized civil society, it turns out to be very much inspired by the same forces that have given rise to the empire of capital that it wants to overthrow.

Rosanvallon's case may seem to leave open the status of other forms of liberalism, notably political liberalism. And one will notice, in fact, a transition in his thought, from a denial that a unified historical vision of liberalism is possible, to the affirmation that it is feasible after all (120, 155). His most recent reflections on the subject of political liberalism may prove especially provocative to Anglo-American readers. The section on rationalism makes clear that a liberalism of Guizot's stripe—the response to willful sovereignty through submission to a putative external and objective reason—is a deeply flawed form of the doctrine understood as a politics. And while Rosanvallon believes that the human rights typically at the core of other forms of political liberalism are essential to democracy, thanks to their role in maintaining diversity and pluralism, the philosophy of political liberties, Rosanvallon says, remains surprisingly difficult to divorce from the pathologies of modernity. It is both necessary and intricate to free it from the threat of depoliticization that haunts modern times.

For civil society, allowed by liberal freedoms, is not simply the realm of pathology. Indeed, Rosanvallon's most recent book, scheduled to appear in English shortly as *The French Political Model*, returns to this central topic of French and modern history as well as of his youthful itinerary. It is especially notable that the argument of the new book departs rather defiantly from the antitotalitarian framework that oriented many of Rosanvallon's earlier studies. To be sure, that perspective's fear of the predatory state emerged in the defense of civil society, and Rosanvallon does not turn a blind eye to the radically antipluralist effects of the Jacobin tradition in French history (beginning with the revolutionary ban on intermediary bodies and partial associations). The pathologies of modernity, while acting in the name of a redeemed and emancipated civil society, often involved its extinction in fact. Instead of stressing the statist and proto-totalitarian extinction of associational life in European life, however, Rosanvallon insists on its silent *strength* (notably, after 1884, thanks to the importance of trade unions). That argument, including his rejection of the "Tocquevillian vulgate" of associational frailty, involves a tacit revision of the perspective staked out in some of the earlier work. "There was little room within this framework for a pluralist democracy of interest," he notes in his essay on the French interpretation of universal suffrage (112); but by the work on civil society, Rosanvallon has come to the view that the refusal of pluralism in France always counted more as an illusion of analysis than as the truth about reality on the ground.[20]

Not surprisingly, Rosanvallon's most recent book returns to narrate historically the agitation in the 1970s on behalf of the democratic significance of civil society that he lived through as a leader in his youth. If its space of freedoms has been among the major sites to enact the political, the place where conflict and dissensus have been practically lived out in allowing the connection of individuals through motley associations, it is nevertheless true that they rarely—before Rosanvallon's own lifetime—won the right to doctrinal recognition and theoretical defense. The overall argument, while making French specificity more precise, also softens any absolute distinction between France and other modern societies, where the modern liberation of individuals, too, could give rise both to the final depoliticizing pathology presented in this section and the vibrancy of democratic association that best incarnates the political as Rosanvallon defines it. Rosanvallon's work on civil society, then, both completes the trinity of pathology—voluntarism, rationalism, and liberalism—and identifies one of the chief historical lineaments of a democracy that would fight free of it.

Democracy After Totalitarianism

As the name implies, antitotalitarianism works by negation. It pioneeringly warns that in modern emancipation—in the voluntarist and collective aspirations of democracy—lay the seeds of totalitarianism. Rosanvallon extended the train of thought by suggesting that in emancipation other dreams of harmony—liberalism and rationalism—could likewise take root. The potential limit of this approach, of course, is that a focus on emancipation's aberrations might seriously underdescribe the diversity of democracy's past incarnations and the variety of its future possibilities.[21] In a word, antitotalitarianism does not tell anyone what to make democracy except by warning about what not to make it. This is so even if, as Rosanvallon argues, the perversions to which modernity is prone are outgrowths—even epitomizations—of its principles and not departures from them.

Approach by negation has been defended, famously, in theology. But democracy, unlike God, is possible to address constructively and positively. And it is plural, too, not singular or unique in its animating principles or incarnating institutions: the critique of its aberrant forms does nothing to distinguish between its non-aberrant ones and may distract from the urgent task of doing so. From the beginning, those subscribing to the antitotalitarian perspective may have relied too much on negation to guide them, as if selecting the right path were simply a matter of eliminating the dangerous ones. As time passed, it came to seem less and less clear whether any positive, programmatic politics could emerge from a style of thought that seemed mostly devoted to the withering critique of utopia, in both its most overt and violent and its less obvious and insidious forms.

But this basic, foundational problem with antitotalitarian politics, which has haunted it, for all its contributions, since its inception, is now joined by a more serious difficulty. It is as if, precisely when the limits of thinking about emancipation through analyzing its perverse and self-destructive forms became clearer and clearer, it became tempting to respond not by searching for a new framework but by extending the weakening doctrine to new ends. Its failure for internal purposes has corresponded, indeed, to its contemporary extension for external purposes. Is there any other way to understand the popularity of antitotalitarian rhetoric—in politics and intellectual life—after September 11?[22]

But the fact is that such attempts to revive the antitotalitarian point of view have involved robbing the concept of whatever depth and plausibility it had, notably in the thought of Claude Lefort, who did the most, along with and after Hannah Arendt, to give it rigor and power in political theory. Most glaringly, of course, violence is an instrument for international terrorism, rather than an enacted regime in which terror becomes the law. For this and other reasons, it is very difficult to generate a plausible interpretation of international terror networks as perversions of emancipated modernity, as Lefort, like Arendt, did with Soviet communism. This is not to gainsay the existence of modernist *elements* in it (the ones Berman, for example, devotes his energies to emphasizing). But those elements are far from the full story.

Whatever the shape such an argument might take in developed form, the antitotalitarian consensus simply has not coalesced, as a matter of fact, around the new war on terror. "Iraq . . . has confirmed *the end of the anti-totalitarian moment*," Rosanvallon wrote in July 2004:

> There has been a strong temptation to see in al-Qaeda a new form of terrorism capable of reconstituting this old western front. But in Europe the anti-terrorist fight has not given rise, at least for the moment, to a political and intellectual front comparable to 1970s–1980s anti-totalitarianism; and the sharp differences between the successive adversaries (Soviet communism and al-Qaeda) make such an outcome unlikely.[23]

The result of the faltering of antitotalitarianism, however, is not that voluntarism, rationalism, or liberalism, as Rosanvallon defines them, receives new intellectual credentials, though their theoretical and practical appeal remains as irresistible as ever. Instead, it prompts the recognition that antitotalitarianism does not provide a sufficient alternative to those pathologies.

Is it an accident that the end of the antitotalitarian moment coincides with the partial exhaustion of thinking about democracy chiefly through its perversions? In any case, far from remaining in his tracks, in recent years Rosanvallon has begun the attempt to turn his exploration of the political to new ends. No doubt the most pivotal lines in Rosanvallon's inaugural lecture at the Collège de France, which deserve to be cited at length, are these:

> The discovery of the limits of the political has thus essentially consisted, at least up to the present, in an exploration of the stormy zones and savage domains into which democracy could lead. This exploration of its abysses remains a privileged way to understand democracy. . . . And yet it is now pressing to note that we are today truly confronted with the inverse problem, with the attrition and no longer the exacerbation of the political. We live

through the ordeal of an apparent dissolution or erasure: the feeling of a decline of sovereignty, the perception of a dissolution of the will, along with a parallel rise in the power of the law and the market. The frontiers of government and administration, of management and politics, are similarly becoming more vague. The diagnosis, no doubt, will have to be improved. But the key is to emphasize that it is now time to approach the political taking these gray zones as a point of departure, making sense of the weakened energies, the paralyzing drifts, and the silent fragmentations. (52)

The shift, one might say, corresponds to one from the margins of democracy to its core. Antitotalitarianism's limit is that it concentrates on exorcising terror from modern politics. Even when it is used to approach democracy through negation, it can have the vice of externalizing one's view and, as a rhetoric for identifying and banishing enemies, distracting from one's own quandaries.

Rosanvallon's current interest in the "attrition" of the political seems designed to keep this perversion of antitotalitarianism—its reconstruction as an externalizing doctrine for targeting others—from occurring. Beginning in the inaugural lecture and continuing in the last section of this volume, Rosanvallon announces his future explorations in democratic theory (and commends to Europe an experiment in democratic practice). One way to read this final section is as a promising and tantalizing attempt to turn toward a democratic theory that would leave behind the exclusive antitotalitarian orientation. And whatever their tentative and promissory status, Rosanvallon's interventions are promising in relation to existing American debates.

Consider his notion of the *pluralization of sovereignty*, for example, which helps see a way past a typical American dilemma between the inviolability of popular rule and the importance of constitutional control by judges. A recent school of progressive jurisprudence has insisted, in a spate of works, on the contingency of constitutional judicial review and judicial supremacy in American history and demanded the return of sovereignty to "the people themselves."[24] Traditional constitutionalists, in response, see the defense of popular sovereignty against judicial review (as one of them put it) as "taking the law out of constitutional law."[25] Rosanvallon's argument is evidently directed against European fears of constitutional control through judicial empowerment of any kind, but it is equally applicable to the contemporary American belief that judicial review has been taken too far. Still, Rosanvallon's insight into the possibility of pluralized sovereignty, which would allow analysis to exit from the contemporary assumption in a zero-sum game, does not yet provide sufficient detail to know when institutional change under the banner of pluralization might abridge popular sovereignty (as Americans often worry) and when it might genuinely enhance it. Certainly both eventualities are possible. Similar observations apply to Rosanvallon's imaginative call for the study of democracy's temporalities, which also joins a budding American discussion, as well as the generalization of emancipation he outlines.[26]

No one, then, should expect finished or immediately applicable answers from this collection, offered as it is in an introductory rather than conclusive mode. It offers an exploration of democracy of the kind for which Lefort once asked without leading to a definite program. This result, however, is not just a matter of a work in progress and a new turn in the making. In a way, the enlightened persistence of the questions is part of the point. Indeed, it is following Lefort that Rosanvallon insists, in some of the most eloquent passages in this book, that democracy is by definition adventurous and unfinished, and that the goal of reflection and action is not to achieve some mythical and utopian "realization" of democracy, but to further deepen its possibilities in full awareness of its insoluble quandaries.

In this way, the volume is intended to lead to the brink of a program. Defining the situation through conceptual reconstruction of its historical antecedents does not suffice, but it is a start.

Caution before the threat of political disaster prompted by anti-totalitarianism, then, joined with a commitment to exploration of the open field of democracy. Patrolling the borders is not enough, for the difficulties are internal too. Such is the open spirit, abandoning the wish for final answers or total closure but also rejecting easy responses and the demonization of enemies, in which to read the essays of Pierre Rosanvallon that follow.

A Note on the Translations

The texts in this book were selected and put in order by the author and editor of this volume together. The translators of chapters 2, 4, 6, and 10—whose names, where known, are recorded in the acknowledgments—deserve robust thanks. I translated the remaining essays and revised the others, in major or minor ways, to ensure accuracy and consistency throughout.

Whatever their origin, whether as independent articles or as prefaces to or parts of books, the titles have sometimes been changed in an attempt to give the volume overall coherence. In addition, the content of the texts have been altered, if only minutely, to allow each to be free-standing. Editorial additions, where deemed useful, have been added in brackets; existing English translations for cited French texts have been noted, cited, and used when easily available, and for texts cited from other languages English references have been substituted when possible.

Certain terms, most of them deriving from Claude Lefort's political theory, have been translated in the same manner throughout. *Le politique* has been translated as "the political," and its meaning is explained in the first chapter; *mise en forme* and *mise en scène* and their variants have been translated as "set-up" and "staging" respectively. The notion of *Le Peuple-Un* or *l'Un*, which originates from Lefort's interpretation of Étienne de la Boétie,[27] has been translated simply as "unified people" to avoid a jarring neologism. Finally, the translations preserve the term "institution" which Rosanvallon, following predecessors, uses often to signify a process—less conscious and instantaneous than foundation or revolution—by which human political collectivities come about. A selective bibliography of Rosanvallon's writings, including English translations where they exist, is appended to the end of the selections.

The author and editor express their gratitude to Alisa Berger for her logistical assistance with the texts, Danielle Haase-Dubosc and the Institute for Scholars at Reid Hall for a wonderfully congenial work setting for pulling the materials together, Andrew Geoffrey Beres for help with the index, and Peter Dimock and his staff at Columbia University Press for their enthusiasm in making the volume possible and bringing it into being.

December 2004

PART I

The Study
of Politics
in History

CHAPTER 1

Inaugural Lecture, Collège de France

I thank you for receiving me in your midst. At this inaugural moment today, I am first of all aware of the responsibility that falls on me as a result of your decision to open your courses of instruction to the most living of the problems of contemporary politics. But I am most conscious of the wonderful opportunity that you have accorded me. It is an opportunity, at a moment I hope to be the midpoint of my career, to invigorate my researches with a new energy, by relocating them in an intellectual milieu unique thanks to the radical freedom it provides— shielded, as one is at the Collège de France, from the pressures of any agenda, freed from any obligation to evaluate and train students, and liberated from the need to present one's credentials in the face of the usual disciplinary barriers. This chance for a new departure therefore has nothing of the ambiguous and melancholy air of summation so inevitably associated with what are called "academic honors," signaling—as they so frequently do— that a work is considered essentially complete. For this reason I can make my own the words of Roland Barthes: "My entry into the Collège de France is a joy more than an honor: an honor is sometimes undeserved, but a joy never is."[1] And it is unquestionably a joy for me to be able to speak with you today about a project at the moment of its continued elaboration, the joy of an activating obligation and a productive duty.

The expression of my acknowledgments must begin with Professor Marc Fumaroli, who presented you with the project of a chair in the modern and contemporary history of the political. It is first of all thanks to the breadth of his interests and the force of his eloquence that I am able to be in your midst this evening.

I must also, without further delay, let one share in these thanks who is no longer here to receive them this evening: François Furet. It was he who, by inviting me to join the École des Hautes Études en Sciences Sociales at the beginning of the 1980s, helped me make the decisive leap at time when, as a young academic, I remained between two worlds, at the margins of the university system, in the rather precarious position of an intellectual maverick. He put me in a position to give a certain unity to my life and realize the dream of every man and woman: to make a profession of his passion. It was under his guidance and that of Claude Lefort, the one a historian and the other a philosopher, that I learned to work beyond academic routines and intellectual fashions. They were for me, both of them, masters and, indissociably, friends and colleagues. The other members of the Centre de Recherches Politiques Raymond Aron, together with whom we undertook to renovate the long decrepit study of the political, know well what I owe each one of them. It gladdens me that this small community of historians, sociologists, and philosophers are able to see the originality of its work recognized through my election. Finally, though the list of those to whom I ought to express my gratitude could be lengthened further, I will limit myself to thanking the great late medievalist Paul Vignaux. In fact it is probably because of the bonds of friendship that were forged at the very beginning of the 1970s with Vignaux, one of the founders of democratic trade-unionism in France, that as a young militant I could have slowly realized as I did, unlike an important part of the generation of 1968, that a life rigorously dedicated to the comprehension of the world fully participates in creating the conditions for its change: that there is a total complementarity between the *vita activa* and the *vita contemplativa*.

The modern and contemporary history of the political, then. The study of the political sometimes has taken place at the Collège de France, tangentially, under more oblique headings. I must, of course, make special mention of André Siegfried, author of *Le Tableau politique de la France et de l'Ouest*; holder of a chair in "economic and political geography," he was one of the pioneers of electoral analysis in this country.[2] The question of power and its genesis, more generally, has figured in the courses of professors who officially taught sociology or philosophy; one thinks simply of Raymond Aron or Michel Foucault, who each, if in quite different ways, meant so much for my generation. And the decisive role that Maurice Agulhon has played more recently in the study of political mentalities and political culture in nineteenth-century France is well known.

This new chair that I occupy today joins this tradition, even if these various antecedents do not constitute a true genealogy. But there are also certain curricula of the nineteenth century at the Collège de France that approach the spirit, if not the content, of the present chair. I think, especially, of Jules Michelet's concern to illuminate the vicissitudes of the present by retracing the genesis of the French state and nation. And one must likewise make reference to Ernest Renan. While he held a highly specialized chair in Hebraic, Chaldaic, and Syriac languages, the great academic at the same time wanted to reflect on collective life in the long term, to enlighten his contemporaries and to challenge them for their blind spots and oversimplifications. The intent of my enterprise is not terribly different, in many respects, from that "philosophy of contemporary history" to which he aspired.

Edgar Quinet, lastly. He, too, entered the Collège de France in 1841 charged with a traditional study. But in his actual courses, that ardent republican moved very quickly onto more dangerous terrain, successively dealing with the Jesuits (together with Michelet), ultramontanism, and then the relationship between Christianity and the French Revolution. I can recognize myself quite well in one of the more famous expressions of this author of *The Revolution*: "French democracy has exhausted its storehouse of ideas, which has to be stocked up again."[3] I eagerly adopt Quinet's program myself, and I feel myself close to his concern to help prepare for the future by rooting reflection on the present in the comprehension of the ordeals of the past. With one appreciable difference, however, which is that such a project can retain its meaning only through being placed in a much larger comparative framework.

This is not the first time, *stricto sensu*, that the word "political" figures in the title of a Collège de France chair. And yet, the object of modern and comporary politics is now taken explicitly as a subject matter and placed at the center of a teaching plan. Notwithstanding the continuities with the past I have just mentioned, the project of a history of "the political" is, for this reason alone, something original. Accordingly, it is best to start with a definition of the object of study.

As I understand it, "the political" is at once *a field* and *a project*. As a field, it designates the site where the multiple threads of the lives of men and women come together, what allows all of their activities and discourses to be understood in an overall framework. It exists in virtue of the fact that there exists a "society" acknowledged by its members as a whole that affords meaningfulness to its constituent parts. As a project, the political means the process whereby a human collectivity, which is never to be understood as a simple "population," progressively takes on the face of an actual community. It is, rather, constituted by an always contentious process whereby the explicit or implicit rules of what they can share and accomplish in common—rules which give a form to the life of the polity—are elaborated.

One cannot make sense of the world without making room for the synthetic order of the political, except at the price of an exasperatingly reductive vision. The understanding of society, in fact, can never be limited to adding up and connecting together the various subsystems of action (economic, social, cultural, and so forth). These latter are, for their part, far from being easily intelligible by themselves, and only become so as part of a more general interpretive framework. Whatever the catalogue of cultural and social facts, economic variables, and institutional logics, it is impossible to decipher society at its most essential level without bringing to light the nerve center from which the very fact of its institution originates. An example or two will suffice to persuade of this fact.

To understand the specificity of a phenomenon like Nazism, it is easy to say that the dissection of the different tensions and the multiple stalemates of German society in the 1930s is not enough—unless one wants to limit oneself to a banal analysis of its origins as simply an exacerbated response to the crisis of the Weimar regime. The truth of Nazism as a pathological attempt to bring about a unified and homogenous people is understandable only if it is related to the conditions of the perverse resymbolization and recomposition of the global order of the political in which it took place. To take another example, closer to the present, the crisis that today is wracking a country like Argentina is not be interpreted simply according to economic and financial factors that immediately present themselves. It takes on meaning only when resituated in a long history of decline linked to the recurrent difficulty of forging a nation founded on the recognition of shared obligations.

At this level, therefore, which one could call "global," is where matters have to be studied in order to usefully approach a good number of questions that haunt the contemporary world. Whether it is a matter of contemplating the possible future forms of Europe, analyzing the transformations of democracy in an age of globalization, guessing the destiny of the nation-state, evaluating the transformations of the welfare state, or discovering the conditions in which the long term in societies so often governed by the dictatorship of the present would be taken seriously, it is always to the key question of the political that the perplexities and disquietudes of today lead back.

In speaking of "the political" as a noun, I thus mean as much a modality of existence of life in common as a form of collective action that is implicitly distinct from the functioning of politics.[4] To refer to "the political" rather than to "politics" is to speak of power and law, state and nation, equality and justice, identity and difference, citizenship and civility—in sum, of everything that constitutes political life beyond the immediate field of partisan competition for political power, everyday governmental action, and the ordinary function of institutions.

The question is thrown into the relief it deserves in democratic societies, that is to say, in those societies in which the conditions of life in common are not defined *a priori*, engraved in a tradition, or imposed by an authority. Democracy, in fact, constitutes the political in a field largely open to the very fact of the tensions and uncertainties that underlay it. If it has seemed for two centuries now to be the unsurpassable principle of organization of any modern political order, the imperative that spread this assured belief has always been both ardently felt and ambiguous in its implications. Since it is at bottom an experiment in freedom, democracy has never been other than a problematic solution for the institution of a polity of free beings. The dream of the good and the reality of indeterminacy have combined in it over the long term. This coexistence is specific to the extent that it is due principally to the fact that democracy is not simply a distant ideal on whose content everyone already agrees, with debate remaining simply as to the means for realizing it. The history of democracy is, for this reason, not simply one of a blocked experiment or a betrayed utopia.

Far from corresponding, then, to a simple practical uncertainty as to how to bring it about, democracy's unmoored meaning is due quite fundamentally to its essence. It implies a type of regime that resists any attempt at unequivocal classification. The specificity of the malaise that has dogged its history stems from this fact too. The train of disappointments and the perpetual feelings of its betrayal that have always accompanied it have stung just as much as the debate over its definition has resisted closure. From democracy's unmoored wandering has followed both a quest and a nagging absence of destination. One must begin with this fact in order to understand what democracy is: the history of a disenchantment and the history of an indeterminacy are bound up with one another.

The indeterminacy is rooted in a complex network of equivocations and tensions that have structured political modernity since its inception, as study of the English, American, and French revolutions shows. There is equivocation, first of all, about the very subject of this democracy, for the people do not exist except through *approximate* successive representations of itself. The people is a master at once imperious and impossible to find. "We the people" can take only debatable form. Its definition is at once a problem and a challenge. There is a tension, too, between number and reason, between opinion and expertise, for the modern regime instituted political equality through universal suffrage at the same time that it has often called for a rational authority to arise whose objectivity implies impersonality. There is an uncertainty, next, about the adequate forms of social power—popular sovereignty struggling to express itself through representative institutions that will not lead to its limitation in one way or another. There is a duality, finally, of the modern notion of emancipation that gives rise to a desire for individual autonomy (privileging law) at the same moment as it prompts participation in the exercise of social power (replacing authority with politics). The duality is one between liberty and power or, put differently, between liberalism and democracy.

Such a conception of the political makes a historical approach the condition of its thorough study. In fact, one cannot make sense of the political as I have just defined it except in recalling, in some tangible way, the breadth and density of the contradictions and ambiguities that run through it. It has been my ambition, therefore, to rethink democracy by following the thread of its history as it has been spun. But note that it is not simply a matter of saying that democracy *has* a history. More radically, one must see that democracy *is* a history. It has been a work irreducibly involving exploration and experimentation, in its attempt to understand and elaborate itself.

The goal is thus to retrace the long genealogy of contemporary political questions in order to make them more thoroughly intelligible. History enters the project not only out of the interest in recognizing the weight of tradition, in order to provide banal "enlightenment" of the present through the study of the past. Rather, the point is to make the succession of presents live again as trials of experience that can inform our own. It is a matter of reconstructing the manner in which individuals and groups forged their understanding of their situations, to make sense of the challenges and aspirations that led them to formulate their objectives, to retrace, in a sense, the manner in which their vision of the world organized and limited the field of their activity. The object of such a history, to put it yet another way, is to follow the thread of trial and error, of conflict and controversy, through which the polity sought to achieve legitimate form. It consists, in a metaphor, in the publication of the script of the play in which different acts of the attempt to live together have been performed. In attempting to take up this red thread, I have been led to return, in part, to follow in the footsteps of the publicists and historians of the nineteenth century—such as Quinet, François Guizot, or Alexis de Tocqueville—who wanted to enlighten their contemporaries in developing what they defined as a history of civilization. I share with them the selfsame preoccupation with writing what one could call a global history.

History conceived in this way is the *active laboratory* that created our present and not simply its background. Attention to the most burning and urgent of contemporary problems can therefore not be dissociated from the meticulous reconstruction of their origins. To start with a contemporary question, to trace its genealogy before facing it anew at the end of the inquiry, enriched by the lessons of the past, has to be the method developed to give indispensable depth to political analysis. It is thanks to such a permanent dialogue between present and past that the process whereby societies are instituted can become legible and from which a synthetic understanding of the world can emerge. The project is identical to envisioning a history that one might call comprehensive, so that intellection of the past and interrogation of the present participate in the same task through being placed in a common framework. It reveals the resonances between our experience of the political and that of the men and women who were our predecessors, giving Marc Bloch's formula its strongest possible meaning: "Misunderstanding of the present is the inevitable consequence of ignorance of the past."[5] It makes structural partners of the passionate concern for relevance and a scrupulous attention to history. It is for this reason a history whose purpose is to recover problems more than to describe models. Its enterprise ends up, in this manner, intersecting that of political philosophy.

The history of *the political* as practiced in this spirit is distinct in the first place, and by its very object of study, from the history of *politics*. The latter, beyond the recovery of the chronological unfolding of events, analyzes the functioning of institutions, unravels the mechanisms of public decisionmaking, illuminates the reasoning of actors and the way they interacted, and describes the rites and symbols that punctuate life. The history of *the political* draws on such sources, to be sure. With all of the subaltern battles, personal rivalries, intellectual confusions, and short-term calculations that it involves, political activity *stricto sensu* is in fact what circumscribes the political and allows it to be carried out. It is inseparably both an impediment and a means. Rational deliberation and philosophical reflections are not dissociable from passions and interest. The majestic theater of the general will is also the permanent stage for scenes borrowed from the more daily comedies of power. So it is not through taking refuge in the supposedly tranquil sky of concepts that one could really claim to understand the sources and the difficulties of instituting the polity. Those cannot be grasped except through study of ordinary contingencies, always coated as they are by the veneer of events. This has to be acknowledged. But it is necessary to emphasize forcefully, all the same, that one cannot remain at that level to reach the enigma of the political. How could one understand the structural instability of a regime, for example, by contenting oneself with narrating the ministerial crises that take place in the visible foreground?[6]

In a more general way, one should take into account that the history of the political as I try to practice it likewise draws on the results of the different social sciences; and that it intends, moreover, to unify their variety, even if it is especially interested in a set of facts and problems that occupy their traditional blind spot. To make clear what I mean, and to avoid excessively abstract methodological considerations, it is more useful to proceed through several examples in order to suggest how my approach is distinguished from the disciplines of social history, political sociology, political theory, and finally intellectual history.

Social history, first. It places the accent on the interpretation of conflicts of power and oppositions of interest. It furnishes an explanatory grid that allows the link between positions and actions in the specifically political field—that of elections or partisan affiliations for instance—and the cultural, economic, or social variables that characterize different groups to be perceived. The problem, however, is that this approach takes only a portion of reality into account. Consider, in this regard, the example of the fight for universal suffrage. A social history could retrace the conflict between the "impatience" of the people and the "fear" of the elites and could describe the strategies of the forces in play. One can, in fact, analyze the movement for electoral reform that punctuated the July monarchy in this way. But such an interpretation would be partial. It makes little sense, in fact, of the position of the *ultras*, the legitimists, who presented themselves at the time as champions of universal suffrage. It also fails to explain the vacillation of a whole part of the republican camp, perceptible in the defense that some of its members made of mediated suffrage or even the hesitation of others even to use the term universal suffrage (the prominence of the alternative watchword of "electoral reform" implying an uncertainty about the immediate *goal* to be achieved, and not simply tactical prudence). History in such a case is thus not only marked by a conflict between high and low in society, but is also structured by an implicit tension about the very notion of political suffrage: a tension, namely, between suffrage as a symbol of social inclusion, the sacralization of equal citizenship (which, therefore, gives rise to the imperative of its universalization), and suffrage as an expression of social power, a form of social governance (which, in contrast, forces a confrontation with the relation between number and reason and between entitlement to vote and capacity to vote). This last history, which one could call "internal," also has to be retraced.

Sociology, for its part, proposes to "disenchant" politics, to make manifest the real social mechanisms that structure its field, at some distance from whatever doctrines are proclaimed there and thus from the discourses of actors and the advertised functioning of institutions. At the beginning of the twentieth century, several pioneering works laid down the framework of the discipline. Roberto Michels, first, developed a meticulous theory of the conditions in which oligarchic power arises in democratic organizations. Moisei Ostrogorski, in another foundational work, showed how the rise and extension of political parties leads in practice to the transformation of the meaning of representative government from top to bottom.[7] The work of Max

Weber, among many others still, could be added to the list if it were a matter of charting the formation of the discipline. No one could dream of contesting its academic fecundity and its civic importance—the "public pessimists" (in Michels's expression) whom I have just mentioned have been enormously useful teachers of lucidity. I myself helped make certain of their works available again in the 1970s.[8]

But something escapes this approach, too. Take, for example, the analysis of the real functioning of representative government that occupies the center of most of these works. Political sociology indeed "unmasks" the way power is arrogated and the forms of manipulation that develop in the shadow of the representative mechanism. But it does not interest itself in understanding what amounts in some sense to the heart of the problem of modern representation: the quandary of the representability of democracy. By sacralizing the will against the order of nature or that of history, modern politics entrusts power to the people at the very moment that the project of emancipation that it furthers leads in parallel to making the social more and more abstract. The development of juridical conventions and fictions is, in this way, driven by the concern to achieve an equality of treatment and to institute a common space among men and women who are very different from one another. Such abstraction is in this sense a condition of social integration in a world of individuals (whereas in traditional society concrete differences were a factor of insertion, the hierarchical order basing itself on the principle that differences were to interlock with and complement one another). Democracy is thus a regime of fictionality in a double sense. Sociologically, first, since it involves the symbolic creation of an artificial body of the people. But technically, too, for the development of a rule of law presupposes the "generalization of the social," its abstraction as it were, in order to make it governable according to universal rules. If in democracy this formalism is thus a positive principle of social construction, it makes the constitution of a tangible people more uncertain at the same time. Accordingly, a contradiction arises between the *political principle* of democracy and its *sociological principle*: the political principle consecrates the power of the very collective subject that the sociological principle tends to make less coherent and whose visibility it tends to reduce. It is from the point of view of this other "internal contradiction" that the history of the political as I understand it frames the question of representative government. It *also* studies, for example, the history of electoral techniques as a succession of attempts to address this founding deficit of representability.

It bears noting too that the approach I am outlining offers the possibility of going beyond a certain structural contradiction to be found in political sociology and in the social sciences quite generally: the terms in which they make sense of social functioning in effect lead to thinking about it in its steady state—according to its regularities. But to understand change, one needs other concepts. The history of the political can combine the two dimensions, reconciling structure and history. (One might note in passing that it was this formal promise that for a long time was one of the principal reasons for Marxism's analytical appeal.)

It is worth discussing next how my project differs from that of *political theory*, at least as it is usually understood today. The works of John Rawls and Jürgen Habermas which, in the 1970s and 1980s, gave a new centrality to this approach can be cited as convenient examples of what I mean. Their basic trait is to be essentially *normative*. They explain what rational deliberation ought to look like, what popular sovereignty demands, what the universally recognized principles of justice are, or those on which any legitimate legal rules ought to be based. Everyone knows the salutary role that such works have played in restoring to their deserved relevance questions that the social sciences dismissed as useless. They have constituted the heart of an undeniable renovation of political thought, leading some for this reason to speak of the 1970s as the period of a "return of the political." But these intellectual enterprises have, yet again, missed something; in this case it is the aporetic essence of the political that suffers the neglect. That their essentially *procedural* concerns generally led them to a close affiliation with legal or moral philosophy testifies to this fact. It is easy to see, in such authors, that the deployment of a rationalizing vision of the establishment of the social contract leads them to "formalize" reality. The person who, in Rawls's theory, makes choices under the veil of ignorance adopts a more universal and rational view the more he sheds himself of information about the real world. Reason is available in this framework only on condition of abstraction, according to the extent distance is won from the sound and fury of the world.

Basing oneself on the complexity of reality and acknowledging its aporetic dimension, in contrast, leads to interest in the very heart of the political. For this reason, it is necessary to come to grips, first of all, with the problematic character of the modern political regime in order to understand its movement and not hope to dissipate its enigma through an imposition of normativity, as if a pure science of language or law could provide men with the reasonable solution to which they would have nothing to add but conformity. It is also, for similar reasons, to go astray to think that one can exorcise complexity in movement of the democratic adventure through any typological exercise. What is interesting is not the distinction of many different kinds of representative government from one another or the attempt to classify the positions of actors or the characteristics of institutions according to well-defined cases. The point, rather, is to take the permanently open and tension-filled character of the democratic experience as one's object. The proposal is not simply to oppose, in the banal manner of the past, the universe of practices to that of norms. It is to take the constitutive antinomies of politics as the point of departure, antinomies that reveal their nature only in their historical development. If one takes social justice as an example, the goal would be to show through a history of the welfare state how perceptions of the extent of legitimate redistribution practically evolved, and then what the determinants of these perceptions were. In this way, the starting point would have to be the contradiction that set up the matrix of the problem: on one side, the principle of citizenship imposing the recognition of an "objective" social debt; on the other side, the principle of personal autonomy and responsibility leading to the appreciation of the importance of "subjective" individual behavior. Only this history, once again, could clarify the "concept" under study in the case. History is, for such reasons, both the *subject matter* and the *necessary form* of a total interpretation of the political. Political concepts (democracy, liberty, equality, and so forth) can be understood only through the historical work of their testing and the historical search for their clarification. I therefore feel close to the project of "empirical phenomenology" that Anne Fagot-Largeault evoked in her recent inaugural lecture.[9]

The history of the political is situated, fourth and finally, at a great distance from intellectual history. The two kinds of history, to be sure, are interested in the same kinds of touchstone works. But in the history of political, these works are no longer taken by themselves, as simple autonomous "theories," the imposing wreckage of failed voyages since left on the shores of the past. They are analyzed as elements of a more global social imaginary. They are its remnants that now have to be placed back in a general framework of interpretation and exploration. Representations and "ideas" amount in this perspective to a structuring material of social experience. Far from being taken on their own, in narrow genealogies, placed in the closed circle of doctrinal proximity and distance, these representations are understood as real and powerful "infrastructures" in the life of societies. At a distance, then, from a disincarnated vision that would falsely liberate itself from taking into account the forces that shape the framework of human action, the goal is rather to enrich and complicate the notion of "determination." It is a matter of taking hold of all of the "active" representations that orient action, impose on the field of possibilities the limits of the thinkable, and demarcate the ground on which contest and controversy can take place. "Like the Roman *fētiālēs*," Michel de Certeau once suggestively noted, "stories 'go in a procession' ahead of social practices in order to open a field for them."[10] I would like to make this formula my own. Narratives and representations have precisely this positive function of opening "a *legitimate* theater for practical *actions*."[11]

In contrast to the history of ideas, then, the subject matter of the history of the political, which I would call "conceptual," cannot be limited to the analysis of and commentary on great works, even if these can often justifiably be considered "moments" crystallizing the questions that an era poses and the responses that it attempts to these questions. The history of the political borrows, especially, from the history of mentalities the concern of incorporating the totality of the elements that compose that complex object that a political culture is: the way that great theoretical texts are read, the reception of literary works, the analysis of the press and movements of opinion, the life of pamphlets, the construction of transitory discourses, the presence of images, the significance of rites, and even the ephemeral trace of songs. Theorizing the political and doing a living history of representations of life in common combine in this approach. For it is at a "bastard" level that one must always come to the political, in the tangle of practices and representations.

Only under the conditions of its *experiential testing* can the political be deciphered. Its history for this reason demands first of all attention to its antinomies, analysis of its limits and tipping points, and examination of the disappointments and the disarray to which it can lead. The work I have done accordingly takes as its privileged object the lack of fulfillment—the fractures, the tensions, the limits, and the oppositions—that have been emblematic of democracy. The content of the political in fact is not possible to apprehend except in those moments and situations that make clear that democratic life is not one of distance from some preexisting ideal model but one of the exploration of a problem to be resolved.

I have already made brief mention of some of the structuring antinomies of which democracy is made and which I have had occasion to study. But there are many others that have to be taken into consideration. I think especially of those one could classify as "contradictions of form." And they have hardly been explored up to now. Notably deserving of detailed examination is what I call the problem of the "organizing third." I mean by this phrase the fact that collective expression is practically inconceivable without the intervention of a certain exteriority. There is, for example, no possibility of elections without the existence of candidates, who limit in advance the choice of the citizens even in allowing them to choose. The *logical* impossibility of direct or immediate democracy has been the subject of many discussions over the last two centuries, discussions whose history deserves to be reconstructed. It would lead to a better appreciation of the meaning to be attributed to the necessarily reflexive character of representative democracy, and it would permit a new appreciation of the foundations of democratic legitimacy.

But I would especially like to draw attention to another contradiction of form—one that has not, in my opinion, been adequately taken into account: I mean that of the relation of democracy and time. The study of the political has, in general, focused on the analysis of actors, procedures, and institutions, thereby taking temporality as a basically neutral element (as duration). But if democracy is a regime of the self-institution of society, it seems necessary to understand time as an active and constructive dimension. For politics is also the set-up of social time, marked simultaneously by memory and the impatience of the will; it combines rootedness and inventiveness. I would like, in this case as well, to try to understand democracy on the basis of an analysis of its aporias, taking as my point of departure a distinction between time understood as a resource and time understood as a constraint. In the late eighteenth century Edmund Burke and

Thomas Paine posed this problem in an exemplary way in their great debate on the rights of man. Paine formulated the modern program of radical emancipation when he set Burke in his sights: "There never did, there never will, and there never can exist a parliament, or any description of man, or any generations of men, in any country, possessed of the right or the power of binding and controlling posterity to the *'end of time,'* " he wrote. "Every age and generation must be as free to act for itself, *in all cases*, as the ages and generations that preceded it."[12]

For the American or French revolutionaries, the affirmation of the general will presupposed a permanent capacity—or at least a generational one—to invent the future, with the result that what one generation freely chose cannot become an inexorable destiny for those that follow. Whence the debate, central on both sides of the Atlantic in the eighteenth century, over the correct way to think about a constitutional text, so that it does not take the force of what would come close to a binding constraint. (The problem is still alive today, as the terms in which the question of the democratic pedigree of constitution control is often approached would seem to suggest.) All democracies have thus evinced the same worries as Karl Marx when he railed against "the tradition of all the dead generations [that] weighs like a nightmare on the brain of the living."[13]

The attraction for the short term that many deplore today does not stem simply from a kind of acceleration of history artificially sustained in a fickle media-driven world. It is rooted, rather, in a structural phenomenon. In order to confer tangible power on the general will, democracy is constantly tempted to award legitimacy to "the caprice of the moment" (in Renan's phrase), an imperative that imposes itself as a destructive master. From another angle, law—considered by everyone as a necessary agent of protection—can take form only by introducing a longer temporality in common life. It is equally patent that we live in a world in which economic vitality depends on the capacity to consider public interventions over longer and longer periods of time and in which, too, taking environmental problems seriously commits one to thinking in temporal horizons that are incompatible with those of electoral cycles. Democratic time is thus susceptible to two kinds of temporal difficulties: excessive immediacy for the concerns of the long term and excessive duration for the urgencies of the moment. In both cases, the pertinence of the notion of the general will finds itself open to question.

Such tensions of temporality have nourished and deepened a whole set of perplexities and conflicts. Positions can easily oscillate between two equally troubling extremes. On the one hand, one finds a radically instantaneous interpretation of democracy—an interpretation that could fall prey to an executive power capable of freeing itself from ordinary constraints in the name of exceptional situations. On the other, there is the opposite position, which would empower experts—allegedly possessing unique insights into the issues at hand—who alone would be considered competent to "represent" social interests over the long term. The long history of such conflicts illuminates numerous contemporary alternatives of this kind. It also can open the way to a renovated understanding of democracy as a conjunction of temporalities. The *subject* of democracy, I would like to show, has to be understood as one indissociably juridical (the people as citizens and electors) *and* historical (with the nation linking memory to the promise of a shared future).

But the *forms* of democracy have their own connection to the plurality of temporalities. At some distance from any univocal approach, which might concentrate on the procedure of electoral legitimation alone, it is better to emphasize how the perspective of a more complex body of forms of sovereignty (from a simple decision to protest to the memorial institution of the general will in a constitution) works in tandem with the understanding and analysis of the multiplicity of temporalities that constitutes the human experience.

To add to all of these different aspects of democratic indeterminacy there is also the permanent crisis of political language.

And it is, alas, all of the essential notions—equality, citizenship, sovereignty, the people, and so forth—whose definition is so problematic. Significantly enough, the drama of language's breakdown already seemed to occur in the French revolutionary years. At the moment that he launched the *Journal d'instruction sociale*, together with the Abbé Joseph Sieyès, the Marquis de Condorcet stated, for example, that "the alteration of the meaning of words indicates the alteration of things."[14] One of the most perspicacious observers of the Terror could note of Maximilien Robespierre and his associates, too, that "they deprived all the words of the French language of their true meaning,"[15] while Jacques-Pierre Brissot, for his part, violently attacked those he called "thieves of names."[16] It is for such reasons that Camille Desmoulins could make it his program in *Le Vieux Cordelier* to champion freedom of the press, with the possibility of challenge to words and things that it implies, as the touchstone of the democratic experience: "It is in the character of the Republic," he put it at the time, "for men and things to be called by their name."[17] In contrast, ideology is the most nakedly perverse manifestation of a calculated or consensual divorce between words and things. It comes down in the end to the attempt to deny and dissimulate the contradictions of the world through the illusory coherence of doctrine. It breaks free of reality in staging a fantasmic order and in following a path in which clarity is forced.

The work of the historian is, there too, to bring to light these questions and endeavors in order to grasp the movement of democracy in its most problematic dimensions. To this extent, his way can intersect with those whose job it is to explore words and to tame an opaque reality with the tool of language. If literature and poetry have the function of opening us up to the presence of the world by the devices of language, there is reason for them to take on a more expansive purpose in the midst of the uncertainties of the democratic age. The novelist and the poet are, each after his own singular fashion, those who survey the ambiguity and clear the silence of language; they remain open to the contraditions of the world and never allow concepts to exhaust the density of the real. The history of the political joins in concert with literature in the interstices of the social sciences. They work together in a related movement of deciphering the world. I note the place that writing had among a number of nineteenth-century historians; Michelet, among all of them, knew best how through his language and style to say most sensitively what his documents sometimes had trouble expressing on their own.

A history of aporias, then, but also a history of limits and boundaries. For it is in fact at its moments of gestalt switch, at the points at which it turns back on itself, that the question of democracy is clarified each time anew in the most startling ways. From Hannah Arendt to Claude Lefort, a complete renovation of the conceptualization of the political took place between the 1950s and the 1970s, taking the recognition of totalitarianism as its point of departure. Against purely descriptive approaches, which saw only the aggravated resurgence of dictatorship or tyranny, the originality of these authors was to show that the regimes in question had to be understood as deviant forms of democratic modernity—as its negative fulfillment, in a sense. And one must understand the effective fantasy of a power that could fully absorb society—the key characteristic of totalitarianism—as corresponding to a utopian extension of the representative principle. It involved the desire to bring about, artificially and at the same time, a society perfectly legible in its unity and a power supposed to be completely identified with it, with the goal of reabsorbing in its very origin the gap between the social and the political. The motivating energy of the totalitarian enterprise derived from this pretension, which continued in the utopia of calling into existence a power wholly confounded with society and absolutely indissociable from it. Totalitarian power is, for this reason, commanded by an imperious logic of identification. In radicalizing the notion of the class party and in finally erecting it as an absolute, it hoped to surpass the founding aporias of representation and to institute a power that would provide "real representation" of society. It is the party that put in place that imaginary chain of identification that led to thinking of the political direction and even the first secretary—whom Alexander Solzhenitsyn called the "Egocrat"—as the perfect incarnation of the people. The party eventually went beyond the function of representation: it became the very substance of the people.

The discovery of the limits of the political has thus essentially consisted, at least up to the present, of an exploration of the stormy zones and savage domains into which democracy could lead. This exploration of its abysses remains a privileged way to understand democracy. Research in these directions, for this reason, still has to be pursued; contemporary events provide further encouragement to do so, and I plan to play my role in this endeavor. And yet it is now pressing to note that we are today truly confronted with the inverse problem, with the attrition and no longer the exacerbation of the political. We live through the ordeal of an apparent dissolution or erasure: the feeling of a decline of sovereignty, the perception of a dissolution of the will, along with a parallel rise in the power of the law and the market. The frontiers of government and administration, of management and politics, are similarly becoming more vague. The diagnosis will have to be improved, no doubt. But the key is to emphasize that it is now time to approach the political taking these gray zones as a point of departure, making sense of the weakened energies, the paralyzing drifts, and the silent fragmentations.

The turbulence of the contemporary world should not, however, incite anyone to reflect solely on the *limit forms* of the political. For it is also today the *space* of the political that finds itself in dire straits. The question has been studied for twenty years now, by numerous authors, based on the recognition of a growing dissociation and differentiation of the relations of power and territory once securely anchored in the figure of the sovereign state. The various works of political science or legal study on the dissolution of sovereignty *externally* and its dissemination elsewhere are well known. Not enough attention has been accorded, however, to the concomitant tendency through which nation-states have become more fragile *internally*, thanks to the weakening of the social contract and the narrowing of collective identities.

The acceleration of secessionist movements is the most remarkable clue to the trend. The number of states has grown at the same time as the source of such multiplication has changed. The numbers are eloquent. The 44 states of 1850 had only become 60 by the eve of World War II. The process of decolonization of the 1950s and 1960s and the breakup of the Soviet sphere, in the largest sense, after 1989 were the most important causes of the multiplication of states: they had reached 118 as of 1963, and 197 in 2000. The movement has continued, sharpened in many cases thanks to ethnic and religious conflict.

Specialists in international relations have looked into the phenomenon from the point of view of their discipline. But it is also useful to analyze it by connecting it to the process of ethnic segmentation and the reality of "social secession" that seems to play a growing role. A number of national splits, in fact, have occurred when, in the face of the need for redistribution to master differences, existing populations have simply refused to coexist any longer. These mechanisms of the *retraction of the political* correspond, in this way, to a test of the limits of the social contract whose dimensions it is now urgent to measure. The decisive phenomenon is not always clearly perceived. The genuine paradox is that the contemporary decline of the nation-state—as a *social form*—is occluded by the multiplication of nation-states as *sovereign entities*. The conflicts over distribution that normally are resolved through "internal" *social compromise* are transformed in certain cases into conflicts of identity that are "externalized" as a *partition of nations*. The older logic of winning and defending rights through aggregation has, in other words, often now become segregative. The blossoming of nationalism today testifies, correspondingly, to the retreat and not the spread of the historical form of the nation. For nations once considered as *reduced universals* is now substituted a new sense of nations restrictively conceived as *enlarged particularities*. This is a phenomenon that cries out for precise analysis, at least if one wants to combat its deleterious consequences. It is therefore pressing to articulate an "internal" analysis and an "external" analysis of the political, to open the approach in terms of international relations to research conducted from the perspective of the social contract's content and the forms of collective identity and solidarity still felt to be pertinent.

Antinomies and limits, in sum, but also disappointments. For it seems to me necessary to proceed yet further and open up a third mode of inquiry into the political, involved in the exploration of democratic disappointment. A whole series of contemporary debates coalesce, in fact, around the diagnosis of a transition felt to be dangerous: the decline of the will, the unraveling of sovereignty, the disaggregations of forms of collectivity, and so forth. Such debates, it bears repeating, are by no means unprecedented, even if with each reappearance they are formulated in new ways. It is first of all thanks to the impossibility of dissociating *the political* from *politics* that a certain kind of disappointment with the modern regime comes about. For it is never simple to separate the noble from the vulgar, the great ambitions from the petty egotistical calculations, the trenchant language of truth from the sophistry of manipulation and seduction, the necessary attention to the long term from submission to the urgencies of the moment. If the frontier in each case has to be a subject of reflection and an object of discovery, it remains in movement and in fluctuation, determined as it is in part by the prism of interests, captive to differences of perspective.

There grows up around the political, as a result, a longing that in a certain sense is impossible to fulfill. It is often as if there were at the same time too much and too little of politics, a fact which combines an expectation and a rejection. The desire for politics flows from the aspiration for the collectivity to be its own master, and the hope of seeing a community take form in which a place is made for each person. At the same time, there is a rejection of sterile conflicts and the search for a simply private happiness. It is easy to feel at once what feels like an exasperation before an excess and a nostalgia before what feels like a decline. Politics often seems simultaneously like an irritating residue, to be eliminated if possible, and like a tragically lacking dimension of life, a cruelly absent grandeur.

I hope to devote myself to retracing the history of this disappointment as well as that of various attempts to surmount it: the search for *rational politics* on the one hand, and the exaltation of *cultures of voluntarism* on the other. The plan in this regard is to conceptualize democracy based on an analysis of the feeling that it is absent. From Pierre-Louis Roederer to Auguste Comte, from Auguste Jullien to the Count Henri Saint-Simon, one can follow the formulation in the first quarter of the nineteenth century of a social science, a science of order, or a positive politics that would allow the passage from the difficult government of men to the supposedly peaceable administration of things. Against the grain of such scientistic utopias of a radical deep freeze of the political, allowing its dissolution in a happy ending, there have also occurred the periodically expressed aspirations for its exaltation, in the form of a whole series of cults of the will. The history of these cycles remains to be taken up. This history undeniably possesses a dimension one could call "social." Memories of the Terror often overdetermined the horizon of all those, after Thermidor, who aspired to an impersonal government of reason; conversely, it was the narrowness and irresolution of routine regimes that, a half-century later, nourished calls in 1848 for a creative voluntarism. But one cannot stop with this oversimplifying approach, if only because the same forces often led the simultaneous expression of both moods (in twentieth-century communism, for example, the praise of supposedly authoritative experts in management went together with the most exacerbated voluntarism). It is also necessary to show that disappointment is born from the difficulty of making the democratic ideal a living force in quotidian reality: democracy has been prey in turn to fear of conflict and to anxiety about its absence, torn between the aspiration to individual autonomy and the quest for participation in life together.

Contemporary debates about the disappearance of the political could not, therefore, be understood solely thanks to the analysis, admittedly sketched quite briefly, of the forms through which sovereignty has been disseminated and its ingredients resynthesized. They would have to be placed, in addition, in a continuous history of democratic disappointment which is only, perhaps, the other face of a history of the hatred of democracy, a hatred that sometimes masks itself in the claim that it solely objects to the dominance of its so-called "liberal" or "bourgeois" form. The project would involve, to put it differently, the composition of a negative history of democracy.

This task I have been outlining of a history of the political takes on all of its importance at this dawn of the third millennium, at a moment when everyone feels the growing disquietude of "history biting from behind," in a famous [Trotskyist] line.[18] It will suffice for my purposes now, in a rapid sketch, to recall the conditions in which economic globalization has modified the space of democracy and made the search for the general interest more difficult; to measure the emergence of a universe in which forms of "governance" have substituted more and more, in a burst throughout the world, for the legible and responsible exercise of sovereignty; to record the disturbances caused by the compression of media-driven time; to bear in mind the conflicts linked to the renaissance of national identity; and finally to evoke the problems suggested by the entry into a framework in which the weight of forces as ungraspable as they are menacing becomes more obvious each day. It is around pressing observations of this nature that numerous projects of research in the social sciences are organized today. The history of the political, in the way that I have attempted to sketch its contours today, offers a specific contribution, I think, to the clarification of these questions in restoring them to the longer and enlarged perspective that they deserve. It must also allow the widespread temptations of the day—to take refuge in the position of disabused retirement or to abandon the government of the world to the pretended sufficiency of market operations or the exclusive power of law—to be overcome.

"In scientific matters," Marcel Mauss noted, "it is impossible to proceed too slowly; while in practical matters, one cannot wait."[19] I have taken care not to forget this essential distinction, which one could not transcend without consequences. The moment one intervenes in universally debated problems in the contemporary world, there is a great risk that the difference between patient labor and hasty commentary, between science and opinion, will dissolve before one's eyes. But for the modern and contemporary history of the political, there is no way beyond this risk, no hope of discovering a zone of inquiry protected, thanks to some means of inaccessibility, from the movements of life. Its ambition, rather, is to descend in the civic arena to offer it a supplement of intelligibility and a dose of lucidity. It owes to itself the project of offering a calm and critical reading of the world where too often the clamor of passions, the flexibility of opinions, and the comfort of ideologies rule. The most rigorous academic work and the most patient acts of erudition can in this way participate directly in the activity of citizenship, born as they are from confrontation with events, and always remaining tethered to them. I hope to enroll myself to this extent, with modesty but with the firmest determination, in the line of all of the scholars who were the most indefatigable citizens, precisely through their works, incessantly joining together—in Romain Rolland's phrase, one popularized by Antonio Gramsci, who served as a longtime guide for a whole sector of my generation—the pessimism of the intellect with the optimism of the will.

Reflecting on what made the courses that he gave within these walls special, Michelet noted: "It is not really teaching that occurs here, to be perfectly precise. It is the examination of high questions, in front of the public. One speaks, not to students, but to equals."[20] There is probably some part of illusion in such an approach to a public course, which is not equally possible from discipline to discipline. Yet it provides a healthy reminder of the experiential test to which the kinds of words risked in this forum are submitted. And it is, one might say, precisely in such a test that is to be found the source of the joy that I mentioned at the beginning of this lesson, without yet being able to define it. It is that of participating in a scholarly utopia, one that exists for the sake of the polity's reinvigoration.

CHAPTER 2

Toward a Philosophical History of the Political

The past twenty years or so have witnessed a "return of the political," a phrase now hackneyed by overuse.[1] Such a return can be explained by the concurrence of two factors. First, it belongs to a moment in history: that of the rediscovery of the centrality of the question of democracy and of its problematic nature. Until the end of the 1960s, the vision of a central ideological divide served to organize intellectual space around the opposition between the two prevailing visions of the world: the Marxist and the liberal. The advocates of classical parliamentary democracy and the champions of "real" democracy both believed that the model whose merits they proclaimed corresponded to a fully realized ideal. In the 1970s, a new version of the critique of totalitarianism caused these convictions to be broken, allowing deeper analyses of the problem of democracy. Since the end of the 1980s, the need for a new social contract, in a context characterized by the rise of nationalism and the crisis of the welfare state, has prolonged this search, thus contributing to making the question of the political central once again. But the "return of the political" also has a methodological cause. It has gone hand in hand with the disenchantment with the social sciences that became apparent in the 1980s. With sociology or anthropology facing a kind of exhaustion, philosophy often seemed to offer a better way to both understand and formulate the difficulties of contemporary societies. It is within such a context that the emergence of what I call the philosophical history of the political is best appreciated.

This essay defends this new approach by making explicit the methodological elements and the underlying intentions of a number of my own publications, in particular *L'État en France* (1990) as well as *Le Sacre du citoyen* (1992).[2] One threshhold point, however, comes first of all. The definition of a new philosophical history of the political rests on a definition of the political domain different from the one generally assumed by political science. For this inherited field, politics constitutes a subset of the social system as a whole. Max Weber, for instance, considered the political order, understood as the exercise of the monopoly of legitimate violence, to be different from the economic or the social order. Each sphere of activities is subject to institutions and regulatory principles of its own. One could mention many other definitions of what politics is, of course. But what characterizes the social sciences is that they view it in terms of its specificity: what distinguishes the political domain is the particular quality of power as a means of shaping the organization and the hierarchy of the social fabric.

Against this usual definition, the philosophical history of the political implies (as Claude Lefort has put it) "the notion that relations between human beings and the world are generated by a principle or body of principles."[3] Seen from this angle, it is not simply a matter of drawing a line between the political and the social, taking the symbolic dimension characteristic of society as the point of reference. If setting the political within this symbolic framework is hardly contestable (it leads, one can note in passing, to viewing the relationship between the political and the religious as fundamental), more precision is nonetheless required. But the very illuminating observations of Lefort help here, too, by defining the political as the set of procedures that institute the social. Interpreted in this way, the political and the social are indissociable, since the latter is given sense, is set up, and is staged by means of the former.

This definition of the political rests on a double premise. The first is the classical acknowledgment of the problematic nature of drawing up the rules whereby the community can live in peace, thus avoiding discord and its own ruin in the shape of a civil war. On this point, one can recall Aristotle's classic definition in his *Politics*: "All men think justice to be a sort of equality. . . . But there still remains a question: equality of what? The question is an aporia and calls for political thought."[4] Understood in this way, politics defines a sphere of activities characterized by irreducible conflicts. The political stems from the need to establish a rule outside the ordinary, and one that cannot in any way be derived from a natural datum. The political can therefore be defined as the process that allows the constitution of an order accepted by all by means of deliberation about the norms of participation and distribution. "Political activity," as Hannah Arendt observes in a similar vein, "depends upon the plurality of human activity. . . . Political activity is concerned with the community and with how being different affects the respective parties."[5]

Such a "classical" definition of the political is still relevant. But it should also be stressed that it acquires a wholly new meaning in modern society. In Aristotle's thought the problematic character of participation and distribution is kept within bounds by the belief in a certain natural order of things and society. In his view the system of differences is in part something already given. But modern society involves the extension, and one might even say the unleashing, of the political—and for two reasons.

The transition from a corporatist to an individualist society gave rise, in the first instance, to a kind of enormous deficit of representation. So the political is called upon to be the agent that "represents" a society to which nature no longer gives immediate form. According to Karl Marx, in the Middle Ages the social estates were immediately political.[6] In modern societies, on the other hand, positive steps have to be taken in order for the representation of society to be instituted. Visible and tangible appearance has to be given to the society of individuals, and the people must be given a face. This imperative of representation therefore distinguishes modern from ancient politics. At the same time, one must draw attention to a second fundamental difference, one that stems from the principle of equality and is related to the advent of a conventional vision of the social (one implied by the equality of individuals as legal subjects). In modern society there are no longer fixed limits that either nature or history can impose on the work of equalization. Modern society is characterized by a revolution of equality that spells the end of all attempts to legitimate differences by appeal to a natural order of any kind. Social life is characterized by two processes, consisting not only of new claims for economic equality but also of the narrowing of anthropological differences. These two aspects of modernity lead thus to a considerable enlargement of the practical domain of politics in comparison to the Aristotelian vision.

Placed in this perspective, the aim of the philosophical history of the political is to promote an understanding of the way systems of representation, which determine the manner in which individuals or social groups conduct their activity and conceive communal life, are formed and evolve.[7] On the assumption that these representations are born of a process whereby society constantly reflects on itself, and that they are therefore not exterior to the consciousness of actors, the philosophical history of the political aims primarily to relate how an epoch, a country, or a social group may seek to construct responses to what, with greater or less precision, they perceive as a *problem*. Second, it seeks to provide a historical account of the effort occasioned by the permanent interaction of reality and its representation by defining historico-conceptual fields. Its objective therefore is to identify the *historical nodes* around which new political and social rationalities organize themselves and representations of public life undergo change, in relation to the transformation of institutions and forms of regulation and connection. It is a *philosophical* history because it is through concepts that organize society's self-representations—such as equality, sovereignty, democracy, etc.—

that the intelligibility of social life and its change is made possible. Such a definition, finally, explains why two great historical "moments" are privileged by this approach. One is the loss of the autonomy of the social order understood as a corporatist body. The history of the political in this case is interested in the unraveling of an organic representation of society. The second is the democratic period that followed. These two great moments are very different from each other. One is the era of the birth of modern political forms, of the state, together with the emergence of the individual; the other is, more directly, the history of what one may call the "democratic experience."

Contrary to the classical history of ideas, the material for this philosophical history of the political cannot be limited to an analysis of and the commentary upon the great texts, even though such texts, in certain cases, can justifiably be considered as poles around which the questions raised in a period of history as well as the answers that it sought to offer crystallized. The philosophical history of the political borrows from the history of mentalities the concern to incorporate the entirety of those elements that make up that complex object that any political culture is: the manner in which great theoretical texts are read, to be sure, but also literary works, the press and the movement of opinion, pamphlets and formal speeches, emblems and signs. More broadly still, the history of events and institutions has to be taken into account, so that, to this extent, no subject matter is really exclusive to this type of history of the political. It consists, then, in gathering together all those materials drawn upon, each in separate ways, by historians of ideas, of mentalities, of institutions, and of events. For example, the relationship between liberalism and democracy during the French Revolution does not simply consist of a kind of high-level debate between Rousseau and Montesquieu. One must make the effort to grasp what those who used these authors as authorities actually read in their works, study the mass of petitions sent to the National Assembly, immerse oneself in the world of pamphlets and satirical tracts, re-read parliamentary debates, and follow the proceedings of clubs and committees. It is also necessary to study the history of words and the development of language (the word "democracy" did not mean the same thing in 1789 as it did in 1793, for example). This kind of history is naturally pluralistic.

How does one analyze the multiplicity of these various levels? It is an important question because often the history of the political (when it is confused with the history of ideas) is reproached for being simply a history of the great writers. How to manage the rivalry between histories "from above" and "from below"? Here one must attempt to reanimate the meaning of the classical texts. If a certain number of texts appear to be crucial, they are so not just as expressions of thought, but also because they represent a philosophical and conceptual formalization of a specific historical, political, or philosophical moment.

The point is not to carry out a reading of *The Social Contract* in the style of Leo Strauss—as a strictly philosophical contribution. It is more interesting, rather, to show how *The Social Contract* represented one response to the problem of constructing the social order in the eighteenth century. If great texts enjoy a particular status in this history, it is because their peculiar quality is precisely that they capture the dimensions of a problem. But obviously one cannot restrict oneself to the great texts. If, for instance, one wants to understand how a vision of modern political representation originates, one cannot simply infer it from the Abbé Joseph Sieyès or Antoine Barnave alone, or even from the opposition between the archaic vision of representation of Montesquieu's vision and its radical critique in Rousseau's thought. For it is also necessary to analyze the way society at large addressed the same question, looking at pamphlets, iconography and songs. When I wrote *Le Sacre du citoyen*, I therefore tried not to separate the use of classical texts from that of material of a less "noble" intellectual origin. I sought, for example, to place the analysis of iconographic documents alongside a classical commentary on different texts.

In this sense, the philosophical history of the political represents an attempt to give new meaning to Fernand Braudel's project of a *total history*. One must in fact move in the direction of a "total political history" in order to make sense of the political in all its complexity. Today the avenues by which history can renew itself are many. In this respect, contemporary debates on the frontiers between history and fiction, on the renewal of the biographical approach to the social, and on the renovation of microhistory are all significant. History lives off these methodological debates. The new philosophical history of the political must be understood within the framework of these major innovations within the discipline. It is this new history that takes over, in a different form, the old project of a total history: a history that refuses to separate, as a matter of principle, the different instruments of the various historical specialties. In this sense, the history of the political can draw from cultural history, from social history, from the classical history of political institutions, and from the history of ideas. What gives it unity, however, is not just the variety of instruments that it can bring to bear but its very object; it is the peculiarity of this object that distinguishes it from the other fields of history.

The originality of this philosophical history of the political, then, lies in both its approach and its content. Its approach is at the same time interactive and comprehensive. It is interactive because it analyzes the way the institutions and the events of a political culture combine to establish more or less stable political forms. It charts the convergences and divergences, the false starts and the blind spots, that characterize the creation of political forms and determine what makes them equivocal or ambiguous (or indeed what allows them to succeed). The philosophical history is also comprehensive, because its central objective is to understand an issue by placing it within the context of its emergence. Under these conditions it is impossible to maintain an objectivist approach presupposing that the historian can survey and control a passive object from without. The comprehensive approach seeks to apprehend history in the making, while it remains full of potential, before it becomes actualized in its completed and seemingly necessary form. "Understanding" (*Verstehen* in Max Weber's sense) in the field of history implies reconstructing the way actors made sense of their situations, rediscovering the affinities and the oppositions from which they planned their actions, drawing the genealogies of possibility and impossibility that implicitly structured their horizon. It is a method, in a sense, based on empathy, because it presupposes the ability to address an issue by putting oneself within the situation from which it emerged. But it is naturally a form of empathy limited by the very distance that may allow one to understand the blind spots and the contradictions of actors and authors: a controlled empathy, so to speak.

These general comments on the definition of the content and the approach of a conceptual history of the political are not meant as a rejection of the traditional methods of the histories of ideas, of events, and of institutions—or of the more recent history of mentalities. Rather, they suggest a reassessment of their subject matter from a fresh perspective. Such a reassessment may in some instances entail the risk of reviving old approaches, particularly the history of ideas. This field has for so long been forsaken by French academics that it was often necessary to start from the most traditional historical reconstruction before attempting a more conceptual account of it. It is important, in this regard, to understand the connection between the history of the political and what has come to be known as the *Annales* school. The gap between the two that developed in the 1980s had an exaggerated appearance following from the inevitable sense of rediscovery that came from the reappraisal of a field of scholarship that had been neglected for far too long, so that the return to an earlier tradition of the history of ideas could briefly seem tantamount to a new approach to the political. The moment when the senses both of recovery and of innovation seemed to combine, however, is now at an end, and it is clear that the history of the

political is one that fits into a perspective of extension and renewal of the French historical school, rather than breaking away
from it altogether. The way forward is still uncertain and experimental. I can therefore well understand that this attempt can
sometimes give the impression that it is one that opposes a "top-
down" to a "bottom-up" history. This impression, however, remains the main obstacle in the way of the development of this
ambitious project, whether it is considered in terms of its aims or
its methods. A new path needs to be discovered to allow the
philosophical history of the political to avoid becoming either a
simple history of ideas, even an improved one, or mere political
theory.

Far from being isolated from other fields of historical research, the history of the political is, on closer inspection, easily
reconciled with them. In any case, certain traditional historians
have themselves turned more and more to the political, as part of
the intrinsic development of their own approaches. This is so in
the case of social history, if one considers, for example, Jacques
Julliard's work.[8] The same is true for the history of symbolism,
as Pierre Nora's undertaking in Les lieux de mémoire reveals.[9]
L'histoire de France, published by Le Seuil and edited by André
Burguière and Jacques Revel, has also made for a fruitful exchange.[10] The conditions for a productive dialogue, indeed for
collaboration among historians, philosophers, and sociologists,
have thus steadily emerged. Work with jurists has widened still
further the possibilities for exchange. By its very nature, the
study of the political requires taking diverse paths and the dis-
mantling of narrow disciplinary boundaries.

I have described the sense in which the philosophical history
of the political revives intellectual history while integrating it
with other approaches. And what of political theory? My aim,
from this perspective, is to heal the division between political
theory and political history, so as to arrive at a point at which the
two enterprises fuse. The reasons for this ambition are grounded
in the important premise that history must be considered as ma-

terial for political theory, an object of philosophical reflection. Hannah Arendt took this line, observing in *Between Past and Future* that "thought itself arises out of incidents of living experience and must remain bound to them as the only guideposts by which to take its bearings."[11] One of political thought's major features is expressed in these lines: it is shaped first of all by a "relationship at once *necessary, insurmountable and forever problematic* with the experiences and the opinions actually present at any given time in the 'real' politics of polity."[12] In no way, then, can political theory be viewed as a "province" of general philosophy. Rather, it constitutes a particular *manner* of doing philosophy, since its issues arise directly from the life of the community, along with the totality of the arguments and controversies that run through it. From this perspective, it is necessary to insist that there is no political concept (whether democracy, liberty, or any other) that can be extricated from its articulation in history.

Understood in this way, political experience is indeed the subject matter of political theory, but it also follows that this subject matter is always in motion. Doing the history of politics thus turns out to mean reconstructing a search in which we, too, remain immersed in a sense. In fact, democracy is always at one and the same time the clear solution to the modern problem of the institution of society as well as a question forever left unanswered, in the sense that no conclusive and perfectly adequate response can ever be provided to it. The philosophical history of the political involves, therefore, a constant rethinking of the antinomies constitutive of the modern experience. What is called for is an attempt to unravel the historical thread of investigation and interrogation so as to understand history as it is made in a kind of collective experiment. In the end it is a matter of writing a history that one could term comprehensive.

The comprehensive approach depends on the premise that there is something enduring and constant between the situation of the author or actor under study and our own situation. For the

Weberian sociologist, such a constant is that of human nature. In the case of a conceptual history of ideas, it is a function of our sense that we continue to be immersed in the questions whose path we are historically reconstructing. In this sense, the work of the historian can open the way toward a new type of intellectual commitment. To be sure, this engagement cannot involve transferring the preferred ideology or *a priori* assumptions of the present into a text or position from the past, nor is it a matter of reviving social groups or thinkers with whom the interpreter happens to sympathize. The aim, rather, is to turn conceptual history into a resource for understanding the present. The proposal is banal at first blush, some will justifiably say: the study of the past is always inspired by the need for light in the present. But considered more closely, matters are not quite so simple.

Many history books seek in fact rather to reinterpret history in terms of the present or even of the future as they imagine it. Such an inversion of the task of comprehension seems to me to be particularly striking in the field of political history. Take as an example the political history of the French Revolution. Alphonse Aulard's book, which still remains the classic work of reference on the subject, offered an analysis of the political movement of the Revolution by constantly relating speeches and political institutions of the period to what he took to be the fixed and established democratic idea.[13] Thus he traced the advances and the setbacks of democracy between 1789 and 1799 by reference to his own vision of democracy (government for the people and through universal suffrage). He makes judgments on this period by taking his present as the fixed point of reference. This sort of gradualist and linear history, with democracy equated to universal suffrage, takes as an extrahistorical given and an indisputable fact what is actually the shifting terrain to study: the gradual equation of the idea of democracy with the idea of the vote during the period. Aulard wrote as if the democratic idea already existed *from the outset*, prevented from full realization only by the ambient circumstances, the insufficient discernment of the actors involved, or the impact of the class struggle between the people and the bourgeoisie.

History read this way is always simple: it is the territory where opposing forces clash (action versus reaction, progress versus conservation, modern versus archaic, bourgeois versus popular). Their outcome explains the advances and the setbacks that the idea—itself insulated from history—enjoys or suffers. The past is judged from the standpoint of a present that is not itself historicized. Under these conditions, history becomes a genuine obstacle to the understanding of the present. The philosophical history of the political in its comprehensive form allows, in contrast, for dispensing with the barrier separating political history from political thought. Understanding the past and interrogating the present are part of the same intellectual agenda. The sort of philosophical history I am outlining also provides a meeting ground between commentary and scholarship, undertakings that are often portrayed as mutually exclusive. Scholarship is the vital condition of understanding of historical processes (the amount of information to be gathered and of texts to be read is, indeed, considerable when carrying out a comprehensive study), while commentary as a form of intervention in the present remains the motor driving the impulse to know and to understand. It is not an "engaged" history (understood as the simple projection of personal preferences and passions in the guise of scholarship). And it is not a Whig history (one that presents the past as the slow preparation for the realized present). Rather, it is a history of the *resonances* between our experience and that of past actors.

This way of conceiving the historian's craft should lead to a reconsideration of *the relationship between intellectual labor and civic and political involvement*. The strength of this history of the political is that it conceives academic life in such a way that it becomes an integral part of the civic experience. It suggests, in effect, a new form of engagement. Such engagement is no longer determined by the *position* of the intellectual (the authority conferred upon him by his specialized knowledge); it is of a more substantive kind. In a certain sense, it is the very nature of intellectual labor that amounts to political engagement. If concern with civic life may take forms other than ordinary political combat, or the adherence to certain values or utopias, then it can also be thought of as the capacity to lucidly discern the aporias of the circumstances in which individuals find themselves and the questions that arise from them. If so, the work of the political historian is part and parcel of this civic process. Knowledge thus becomes a form of action. To such an extent, intellectual labor is a form of political practice. It is political understanding that, thanks to its contribution to the elucidation of the aporias of politics, participates in the attempt to define what properly belongs to the political domain. What is at stake here is the connection between erudition and involvement. The philosophical history of the political is able simultaneously to forge instruments of understanding and tools for practical involvement. The aim is to reach the point where the distinction between knowledge and action vanishes. It means participating in the process through which society might no longer separate knowledge about itself from intentional action on itself.

The project for a philosophical history of the political is thus based on a strong thesis. It claims to rebuild the relationship between intellectual labor and political life along new lines. Intellectual labor is not a form of "capital" available for reinvestment in another field thanks to the degree of visibility secured by academic fame (which by itself confers credibility to political discourse). Rather, it is the *very content* of the intellectual labor that has a civic dimension. To speak more personally, it is for such reasons that I do not detect any clear difference between what I write as part of a more direct political or social involvement and my more academic publications. Of course, there is a difference between an essayistic intervention and a developed work. But the essay is informed by the serious intellectual investment of the latter. Naturally there are very different levels and forms of writing. One can write as a scholar or as an essayist; one can also express oneself at different levels of complexity, by handling a quite varied range of sources. But I contend that one should not consider the short interpretative essay as fundamentally separate from the thick scholarly tome with the stamp of erudition, on condition, to be sure, that the same scholarly purpose nourishes both. For myself I endeavor to mix both genres. In this respect there is an experimental nature to my work. But above all, I try to write books about politics of a different kind in order to find ways of drawing together an interested concern for civic matters and academic work. This position, I readily acknowledge, is that of a small minority within academia, but this does not seem to me to make it less worthy of defense.

Having outlined this "program," I should now attempt to answer a certain number of objections often aired against this approach, and to try to define with more precision its relation to other powerful scholarly practices. One of the main objections to the philosophical history of the political has been put forward by the historian Roger Chartier, who has criticized this "return of political" as a trite, idealistic attempt to restore the old philosophy of the free subject, whose luster had been somewhat tarnished by the social sciences.[14] In his judgment, the philosophical history of the political mistakenly fails to distinguish between the discursive and the nondiscursive. Such a criticism would appear justified in the old campaign of the social sciences against the antiquated history of ideas. But it is the essence of the philosophical history of the political to consider that social representations cannot simply be assimilated to the order of ideology; they cannot be reduced, either, to prejudices reflecting a given state of social relationships. The philosophical history of the political maintains that beyond ideologies and prejudices there are positive representations that organize the intellectual field within which lies a certain range of possibilities at a given historical moment. These representations need to be taken seriously: they constitute real and powerful infrastructures in the life of societies. In contrast to an idealist vision, which disregards the economic and social determinants structuring the field of human action, this approach sets out to enrich and make more complex the notion of determination. Alongside "passive" representations, it is consequently necessary to take into account all those "active" representations—ones that determine the questions of the moment, shape practical responses to them, and give boundaries to the field of possibilities by establishing the parameters of thought and action.

Far from taking a principled stand against social history, then, this philosophical history of the political follows its very same program while adding to it. The "ideas" that it takes into account constitute an essential part of reality, provided these ideas are defined as I have outlined above. One can even argue that the approach takes as its object the most intimate and decisive matters of social experience. Indeed, in modern society the forms of collective life exist in a permanent and constitutive tension with representations, since the structure of society is no longer a product of either nature or history, but needs to be continuously constructed and criticized.

I do not reject, for such reasons, the endeavor of social history, preferring instead the company of great writers or parliamentary orators rather than the silent and long-suffering masses. And I do not at all disdain material history (which indeed I practice in my work). For example, it is important to trace the evolution of the hand-written ballot form or to be interested in the history of the voting booth (the so-called Australian ballot). But the facts of social history reveal their meaning only when they are placed within a context and inserted into a more conceptual kind of history, which for its part is not just an analysis of the great writers, even though the latter often represent a privileged window of access onto the political culture of their time. The relationship between social history and conceptual history is parallel to that between ordinary and revolutionary periods. The conflicts between the forces of progress and reaction, between the people and the elites, between the ruled and the rulers, the clash of vested interests and prejudices, constitute the everyday side of history, an everyday scenario tirelessly repeated and revisited through successive forms of obedience or domination and freedom or oppression. But this ordinary pattern acquires a meaning only when relocated within the process of transformation of institutions and ways of thinking. Otherwise, there is an ever-present threat of anachronism, which may creep in and affect our judgment. The philosophical history of the political aims to unite both ends of the spectrum. By seeking throughout to identify the intersections between the conflicts of men and women and their representations of the world, this philosophical history conceives politics as that terrain where society is at work on itself. The aims and methods, to recall the point once again, are indissociable.

It is not therefore just a matter of doing a simple history of ideas, but rather of understanding the conditions under which the categories that reflect action are both constructed and transformed, to analyze how issues come about, how they impact the social order, tracing a framework of possibilities, delineating systems of opposition and types of available challenge. In fact, political history should not be understood as a more or less linear development, featuring a succession of conquests and defeats leading to an end of history, with democracy celebrated or freedom organized in conclusion. In a sense, there is no possible Hegelian history of the political. This approach is not only called for by what could appear to be a simple requirement of method; it also follows from the very essence of the political, which is defined by the entanglement of the orders of concepts and events, by the effect of the social upon the intellectual, and by the permanence of the need to invent the future by the distinction the old from the new.

The question of the relationship of my approach with the work of Michel Foucault is also worth raising. On this point I wish to be very clear, for the project of the philosophical history of the political recaptures Foucault's own original intention, as it was manifested clearly, or so it seems to me, both in *Madness and Civ-*

ilization and perhaps even more so in *The Order of Things*.[15] Foucault, as his category of *epistēmē* illustrates, was also interested in capturing "political rationalities" from a total perspective. But, in my opinion, Foucault remained captive of too simple an understanding of the political. He understood the political in physical or biological terms: opposing forces, processes of action and reaction, and so forth. In this respect, Foucault remained the prisoner of an excessively narrow approach to the phenomena of power. For him, the political amounted to the struggle for emancipation. His premise is the rationality of domination. In his view the analysis of power exhausted, in some sense, the question of the political, which is almost entirely understood in terms of strategic action. Although this aspect of the political is undeniable, it is perhaps not even the most important. The political field is not only organized by clearly determined forces (passions and interests). It is also the territory of experimentation and exploration. In sum, one can say that democracy is not just a solution, whose development is reducible to a confrontation—at times brutal and at times subtle—between progress and reaction (Foucault did a great deal to throw light on the subtle aspect). Democracy is also a *problem*, felt as such by the social actors. Accordingly, though I share Foucault's interests, his concern to burst the narrow limits of his discipline, and his hope to be at one and the same time historian, philosopher, and citizen, my work is nevertheless set within the framework of a different understanding of the nature of political experience.

Finally, I can clarify the approach of the philosophical history of the political by reference to the contextual history of ideas as Quentin Skinner famously defines it. Author of the excellent *Foundations of Modern Political Thought*, Skinner has sought to transcend a specific methodological dilemma, one especially pronounced in the Anglo-Saxon countries.[16] The conflict is between a philosophical reading of the major authors, based on a view of texts as something both complete and self-sufficient, and a historical reading, smacking of Marxist undertones, that tended to turn political writings into mere ideological products, born of circumstances and fully determined by them.[17] Together with his plan not to restrict himself to the major authors, Skinner, on whom J. L. Austin's work made a strong impression, sought to read the texts as linguistic acts set in conventionally recognizable fields of meaning.[18] Skinner reads texts as discourses whose aim cannot be understood unless their authors' intentions are contextualized within the set or sets of prevailing conventions.

This is an approach that has led to a major renewal of the history of ideas and has made possible a dialogue between historians and philosophers. But its stimulus to innovation, in my view, has been limited by a failure to see any difference between defending the timelessness of philosophical quandaries and defending their persistence. The terms within which the methodological debate on the history of ideas has been carried out in the United States and in Great Britain led Skinner to damn as *philosophia perennis* all attempts to establish a relationship between past and present issues.[19] (This criticism implies the possibility, I would note in passing, on envisioning modernity as a field with relatively constant features. To bear out the contention, however, would require a discussion of pertinence of the concept of "modernity" in political thought.) The conditions under which Skinner developed his criticism of the traditional history of ideas, then, have prevented him from taking the decisive step toward embracing a philosophical history of the political. But his contribution remains invaluable, and I readily acknowledge my debt to him.

A word in conclusion. The philosophical history of the political has no recipes that can be mechanically applied in order to write a book realizing the aspirations underlying the program—at least, no recipes with better instructions than in a necessarily clumsy declaration of intention of this kind. Every work of scholarship is no more than a fragile attempt to produce, through the act of *writing*, a dose of intelligibility—in the realm of the political perhaps more so than in any other.

PART II

The Voluntarist
Drive to Unity

CHAPTER 3

Revolutionary Democracy

The sovereign people? During the French Revolution, it was the order of the day as a political principle before its meaning was defined sociologically: in this concept, indissociably imperious and vague, the life-giving principle of democracy can be found. It is imperious because all power must flow from it. But it is vague because it is anonymous. And this anonymity is striking already in the iconography of the revolutionary period. Only rarely do the people appear in it as a collection of individuals or of identifiable groups. Faceless, the people most often take the form of compact mass, ordered according to a geometrical principle or symbolized by an action.

In all the representations of the Festival of the Federation, in July 1790, commemorating the first anniversary of the storming of the Bastille, it is simply one among other elements of the picture, which attempts more to express a feeling—that of a peaceful force—than to stage a population. In a number of the engravings that depict the taking of the Bastille, the people becomes an actor erased by the movement that animates it, reduced to a forest of rifles or brandished pikes, a direct force, wholly identified with its materiality. As the Revolution progressed, indeed, the abstraction of the representations of the people continuously grew. In the end it was evoked only symbolically or allegorically: the strength of a Hercules with his uplifted club,[1] the haughty presence of the inquisitorial eye, or the display of a Phrygian cap on the end of a pike.[2] An obscure principle from which everything nevertheless derived, it ultimately became unrepresentable: it became "the Yahweh of the French," as a famous engraving proclaimed.[3] It is thus available simply as a word, a pure inscription given over to the meditation of its readers, the silent evocation of an impenetrable mystery. From 1792 or 1793, a growing number of placards limited themselves to inscribing in the triangle of equality the words "sovereign people" that shine with a thousand rays of light, in the manner of those dazzling stars that are too bright to observe except through their reflected effects.

In 1793, the painter Jacques-Louis David threw the permanent gap between the people and its representation into extraordinary relief.[4] On the 17th Brumaire of the Year II, he invited the Convention to erect on the Pont Neuf a giant statue of the French people. In order to symbolize the advent of a new sovereign and the destruction of the old order, David suggested that all the remnants of the statues of the kings that used to adorn the Cathedral of Notre-Dame be gathered to form the base of the new statue. But his allegory would not end with the image of a giant standing and treading with his feet upon the debris of the monarchy. David multiplied the dimensions of his project in order to afford this effigy of the people all of the symbolic density it required: it is armed with a club to suggest its power; it is outfitted with images of liberty and equality gripped in its other hand to recall its republican attachments; there are references to outmoded superstitions to stress the triumph of reason; it is posed on a soil of medals commemorating great events; the texts of the Constitution and the Declaration of the Rights of Man and Citizen are reproduced, and so forth. Even the very substance of the statue, bronze, added to this symbology, since the metal of the colossus was supposed to be forged from the cannonballs of the enemy. The super-accumulation of allegories, however, did not suffice for David to represent the people. "This image, imposing by its forceful yet simple character," he added, "should have engraved in large characters the words *light* (on its forehead), *nature* and *truth* (on its chest), and *strength* and *courage* (on its arms)."[5] It is as if the words had to be added to the signs in order for the people truly to be seen, the work of the imagination admitting its powerlessness to accomplish the task on its own. David's project—which the Convention adopted but that never came to fruition except in the ephemeral form of a plaster model—shows in an exemplary fashion how the concept of the people struggled to incarnate itself in the revolutionary years.

The challenge of figuration traversed the entire period. It is to be noticed just as much in the theater as in the organization of festivals. When Marie-Joseph Chénier wanted to make himself the playwright of the Revolution, he hoped first of all to illustrate and celebrate the appearance of the people as the central actor of history. But though everyone on stage in his plays refers to the people, the people never appears. In most of his tragedies, the people is only evoked or invoked by other characters. While in two or three plays the list of the *dramatis personae* even includes "the People," the books lack directions for staging the protagonist. The people is simply an abstract and collective character, deprived of life and of theatrical plausibility.[6] The same defect marked the organization of the revolutionary festivals consecrated to the new sovereign: the Festival of the French People instituted in 1793 by the Convention and the Festivals of the Sovereignty of the French People and of the Regeneration of the French People put in place by the Directory in 1798 and 1799. The authorities, one senses, were preoccupied by the difficulty. "The goal of the Festival of the Sovereignty of the People involves political and metaphysical notions that it is important to make tangible," François de Neufchâteau, then minister of the interior, noted in the Year VII, in a circular sent to prepare the celebrations.[7] But the programming for the festivals shows the difficulty of living up to this order. Though it was planned for the statue of the People to be constructed as a crowned adolescent, the circular says nothing about the statue of the Sovereignty of the People, supposed to tower above it. Words, in this

case too, were the fallback, since one finds the suggestion to create banners with citations from *The Social Contract* and to throw
Edmund Burke's works on the ground to be trampled.

The notion of the people appeared in this framework as
wholly absorbed and expressed by the determinants that are associated with it. In 1789, and even more in 1848, it existed only
when thought of as a "whole," an "all," or a "unity." The *people
as totality* is not simply celebrated by Alphonse de Lamartine,
the great preacher of social unanimity as an ideology, since all
opinions united in this concept as the central actor of democratic
revolution.[8] "The voice of the people is the voice of god," several
posters proclaimed. In his notes from the spring of 1848, Victor
Hugo, too, could see the people only as a mass: "great people,"
"throng of the people," "columns of the people," "flood of the
people" were the expressions that come spontaneously to his
pen.[9] Its face is as if dissimulated and absorbed by what it expresses. Understood in this manner, the people is not simply a
political subject, but also a quality of social life: the people is always the emblem and the name of a collectivity redeemed from
appearances, saved from all determination, and isolated in its
original principles.[10]

So it is first of all the *people as a principle* that democratic
modernity affirms. A principle and a promise at the same time,
one that symbolizes through the simple presence of the word the
constitution of society as a bloc and one that universalizes the
national entity.[11] It is the truth of the social bond: it refers to a
political proposition before it is a sociological fact. What results
is an inevitable tension between the values that it incarnated and
the reality that it evoked, a political density and a sociological
flux in combination. It had an evident historical force even as its
nature appeared to be problematic. One might almost speak, in
this regard, of "the people's two bodies."[12] As a nation, the people is, whatever its abstraction, a whole and dense body, living according to the principle of unity that it expresses; but as a society, it is, by contrast, without form, a body both fugitive and

improbable. The specificity of French democracy can be understood thanks to this tension. French modernity superimposed political abstraction on sociological specificity. It exacerbated the distance between the two peoples, the nation in its abstraction and the society in its indeterminacy, and the political sphere had the permanent tendency to substitute itself for the social one. Hence, too, the ambiguity of this democracy that entered precociously into the attempt to integrate a great number in the abstract body of citizens (through universal suffrage), at the same time as it seemed to blithely accept situations of economic and social exclusion, as if the symbolic affirmation of popular unity alone sufficed for the realization of that unity.

Yet the tension between the order of the symbolic and that of the real remained even more fraught because the semantic content of the term "people" continued to be indeterminate for so long. In the eighteenth century, the article on "the People" in the *Encyclopédie*, drafted by Louis de Jaucourt, signaled with embarrassment "a collective noun that is difficult to define, since different ideas of it are at work depending on the time, place, and nature of the government."[13] The meaning of the term "people" fluctuated during the era, referring sometimes to the notion of the laboring class (an economic concept), and at other times to that of the populace (both a social and moral concept) or to that of the nation (a political concept). The lack of determinacy remained quite palpable during the revolution. It is evident during the June 1789 debate on the name of the assembly: inherited precautions and instinctive hesitations combined to lead the delegates to avoid the title of "assembly of the French people" and to give preference to "national assembly." "The word 'people,'" the Marquis de Mirabeau recognized at the time, "necessarily means too much or too little. . . . It is a word open to any use."[14] Certain delegates went so far, for such reasons, as to propose controlling the social use of the expression. In July 1791, in *L'Ami des patriotes*, Adrien Duquesnoy wrote: "If the false use of the word 'People' has been for the mischievous a pretext and a means, it has been an excuse for the simple and the credulous. It will soon be time for the Assembly to put an end to this cause of disturbance, and to recall to order with great severity anyone who uses the word 'people' in any other meaning than that which it should have."[15]

In the final analysis, the people is always both a power and an enigma. As a power, it is the source of all legitimacy; as an enigma, it presents no easily identifiable face. The latter dimension, however, remained secondary during the Revolution, so spontaneous was the assimilation of the people to the nation, a necessarily abstract form of the social totality. The people emerged clearly as an enigma only in the nineteenth century, in the double form of a menacing crowd and an unfathomable society. The fear of the people as an inorganic mass, the creature of actions and expressions both unpredictable and unmasterable, traversed the century. It marked the bourgeois of the 1830s, who conjured up the specter of the dangerous classes and barbarians who encircled them in the suburbs,[16] and later those of June 1848 or their equivalents at the end of the century, who feared the prospect of a social revolution. But the enigmatic character of the people stemmed also, and more fundamentally, from a kind of sociological uncertainty. The advent of a society of individuals made society difficult to apprehend even in the eyes of its own members. The publicists of the beginning of the nineteenth century, for example, all shared the same perplexity facing what they called "society reduced to dust." "French society is an enigma for the rest of Europe," Charles de Rémusat noted in 1826, while François Guizot spoke during the same period of the "obscure" dimension of democratic society.[17] The idea of the people remained divided between negative references to the mob—which Hugo saw as better understood as "traitor to the people"—and the confrontation with the wholly unrepresentable character of the new individualist universe.[18]

The people is like Janus: it has two faces. It is at once a danger and a possibility. It menaces the political order at the same time as it grounds it.[19] The undecided and vague character of the people in the nineteenth century combined a sociological incertitude and a philosophical perplexity. The sociological confusion made it a subject of obscure contours, which Hugo magnificently evoked in Les Misérables, observing that "the deeper we sink, the more mysterious are the workers."[20] For its part, the philosophical perplexity related to the very meaning of democracy, a regime that simultaneously is given as a solution (to the problem of foundation in a secularized world) and as a problem (the opaque character of this same foundation).

The transition from a corporatist to an individualist society makes society less representable. For how to give a form—one open to description and recognition—to an agglomeration of individuals? Whence the central problem: it is at the very moment that the principle of popular sovereignty triumphs that its face, in a sense, becomes problematic. Paradoxically, it is when representative governments are put into place that the meaning of representation is obscured. A disconnect, as a result, occurs between the right to vote as a personal right and as a condition of the production of social identities. By the same token, the very concept of representation is disarticulated: the two functions of figuration and delegation no longer overlap. Only the latter retains its clarity. Power and formalism work in tandem under these conditions. The unprecedented means of intervention that the collectivity gains are at the same time put in question, as if the newly elusive character of the subject of power secretly undermined its essence.

In this contradiction, democratic disappointment has one of its deepest roots. The French Revolution serves as a privileged terrain of observation for grasping its mechanism. For it in effect exacerbated the tension between the juridical principle of the vote and the sociological principle of identification. But, at the same time, it masked the contours of the tension, since the course of events made an abstracted and fused vision of the social possible and acceptable for a time. The French Revolution, as everyone knows, exalted the principles of unity and indivisibility.

Those words—and the preoccupation that disseminated them—were everywhere to be found. The Abbé Sieyès sounded the belief constantly: "France is and must be a single whole."[21] This celebration of unity corresponded to different preoccupations. It participated, doubtlessly, in an imperative of a political order first and foremost: to be unified in order to be strong, to overcome the weight of habit and the maneuvers of enemies. But it also referred, more profoundly, to the entire vision of a break with the old social order. Figuring society in the form of unity allowed radical difference to be thought. The opposition of old and new is most manifest when it is imagined almost physically as the confrontation of the homogeneous and the heterogeneous. The principle of unity combined opposition and power. It alone allowed the erection of a force able to reverse what people called in 1789 "the gothic colossus of the ancient constitution."[22]

The nation and the National Assembly together incarnated this alternative power. In contrast to the qualification of "third estate" which always implied finitude and subordination, the two new notions of the nation and the National Assembly connoted the advent of a completely new order. "By substituting the phrase 'National Assembly' for that of 'Third Estate,' Sieyès cut the Gordian knot of ancient privileges," one member of the Constituent Assembly explained.

> He separated the present age from those that preceded it; in place of three orders—sometimes divided, sometimes united, but always on the verge of dissolving—he presented the indivisible body of the nation, made indissoluble through the perfect reunion of all individuals in order to make its mass carry everything along. The phrase "National Assembly," finally, was like one of the words used in magic to alter the appearance of the world, and to make an invincible colossus spring forth from the earth.[23]

In 1789, the nation designated a homogeneous and complete totality, understood as the perfect antithesis of the corporate society. "The nation," Toussaint Guiraudet wrote then in a penetrating essay, "is not made up of orders; it is an aggregation of individuals."[24] Elsewhere it is affirmed that "the constitution recognizes only one corporation, that of all Frenchmen together,"[25] while Sieyès defined the nation as "the great body of the citizens." But how to constitute it and make it visible, in order that form and coherence can be given to a simple assemblage of equal individuals? It is to address this problem that the members of the Constituent Assembly assigned a central role to the work of abstraction, understood at once as ascesis and pedagogy. Sieyès well described its direction in stressing three modalities of realizing this unity: *adunation, regeneration,* and *representation.*[26]

Sieyès coined the word "adunation." It means the process (etymologically, one through which the nation is built) that forges social unity, men making the nation together, sublimating their differences in order to stop viewing one another except as co-equal citizens. It was during the great debate of autumn 1789 on the division of the realm that the term was first used. What Sieyès and the members of the Constituent Assembly wanted to erase were all the former administrative, geographical, or professional distinctions that recalled the old order of things. Hence the extreme importance they accorded to the new departmental partitioning.[27] "For a long time I have felt the need to submit the map of France to a new division," Sieyès wrote at the time. "If we miss this opportunity, it will not return, and the provinces will retain their fraternities, their privileges, their pretensions, and their jealousies eternally. Then France will never achieve that political *adunation* so necessary for a great people governed by the same laws and the same forms of administration."[28] The object was to discover a purely mechanical rationale for dividing France, one that would imply no real opposition and no actual distinction. It would rely, rather, upon a completely artificial basis, derived almost from an arithmetical principle. The reason, of course, was the need to break with the past, to allow a new perspective on things by erasing the categories that were still obsta-

cles to thought. But the objective served an even greater ambition: it appealed to the utopia of an unprecedented substitution
of the whole of society for its fragmentary parts, one that would
then permit only instrumental, and wholly neutral, division.[29]
The goal? It is clearly announced: "to ground the local and particular spirit in a national and public spirit."[30]

The citizen came to be newly defined, as part of this process,
by his distance from civil society, since the latter gives tangible
flesh to differences.[31] "Democracy," Sieyès observed, "is the
complete sacrifice of the individual to the common good, that is,
the submission of the tangible person to the abstract person."[32]
It is not really the purpose of political society, then, to reproduce
society—to "represent" it, as it were—but rather to suggest its
sublimated image, to constitute it in abstract enough a way that
it anticipates a true society of equal individuals. The merit of political society, in other words, is to attain a formalized character
as a positive utopia (rather than an unfinished or betrayed version of reality).[33]

The nation is therefore to be understood in the discourse of
the time as a society redeemed from its shadows, one having
abolished all of its contingent determinations and finally coin-
ciding with its egalitarian foundations. It is a regenerated society,
to use a term constantly deployed during the period itself.[34]
Camille Desmoulins is one of the actors who best described in ef-
fusive language this prospective transfiguration. "Do provincial
distinctions exist any longer?" he asked.

> Do you want to fragment us, to confine us, to lock us up?
> Are we not a great family, a great body, all from the same
> household? Are there hedges and barriers in the spring-
> time field? Do we not find ourselves all under the same
> tent? . . . Saint Paul, who was eloquent two or three times
> in his life, put it admirably somewhere: *All you who have
> been regenerated by baptism, you are no longer Jews, you
> are no longer Samaritans, you are no longer Romans, you*

are no longer Greeks, you are all Christians. In the same way, we have been regenerated by the National Assembly, we are no longer from Chartres or Montlhéry, no longer from Picardy or Brittany, no longer from Aix or Arras: we are all French and all brothers.[35]

The same metaphors and the same Pauline citation are to be found flowing from many pens, implacably testifying of the power of this vision of the nation as the projection and anticipation of a new society.

The work of adunation and regeneration for which the members of the Constituent Assembly hoped and prayed could not simply involve the transformation of the habitual forms of education and imagination. A particular task of representation also had to be shouldered, to give meaning and embodiment to the idea of the nation. It alone could produce the desired unity and indivisibility; it alone had the power to effectively incarnate a concept. "Only representation is the reunited people," Sieyès noted,

> since the ensemble of parties to the association cannot achieve a unity any other way. The integrity of the nation is not anterior to the will of the reunited people, which is only available through its representation. Unity begins in it. Nothing, therefore, is above representation, and it is the only organized body. Dispersed, the people is not an organized body, and has neither a singular *will* nor a singular *mind*—indeed, nothing singular at all.[36]

Representation, in other words, is not understood as a mechanical principle, like that authorizing the delegation of elected authority. It has a creative and instituting capacity unto itself. It is the means to unity and identity. If the fact of voting is a personal right, the subject of representation is not the individual considered in isolation, but the nation as a whole, that is to say the collectivity in its irreducible totality. The only identity that representation produces is that of citizenship, that of belonging to the whole. No particular identity is admissible—or even thinkable— in this framework.

Adunation, regeneration, and representation: in each case the objective is to constitute this "invincible colossus" able to dispel the possibility of the Old Regime's return and to figure the new society of equals. No subtle reasoning is needed to grasp the result: a radical antipluralism, primed to assimilate all differences to the despised category of privilege and to envision all local identities as dangerous causes of division. Hence the problem. For even if the one nation can be imaginatively conceived as a homogeneous totality, or if it can even be supposed that such is its desirable future form, the many divisions and distinctions that still run through society nonetheless remain points of repair—sometimes positive ones—for its members. That one has committed oneself to a vision of a new society does not change society by decree. The French Revolution did not stifle its efforts, outlawing corporations, parties, and all of inherited bodies of the Old Regime, of course. But in spite of trying, it did not realize the utopia of a homogeneous society for which it hankered. For this reason, utopia and reality were to continue their perverse relationship, the order of representations permanently threatening to contradict the immediate data of experience. "The assimilation of men," Sieyès wrote, "is the first condition of the grand national reunion in a *unified* people."[37] The difficulty is that the presupposition of this assimilation turned out to make society illegible and unrepresentable in its complexity. It is in this way that the radicalization of the political abstraction to which the Revolution led has to be understood: it completely disincorporated the social, offering no other identity except for communion with the whole.

The negative and destructive character of such a disincorporation was hardly perceived during the Revolution itself. No dissent was raised, for example, against the destruction of the guilds and corporations, no doubts, even in a hesitant tone. The emancipation of the individual and the freedom of the market seemed to be completely open to definition by tearing down old barriers and obstacles. Abstraction became at once a source of power and a vector of liberation. The construction of the nation of the period, it is true, also demanded combat against the external enemy and the analogous internal enemy to which the nobility came to be assimilated. But the cohesion of the struggle allowed only its positive aspects to be perceptible.

The difficulty of representing the people has to be understood in the perspective of these equivocations and ambiguities. It is the fallout of the gap, an almost constitutive gap, between the people as the legitimate sovereign, in its unity in principle, and the people as an existing society, in its actual complexity. Hence too the dimension of modern political identity that one could justly call schizophrenic: it is torn between the practical diversity of the social body and the political unity that the representative process is charged with producing. "We are a we to which reality does not correspond," as Robert Musil very suggestively puts it.[38] To this extent, the people is always marked by an internal tension: it always appears separated from itself.[39] There is thus a permanent risk that the abstract unity of the popular nation, as the legislature is intended to incarnate it, will be contradicted by the divisions and the differences that practically structure society. Fiction and reality are continuously confronted in the representative process, forming the two poles of a founding and ineliminable tension. It is a tension between a juridical and a sociological principle and at the same time the necessary distance between the figuration of reality and reality itself. It is the difference between the one and the many. Understood on this basis, the crisis of representation results neither from dysfunction nor betrayal: it is consubstantial with its very object.[40]

Only the incandescence of the *event* allows this tension to seem to relax. When the people or the nation were celebrated in 1789—the distinction between the two is not important for these purposes, since the referent is not a sociological reality but rather a historical and political force—there occurred a genuine metallurgy thanks to an event. Under its auspices the people was revealed, for the event allowed it to leave behind ambiguity and obscurity to become pure positivity, *practical power*. For a moment, the visible and symbolic orders coincided. The *people as event* can seem to resolve, for a time, the constitutive aporia of representation. In action, as indissociably lived and narrated, the people is given tangibility by what it makes happen; sociological doubts are silenced by the evidence of behaviors and activities on the move. This explains to a great extent why the crisis of representation was not exacerbated during the revolution: the visibility of the people as actor, whether in the tumult of the street or in the good behavior of patriotic festivals, periodically allowed the possibility of postponing the conceptual and practical difficulties posed by the distance between the representatives and those they represented.

But the saving availability of the people as an event also made possible disaster, a fictional and violent claim of unified representation, as in the Terror's culture of insurrection. In the Terror, politics came to be hostage of an exclusive alternative between an ordinary center and an extreme fringe. It came to seem, in other words, as if there were no space of intervention, negotiation, or conflict between submission to the established order and revolt. Indeed, the very term "insurrection" became wholly banal during the period. As a result of its invocation as a "sacred duty," insurrection became almost an ordinary political category.[41] Albert Soboul showed very usefully that insurrection as the *sans-culottes* spoke about it in the Year II did not necessarily refer to the force of arms, since it could also mean, more vaguely, a whole ensemble of actions of resistance, diverse initiatives, calls to awareness, and attitudes of vigilance, some going so far as to speak of "peaceful insurrection."[42]

Beyond all the semantic variations, there was a general deinstitutionalization of the political at work, and it is indeed in this sense that one may best understand the Terror as a whole. When, on October 10, 1793 (19 Vendémiaire, Year II), the Convention decreed that "the government of France is revolutionary unto peace," it legalized—if one may use that term—this process. "In the circumstances in which the Republic finds itself," Saint-Just remarked, "the constitution cannot be established; it would be immolated by means of itself."[43] In this framework, political life found itself emancipated from all constraint and all form. It became pure action, unmediated expression of a directly palpable will. It incarnated almost perfectly the spirit of the Revolution as Jules Michelet exalted it, "transcending space and time," condensing like a lightning bolt the energy of the whole universe and allowing a dimension of eternity to be perceived in the fugitive moment. It is to such a utopia that the culture of insurrection of these years related.

No one emphasized its burning exigency better than the Marquis de Sade. Through a scandalous and inspiring metaphor, the writer hoped to suggest how the radical transgression of established moral rules alone gives freedom its meaning, likening the shattering of moral customs to that of political institutions. One must read *Philosophy in the Bedroom* (along with its appendix, *Yet Another Effort, Frenchmen, If You Would Become Republicans!*) to best grasp the appeal that a radically deinstitutionalized politics exerted and the meaning that it bore. As much as Jacques René Hébert and his *enragés*, Sade is the great theorist of insurrection. He wrote:

> Insurrection . . . has got to be a republic's permanent condition. Hence it would be no less absurd than dangerous to require that those who are to insure the perpetual *immoral* upheaval in the machinery of state themselves be very *moral* beings, for the *moral* state of man is one of peace and tranquility, whereas the *immoral* state of a man is one of perpetual unrest that brings him nearer to

that necessary state of insurrection in which the republican must always keep the government of which he is a
member.[44]

In this subversion, the Revolution is ready to devour itself, ex-
piring from a radicalism that consumes it.

The Terror could imagine the deinstitutionalization of the
political only in pretending to ground itself *sociologically* and
morally by compensation through an unprecedented kind of fusion between the people and its representatives, one that would
lead beyond the tension between representative government and
direct democracy. The critique of the dysfunctionality of the representative system led the *identification* of the people and power
to seem like the condition of the full achievement of sovereignty.
If in 1792 Maximilien Robespierre indicted representative despotism, in 1794 he legitimated his action based on the presupposition of the fusion between the people and the Convention, the
latter defined *a priori* as a simple "abridged people." The Mountain went so far as to note, in this vein, that they counted as the
"living body of public opinion."[45] The organicist metaphors are,
indeed, continuously present in the political texts of the period.
The Committee of Public Safety addressed the revolutionary
committees, for instance, by saying: "You are like the hands
of the political body of which the Convention is the head and
whose eyes we are."[46] It was thus thanks to a conception of representation as incarnation that the founding aporias of representative government were overcome.[47] Robespierre, as François
Furet justly put it,

> mythically reconciled direct democracy and the represen-
> tative principle, by placing himself at the very pinnacle
> of a pyramid of equivalences whose maintenance his
> word guaranteed day after day. He was the people in the
> sections, the people for the Jacobins, the people in na-
> tional representation; and it was this transparency be-
> tween the people and all the places where one spoke in

their name . . . that it is constantly necessary to institute, control, and reestablish, as the condition of legitimate power.[48]

The thought allowed Robespierre to propose, on the eve of May 31, 1793, "that the people, *in the National Convention,* rise in insurrection against all of the corrupted deputies"—as if the people and the Convention were henceforth a single thing.[49] In the course of the constitutional debate of June 1793, a group of deputies of the Mountain cried out, in this spirit, that "the people is here," pointing to the rows of the assembly.[50]

The people? It is sovereign. One and indivisible, therefore, just like sovereignty is. It existed for the Mountain solely as totality in action, perfectly adequate proxy for the concept of the general will and social practice. It was neither an aggregation of individuals nor a conglomerate of corporations or sections. Saint-Just went so far as to wish that national representation could be elected by the whole people as a body, and accused the Marquis de Condorcet's electoral project of attaining only a "speculative general will."[51] The electoral principle, obligatorily grounded on the expression of a choice or preference by individuals, is thus not central for the Mountain. They tend to transform it into a whole series of dispositions—vote by acclamation or the organization of great assemblies—whose function is to socialize its material organization, with the result that at the limit individual opinions are erased, melting into one single voice. What Condorcet understood as resulting from a meticulously organized deliberative process Robespierre and Saint-Just viewed simply as the expression of a fused people.

Hence the evident impossibility for the members of the Convention to reduce the notion of the people to some sociological definition. It designates neither a group nor a class, but a *moral principle.* For them, democracy draws its coherence and efficiency from a double process of moral conversion of the representatives and of regeneration of the people. "If the representative body is not pure and almost identified with the people, liberty is abolished," Robespierre says.[52] For him, the virtue of the deputies is at once the condition of their resemblance to the people (since the latter is virtuous by nature), and hence of adequate representation, and the corrective factor of potential malfunction of the political system.[53] But the democratic achievement also presupposed, for the Mountain, the existence of a people who deserve their new power. The centrality of the theme of regeneration in their discourse and the call for the advent of a "new man" followed.[54] "It is necessary, in a fundamental sense, to recreate the people in order to render liberty to them," according to Jean-Nicolas Billaud-Varenne's celebrated formula.[55] The Terror therefore came to be understood as the means for "creating a national character that, more and more, identifies the people with its constitution."[56] In this perspective, the people had to be remodeled in a ceaseless double campaign, political exclusion of everything alien from its body and moral regeneration of what remained.

The coalescence of the people in event and insurrection, of course, transcended and outlived the Terror. It is also what gave the revolutionary days of July 1830 or February 1848 their particular tone, allowing the sentiment of a reabsorption of all distinctions in the actions of a unified people—the perfect incarnation of its concept—to re-emerge. Eugène Delacroix expressed it very well in the famous painting of 1830, *Liberty Leading the People*. The people as reality and the people as idea fuse in this painting, suggesting a situation in which the social becomes a pure principle of action. The three features of the symbol of unity (liberty carrying its flag), the representation of classes (the three figures of the street urchin, the worker, and the student), and the undifferentiated mass are in fact superimposed on one another harmoniously, allowing reality to rejoin its representation.[57] One has the impression, before this image, that the people comes into existence through collective action, somehow emerging as both the director and actor of its own destiny. No one has better described this people that accedes to the plenitude of itself in the movement of history than Victor Hugo, when he celebrated in *Les Misérables* the instaurating power of the insurrection, depicted as a "volcano," opposed to the uniquely negative energy of the riot. "It is then," he writes, "that the social masses, the very foundation of civilization, the consolidated group of superimposed and cohering interests, the venerable profile of old France, constantly appear and disappear through the stormy clouds of systems, passions, and theories."[58] It is in the event that the people gathers together to take on a recognizable face and gives itself an audible voice. Many contemporaries celebrated its tangible presence in the springtime of 1848. "The French," so Victor Lefranc summed up, "are the people of the mass uprising. When they act in a mass, a wind kicks them up, a spark electrifies them, a light shines on them, a voice speaks through them."[59] The people is indeed in this case truly universal, a realized promise of social totality, and an immediately active force of sovereignty. But how can it retain a recognizable form, and how to hear its disappeared voice when the event is over and done? There is the whole question of democratic politics.

CHAPTER 4

The Republic of Universal Suffrage

The republican idea acquired a far more complex significance in France after 1830. It no longer designated a particular type of political system that referred only to the memory of 1792 or evoked the government of ancient cities. Identified with the theme of universal suffrage, reference to the republic neatly concentrated a whole ensemble of social and cultural aspirations into a single word. The republic of universal suffrage implied, above all, the search for a society without divisions. Indeed, the central problem of the first years of the July monarchy was that of social division. The onset of industrialization widened schisms in the social fabric at the same time that the disappointment of the hopes raised by the 1830 Revolution aggravated political tensions. Such was the context in which the figure of the proletarian emerged. "The proletarian remains excluded," summarized Auguste Blanqui in 1832. "Cease then, oh noble bourgeois, to repulse us from your breast, for we too are men and not machines," demanded one of the first workers' journals, the *Artisan*,[1] in 1830, while Alphonse de Lamartine wished that the name of the proletariat, "this base, injurious, pagan word, [should] disappear from the language as the proletarian himself must disappear little by little from society."[2]

The demand for universal suffrage, which emerged at the beginning of the July monarchy, was linked to the demand for social inclusion. In 1789, the demand for political equality had derived simply from the primary principle of civil equality; the essential struggle had been waged in the realm of civil rights, around the destruction of privilege and the suppression of legal distinctions between individuals. At that time, suffrage merely extended the new society of equal individuals into the political realm; by 1830, however, social distinctions and differences of status were no longer expressed in the civil domain. The idea of universal suffrage acquired a directly social dimension, while the problem of integration was displaced accordingly: henceforth, the question of equality among men would be played out on the social and political stage. This explains the centrality of the figure of the proletarian after 1830, just as in 1789 all struggle had been organized around the figure of the individual. But the question of universal suffrage was not only subject to a political shift between these two periods; it was also accompanied by new anxiety about the social. In 1789, suffrage had been understood in terms of the dominant abstract universalism; at the beginning of the July Monarchy, in contrast, it assumed a class dimension. In less than half a century, the emergence of the issue of the workers profoundly altered the terms in which social relations were understood. Those excluded from political rights would in future be identified as a social group. "Are the powerful and rich worth more than we are?" asked Achille Roche in his *Manuel du prolétaire*, a question that summarized the basis of his political claim.[3] By 1830–34, reflection on universal suffrage was no longer a general philosophical interrogation of the modern individual citizen, nor *a fortiori* a questioning from above of the relationship between number and reason; it was being expressed *from below*.

Throughout the July Monarchy, the theme of universal suffrage played exactly the same role as had the demand for civil equality in 1789. Both cases reveal the same struggle against feudalism and the Old Regime. The critique of feudalism and the denunciation of the electoral system functioned in exactly the same way during the two periods, the same words and the same expressions returning to denounce caste and privilege. The 200,000 eligible voters were assimilated to the old aristocrats, just as those who were excluded from suffrage became the new Third Estate. Now, however, political monopoly took the place of the former social privileges. The *Journal du peuple* wrote in 1840, "Bad legislatures, bad laws, and the anguish of the proletariat are the results of the monopoly. What then is a free people among whom only 200,000, out of 30 million, are called upon to name their representatives? There is an anomaly here that must end."[4]

Such words spilled forth from all the pens of the day, repeating *ad infinitum* this condemnation of limited suffrage as a remnant of the old figure of privilege in the new France. Thus, the struggle for universal suffrage is a direct descendant of the revolutionary movement. Moreover, it is striking that this same period witnessed the popular reappropriation of the French Revolution. All republicans and social reformers of the period shared the same outlook. It is significant that in 1839, Pagnerre, the publisher of the republican causes, put out a cheap edition of the Abbé Sieyès's *What Is the Third Estate?*[5] Étienne Cabet's *Popular History of the French Revolution* (1839) was enormously successful, and Albert Laponneraye's *History of the French Revolution* was reissued several times between 1838 and 1840. From the earliest days of the 1830 Revolution, the Society of Friends of the People, then the Society of the Rights of Man and Citizen, nourished the memory of the great moments of the Revolution. They circulated the works of Robespierre, Saint-Just, and Jean-Paul Marat, and sold small plaster busts of illustrious deputies to the Convention. Certainly, more radical circles celebrated 1793 and Robespierre's declaration of rights above anything else, but the sense of parallels between the conquest of civil equality in 1789 and the conquest of political suffrage in the 1830s was omnipresent even in the most moderate circles. The term parallel is almost inappropriate if it implies only resemblance; there was in fact a deeper identity between the two movements: in both cases, the principle at stake was that of social inclusion. Hence, the striking specificity of the history of universal suffrage in France.

This convergence was also the source of the divorce between French society and the monarchy. The monarchical idea in France had been overburdened with an accumulation of negative images until, in the end, it came to be associated with every possible form of inequality and social division: fiscal exemptions, social privileges, inequalities of status, electoral barriers, even economic differences. The divorce was definitively accomplished in the 1830s: the monarchy ceased to be conceived of as a simple political regime whose essence might survive its more or less fortunate historical instantiations. Identified with privilege, the monarchical idea would, in the future, represent a totally negative principle, economic as well as social. The image of the monarchy was superimposed on that of the Old Regime just as it was on that of capitalism. The pamphlets and booklets of 1831–35 make this quite clear, in terms that scarcely vary between republicans as moderate as Timon Cormenin and reformers as radical as Laponneraye. The *Lettre aux prolétaires*, which the latter published in 1833, is entirely representative of this Manichaean vision, which led to attributing to the republic every conceivable virtue. "With the monarchy," he wrote, "there are privileged and proletarians; with the republic there are only citizens who possess equal rights, and all of whom participate in forming laws and electing public officials."[6]

The socialist idea, in turn, remained wholly rooted in republicanism, seeming only to implement it in the specific domains of the economic and the social. This becomes very clear upon leafing through the *Revue républicaine* (1834–35), the first publication of the left whose theoretical quality was equal to that of the great liberal reviews. It was in particular Martin Bernard, a printer, who published there two articles with the suggestive title: "On the Means of Bringing the Republic into the Workshop." He wrote:

It is impossible to deny the analogy of the relationship between today's man of the *workshop* and the former

man of the castle, the *serf*. . . . Prejudice has so distorted
the consciousness of the masses that we find the proletarian who well understands that a king is a dispensable
cog in the political order, and yet who refuses to believe
that the same can be accomplished in the industrial
order. . . . In the 18th century, politics displayed the same
character as does industry today. . . . Isn't the workshop a
monarchy in miniature?[7]

These brief phrases say everything, prefiguring Alexandre
Ledru-Rollin and Louis Blanc, Marc Sangnier and Jules Guesde.
The demand for universal suffrage, in its association with the
generic critique of monarchy, formed the original and constitutive basis of modern French political culture. Consequently, in
the 1830s the idea of universal suffrage evoked a form of society
more than it defined a precise technique of political participation;
it was nourished by singularly powerful images and undergirded
by violent rejections, while remaining institutionally vague.

Apart from its demand for social inclusion, the theme of electoral reform catalyzed a whole ensemble of political and economic
claims. Electoral reform played the role of a universal political
remedy, which should provide answers to the great problems of
the moment: the suppression of corruption, the erection of affordable government, respect for the general good, the need for
social peace. Criticism of the electoral system encompassed and
explained all: political monopoly was believed to be the source of
all evils and disturbances.[8]

One of the central themes of republican literature under the
July Monarchy is the association of limited suffrage with corruption. Cormenin ably summarized the argument in his highly
influential pamphlet, *Ordre du jour sur la corruption électorale
et parlementaire*.[9] Corruption, this scourge that ate away at "the
heart and bowels of France," originated, he believed, in the electoral system. As he saw it, individual disorder and the absence of
public morality logically derived from the narrow base of the

electoral system: they simply extended the initial corruption of political representation. "Seeking to sweep away corruption without introducing universal suffrage is to attempt a useless exertion," concluded Ledru-Rollin for his part; "it will restrict evil, but will not eliminate it."[10] Universal suffrage, wrote the *Journal du peuple*, "renders corruption impossible or impotent; it will substitute compact masses for the fat bourgeois cliques, for these minorities of privilege."[11] The people, on the other hand, were essentially incorruptible, in so far as they constituted a social unity. They were not corruptible in the sense of possessing moral virtue, as Saint-Just and Robespierre understood it, but in a more trivial, economic sense: the broadening of suffrage no longer permitted the distorted distribution of public goods, but led almost automatically to equal distribution. "Elections are corrupted with crosses and posts, but one cannot buy the masses," says Stendhal.[12] The number of 200,000 electors was often paralleled to that of 200,000 officials, as if the ministry were implicitly accused of having bought each vote with the offer of a job.

The theme of affordable government almost naturally elaborated upon the theme of corruption. Here again, Cormenin gave a classic formulation in his *Lettres sur la liste civile*, published for the first time in 1832. Throughout the July Monarchy, republicans were convinced that representative government could be nothing more than economic government. Moderates and radicals agreed in their assessment that bureaucracy was not a natural phenomenon, that it was only a perverse effect engendered by insufficiently democratic power. "Be republican because under the republic, you will have no more taxes to pay, the rich alone will pay them; because you will elect your deputies and your officials; because you will have an affordable government": Laponneraye used expressions very much like those of Cormenin in his *Lettres aux prolétaires*.[13] The rejection of the monarchy inherent in this approach was of a very different nature from the rejection characteristic of the revolutionary period. Here the monarchy was not only challenged as a political form: it was also denounced as a social form. The consequence of this was the veritable reinvention of the republican idea in 1848. The republic of universal suffrage that emerged at that time was not a direct continuation of the Marquis de Condorcet's rational republic or of Robespierre's avenging republic. It was inscribed in a new understanding of the relationship between the social and the political.

On March 5, 1848 a decree of the provisional government instituted direct universal suffrage. All men over the age of twenty-one would henceforth be called upon to elect their deputies, without property qualifications or restrictions of capacity. One name symbolized the accomplishment of this revolution: Ledru-Rollin. Since February 22, *La Réforme*, which he advised, had simultaneously demanded Guizot's resignation and the institution of the universal vote. Ledru-Rollin's contemporaries considered him to be the true founder of universal suffrage; Louis Blanc, Adolphe Crémieux, and Victor Hugo would all recall this at his graveside.[14] Throughout the 1840s, he made himself the tireless apostle of popular sovereignty, proliferating pamphlets, petitions, and depositions of legislative projects, at the very moment that the July Monarchy seemed to have disarmed its critics and achieved stability. Ledru-Rollin incarnated an entire generation of progressive writers for whom the republican ideal was inextricably linked with universal suffrage, championing this "sacred ark of democracy" of which Louis Blanc, Jules Ferry, and Léon Gambetta were also singing the praises.

In urging the provisional government to proclaim universal suffrage without delay, Ledru-Rollin only continued his earlier struggle; his role was hardly surprising. More unexpected, however, was the general approval with which the decision was greeted. All doubts, hesitations, objections were swiftly swept away; even as many partisans still believed it to be a proposal for the long term, universal suffrage abruptly imposed itself with a force of truth. Cormenin, charged by Ledru-Rollin with preparing the decree to establish the new electoral system, raised only the question of soldiers' and domestics' rights to vote. But the members of the provisional government swept away his hesitations almost without discussion.[15] Technical objections against the possibility of rapidly reading millions of ballot papers bearing several names each—the principle of the list system had been retained—were quickly dismissed as well. Seizing upon the problem, this Academy of Sciences initially urged caution, calculating, for example, that the reading of the Paris lists by traditional means would take 354 days! But it later revised its opinion, putting its methodological uncertainties to rest.[16]

Not a single voice within the public was raised in protest or uncertainty; no questions were asked; the cautious and the critics miraculously disappeared. Reform was no longer the issue: the principle of universal suffrage was immediately evident in all of its simplicity and radicalism. Acceptance and enthusiasm were also universal; no one even dreamed of discussing or commenting upon means of implementing the new law. Neither the departmental list system, the abandonment of the second ballot, nor the vote for soldiers was contested. These procedures seemed to be simple details, overshadowed by the magnitude of the event. The dominant sentiment everywhere was that something great had just taken place. Every one spoke of universal suffrage in lyrical and emotional terms: country *curés* and bishops, *petits bourgeois* of the towns and great landed proprietors, journalists and intellectuals, conservatives and traditionalists.[17]

How are we to make sense of this striking conversion and abrupt reversal? Many historians have described this "spirit of 1848" as extraordinarily enthusiastic and optimistic, a singular crossbreeding of republican utopias and Christian sentiment; but they have generally done so in order to circumscribe it by squeezing it into the frame of exceptional circumstance, underscoring with a kind of relief the resumption of the "normal" course of history in May, as political and social conflicts intensified under the pressure of the critical economic conditions. And yet, far from constituting a sort of parenthesis in the history of French democracy, the months of March and April 1848 reveal some of its most deep-seated characteristics.

The *Bulletin de la République*, the provisional government's official newspaper, directed by Ledru-Rollin, with the assistance of George Sand, aptly describes the tone of general enthusiasm and the meaning that the inauguration of universal suffrage had for contemporaries. According to the editorial the first number, dated March 13, 1848: "The Republic opens a new era for the people. Deprived of their political rights until now, the people, above all the people of the countryside, counted for nothing in the nation." Universal suffrage was not believed to be a technique of popular power so much as a kind of sacrament of social unity, as the provisional government's *Déclaration* of March 19, 1848, written by Lamartine, made vividly clear. "The provisional electoral law that we have drawn up is the most extensive law of any time or place to call the people to the exercise of man's highest right, his own sovereignty," it stated. "The right of election belongs to all without exception. *From the promulgation of this law, there is no longer a proletariat in France.*"[18] This last expression is extraordinary, revealing the fundamental association between the suffrage question and the issue of social division. Universal suffrage was seen as a rite of passage, a ceremony of inclusion. As the first elections drew near, the *Bulletin de la République* noted thus, "The Republic, which excludes none of its sons, calls you all to public life; *it will be like a new birth, a baptism, a regeneration.*"[19]

For two months, in Paris as well as in the provinces, numerous festivals celebrated the new social unity, while trees of liberty were planted everywhere. Unfortunately, there is no good synthesis of the ceremonies and national festivals of the Second Republic that would permit an assessment comparable to that of Mona Ozouf on the revolutionary period.[20] But the accounts of the main local studies, as well as the readily available iconography, reveal a few general tendencies, most notably their diffuse religiosity. In all cases, it is clear that the essence of this religiosity lay in the celebration of social unity. Numerous engravings represent allegories of fraternity that bring together workers, peasants, and intellectuals, or show parades that unite all trades and social conditions in a single procession. Some testify to extraordinary gestures; in Millery, in the Lyonnais countryside, we see bourgeois serving a table of peasants as a sign of fraternity during a democratic banquet.[21] In Avignon, the representatives of two rival groups pardon one another, and embrace solemnly during a ceremony organized by the local republican committee.[22] On April 20, an enormous festival of fraternity crowned this movement, bringing almost a million people together in Paris. No such gathering had been organized since the Festival of Federation in 1790. In *La Cause du peuple*, George Sand offers an account of unbridled lyricism and shares the general enthusiasm. A rapid survey of the Paris press bears witness. *La Réforme* spoke of a "baptism of liberty"; *Le Siècle* celebrated the unanimity that reigned; *Le National* rejoiced in the hundreds of thousands of voices joined together in a single cry proclaiming "that there was no longer any kind of division within the great French family." Even the austere *Constitutionnel* found warm words to speak of a "real family delight."

The demonstration of April 20 clearly expressed the belief that social division had been overcome by universal suffrage, that unity had been rediscovered. Far from being treated as a condition of pluralism, which permitted the expression of professional differences, or the diversity of social interests, the advent of universal suffrage in France was interpreted as a symbol of national concord and of entry into a new political era. Ledru-Rollin explained this in the *Bulletin de la République* in striking terms that are worth recording:

All living forces of this multiplicitous being that is called the people joined together on the historical stage on April 20 to announce to the world that the solution of all political problems weighs no more than a grain of sand in its powerful hand. Political science is now known to us. It has not revealed itself to a single individual, but reveals itself to all, on the day that the Republic proclaims the principle of the sovereignty of all. This political science will henceforth be one of great and simple application. It will involve nothing more than convoking the people in great masses, the total sovereign, and calling upon unanimous consent to those questions about which the popular conscience speaks so eloquently and unanimously by acclamation.[23]

It is easy to mock such illusions. Since Marx, there has been no shortage of outside witnesses or historians to speak of these sentimental feelings and aspirations toward unity with disdain or condescension. While it is easy and tempting to share their judgment, we must refrain. Far from suggesting a passing rhetorical illusion, or a simple overflowing of good feeling, the statements of Ledru-Rollin express, on the contrary, something profoundly constitutive of French political culture. In their romantic or utopian fashion, they express the essential illiberalism of French democracy. This aspiration to unity was founded on the idea that pluralism was divisive. Certainly, after May 1848, economic difficulties and political confrontations removed all visible consistency from this theme. But the spirit of 1848 did not lose its character of revelation: for a short time, and in its own language, it incarnated the republican utopianism that was the basis of French democracy in the postrevolutionary context. The first universal elections, which took place on April 23, 1848, strikingly illustrate this belief that the object of voting was more to celebrate social unity than to exercise a specific act of sovereignty or to arbitrate between opposing points of view.

By an accident of the calendar, election day fell on Easter Sunday. This coincidence gave rise to a multitude of images and metaphors. Crémieux, a member of the provisional government, spoke of the "day of social regeneration," and everywhere homilies and political declarations alike associated the resurrection of Christ with the resurrection of the people. The sacramental dimension of the advent of universal suffrage was thus reinforced. Lamartine recalled this, using the words of his contemporaries:

> The dawn of salvation rose over France on the day of the general election. It was Easter day, a period of pious solemnity chosen by the provisional government so that the people's work would neither distract nor offer any pretext for shirking the popular duty, and so that the religious reflections, which hover over the human spirit during these days consecrated to commemorating a great cult, make their way into public reflections and give the sanctity of religion to liberty.[24]

The unfolding of the elections themselves helped to reinforce this religious character. Balloting having been arranged to take place at county seats, voters from villages often traveled to the polls together in great processions that crisscrossed the countryside.[25] Many witnesses have described these lay processions, preceded by drums and flags, led by mayors and, in some cases, accompanied by *curés*. Tocqueville gave the classic description in the celebrated pages of his *Recollections*. Significantly, contemporary images often represent the ballot boxes of the occasion placed upon altars that are flanked by republican symbols, as if the box were the political equivalent of the sacred altar, sign of the invisible but active spirit of the people united by the Eucharist of the ballot. This symbology struck a number of foreign travelers.[26] The calm and order that reigned over these first elections can only underscore this dimension of unanimity that was associated with universal suffrage. On the day after the ballot, newspapers commented that all had gone quietly and smoothly. "This first effort at universal suffrage," noted *La Réforme* on April 24, "took place everywhere with great ease—one can even say, with the greatest regularity." Universal suffrage was immediately legitimated. "This test is conclusive," one reads in the *Bulletin de la République*, "and if a few timid spirits still had doubts about the easy and complete application of universal suffrage, those doubts have been alleviated by the admirable spectacle just witnessed in Paris."[27] Almost seven million electors went to the polls on April 23, representing about 83.5 percent of registered voters.[28] Electoral participation had broken all records.

The images of social communion that were tied to the entry of the masses into political life extended into the association of universal suffrage with the idea of social peace. A famous engraving of the period represents a worker with a ballot paper in one hand and a rifle in the other. While putting the former into a ballot box, he pushes away the latter. "This is for a foreign enemy," reads the legend, referring to the rifle; "this is how we loyally fight adversaries at home," it explains, designating the ballot paper. The idea was widely shared at the time that the inclusion of everyone in political life, by the extension of the right to vote, would suppress revolutionary ferment. This theme had already appeared, albeit in a precocious fashion, at the beginning of the July Monarchy period. Charles de Coux, a close associate of Félicité Lamennais, had used this argument in 1831 to justify electoral reform:

> Those who refuse the right of suffrage to the working classes spread a disorder throughout the country that will sweep them away. Deprived of such a right, the working classes can only make their presence felt in the city by entering it as a live force, like a devastating flood or an all-consuming fire. With this right, they will have residence there, something to lose if that residence is violated, hearths to defend, homes for which to plead.[29]

At their strongest, in the campaign of 1839–40, the republicans permanently took up this arithmetic of conflict; they were certain that the universal vote was the only means to truly end revolution. The central committee of Paris from the 1841 session, for example, concluded with this theme. "Universal suffrage, far from weakening guarantees of tranquility, will, on the contrary, have the certain effect of closing the era of revolutions forever."[30] Ledru-Rollin, Armand Marrast, Étienne Arago, Lamennais: all celebrated suffrage during these years as "eminently pacificatory." Seen in this light, universal suffrage has an undeniably utopian aspect; it symbolized the dawning of a thoroughly homogeneous, nonexclusive society, which would constitute a sort of end to history. Social divisions were conflated with geographic frontiers, and the foreigner was construed as the figure who would, from that point on, simply be outside the political community.

Universal suffrage also had a cathartic function; it was a practical means by which politics could be transformed. At the beginning of the 1870s, the founding fathers of the Third Republic would resume the struggle to defend universal suffrage, and denounce the threats that called it into question. Marx is known to have ferociously denounced the "magnanimous intoxication of fraternity" of the spring of 1848 and to have disdained Lamartine, who said that the provisional government had deferred "this terrible misunderstanding that exists between the different classes."[31] But his critique was more than a simple expression of his aversion for moderation. Marx was among those who best understood at that time that the specific character of French democracy found expression in the denial of conflict and division. On this point, he precisely distinguished between French and English political experience. "Universal suffrage, which was regarded as the motto of universal brotherhood," he writes, "has become a battle cry in England. There universal suffrage was the direct content of revolution; here [in England], revolution is the direct content of universal suffrage."[32] The statement well illustrates the particularity of the relationship between the political and the social in French politics. The political sphere was both institution and set-up of the social; it did not function only, as in England and the United States, to guarantee liberties and to regulate collective life.

How to take further this singular characteristic that we have encountered since the revolutionary period? How may we understand the curious amalgam of the aspiration to unanimity and the egalitarian formalism that was associated with the idea of universal suffrage in France? What is at issue here is the manner in which pluralism is understood. All conflict seems to be a threat to social unity because it is understood solely as radical division, like that between the old and new, between the Old Regime and the Revolution. Pluralism is unthinkable without a suspension of the original rupture; it is interpreted as the result of misunderstanding or else as the simple conflict of personal ambitions.

Class conflict itself was, in a certain sense, interpreted in terms of the revolutionary cleavage, of the confrontation between republic and monarchy that stretched across the whole of the nineteenth century. The consequence was the permanent oscillation between the fantasm of consensus and the menace of civil war that structured nineteenth-century political life. There was little room within this framework for a pluralist democracy of interests, just as there was little room for reformist strategy. Universal suffrage was by no means believed to be the instrument of a pluralist debate. Elections were not expected to effect arbitration or choice, at least not as long as the Revolution was believed to be over and the Old Regime definitively abolished. Nor were elections expected to bring social diversity into the sphere of politics. Rather, in 1848, the act of voting was understood to be a gesture of adherence, a symbolic expression of membership in the collectivity. On April 23, there was no distinction between collective arrivals at country seats and individual voting. At that time, suffrage had a power equal to that found in one-party states.[33] Even if events quickly gave popular expression to its dimension of arbitration,[34] the utopia of *suffrage as communion* continued to constitute the limiting horizon of the French representation of politics.

For the same reason, the relationship between "formal" democracy and "real" democracy acquired a very specific character in France. Beyond the always difficult articulation of law and practice and the always impure coincidence of interests and good intentions—which constitute the normal field of democracy—democratic formalism played a role that was both more central and more ambiguous. More than anywhere else, formal democracy in France constituted the *horizon* of real democracy: it was not only its *origin* or juridical foundation. In addition, French democracy endlessly aspired to an abstraction to a realizable form of the political ideal: it aspired to a society without class, without personal conflict, without misunderstanding, freed of all attachment to the past, and eternally devoted to celebrating its unity. Economic competition was soundly rejected for these same reasons, and opposed with regulatory models that were based on collective organization and centralized cooperation. Thus, the same illiberal threat—in the philosophically precise sense of the rejection of pluralism—runs through several dimensions of French culture. Criticism of political parties, denunciation of economic competition, and suspension of social division constituted three facets of the same political vision. In this sense, the spirit of the spring of 1848 remained faithful to the spirit of Jacobinism: only it was a pacified and sentimental version.

The connivance between the Catholic Church and the republican spirit of the spring of 1848 also had its origin here. The clergy blessed liberty trees, and commemorated the victims of the February days, because it was in agreement with the aspirations to unanimity and union that were being expressed in society. Paradoxically, then, the Church accepted in the emerging republic only that which was both its most archaic and its most utopian: its radical illiberalism. Similarly, republicans and socialists made Jesus Christ the "first republican" or "the brother of all proletarians" because of an exactly symmetrical ambiguity, as the iconography of the period profusely illustrates.[35] This also explains the rejection of Protestantism by all the social writers of the period. Cabet or Pierre Leroux, Philippe Buchez or Louis Blanc, shared the same point of view: they hated the individualist and rationalist character of Protestantism, and saw in the Catholic spirit, taken in its broadest sense, the religious matrix of socialism, and the modern republic.

In 1848, the "utopian republic" lasted only the spring. But one cannot judge it by this fugitive appearance. In effect, it expressed, with as much candor as ardor, one of the most profound traits of French political culture: the aspiration to unity and consensus in the political transfiguration of the social bond.

PART III

The Allure
of Rationalism

CHAPTER 5

François Guizot and the Sovereignty of Reason

The Restoration (1814/15–1830) in France was a true golden age of political reflection. After the excesses of the French Revolution and the Napoleonic Empire, all writers began to pose the question of what the proper foundations were of a social and political order that would both achieve stability and protect liberties. From this came a central preoccupation: to allow politics to leave behind the domain of the passions and to enter the Age of Reason, and to substitute for the vagaries of the will the regularities of a scientific order. From all quarters sounded a critique of the dogma of popular sovereignty, accusing it of having created the intellectual framework making the Terror possible. The search was on for a rational government and a scientific politics. Indeed, the idea is so common at the time as to be banal. It is to be found just as much in Auguste Comte as in François Guizot, in Benjamin Constant as in Charles Dunoyer. And it is not even really a novelty. In *De la littérature considérée dans ses rapports avec les institutions sociales* (1800), Mme de Staël had already expressed to a large public the exigency of rationality that the most serious works of the Ideologues obeyed.[1]

Efforts to scientifically ground politics and morality had been deployed in three directions: social mathematics (Pierre-Simon Laplace or the Marquis de Condorcet), social physiology (Xavier Bichat, Jean-Georges Cabanis, or Philippe Pinel), and political economy (Piererz Louis Roederer, the Count Destutt de Tracy,

Jean-Baptiste Say). But these different turn-of-the-century "attempts," as Auguste Comte would later call them, no longer appeared sufficient by the end of the Empire and the beginning of the Restoration. Rooted in the idea of an extinction of the political inherited from the eighteenth century, they simply provided an orienting frame of reference for the new generation that faced the practical task of elaborating institutions and founding a government. Guizot's intervention, along with that of the other Doctrinaires (Pierre Paul Royer-Collard, Charles Rémusat, the Duc de Broglie), must be understood in this context.

Everyone who has ever heard of Guizot associates him with the line "Enrichissez-vous!" (get rich).[2] The famous old aphorism suffices to summarize the man in the memory of most. Guizot (1787–1874) remains the vague symbol of business interests triumphant, as well as of the mediocrity of ambition, and the political blindness, that characterized the July Monarchy. Forgotten, in this stereotype, is that Guizot was also one of the most prolific and important historians and political theorists of the nineteenth century; for almost a century, his enormous number of published works (more than fifty volumes) has hardly been read. As a historian, he has been eclipsed by Jules Michelet, Edgar Quinet, and even Augustin Thierry; as a liberal publicist, by Benjamin Constant and Alexis de Tocqueville; and as a statesman, by Adolphe Thiers. But Guizot is every bit their equal, and the proscription of which he remains the object makes for a singular exception to the contemporary rediscovery of many other political writers of the first half of the nineteenth century.

No doubt, the austerity of his personality, his inflexibility, and the many hatreds that he provoked, have played their part in this oblivion. Certainly one finds in him none of the usual elements that would afford him a favorable place in history. The left, for whom he was the incarnation of bourgeois reaction, held him in contempt. In fact, Karl Marx reserved him place of shame in the "Holy Alliance" haunted by the specter of communism. To his own class he became *persona non grata*—the scapegoat for the collapse of the July monarchy.[3]

But the oblivion that Guizot has suffered has another meaning too. It is as if the man and the work have had to be effaced because of a deterministic philosophy of history—a sociological one (the rise of the bourgeoisie) or an economic one (the development of capitalism)—a stage of which they are then implicitly thought to have simply reflected. The failure of memory thus has a kind of *theoretical status*. Liberalism as an exercise of political reflection and the so-called liberal state as a political form and as a political practice are not thought to have their own independence. They are taken into account only on the condition that they point somewhere else: the difficult emergence of political democracy or the rise of the capitalist mode of production. It is the stages of industrialization and the conditions for the accumulation of capital, the birth of the labor movement and the struggles for economic emancipation and universal suffrage, the forms of repression and social control, the movement of ideologies and utopias, the vicissitudes of class conflict and alliance, that monopolize the attention of historians, economists, and sociologists who study the first half of the nineteenth century.

To this extent, the question of liberalism in French political culture of the nineteenth century is "missing" in contemporary thought. In fact, liberal philosophy is simultaneously, and often in contradictory fashion, understood as a theory of the rule of law and individual liberties, the first attempt at a modern expression of the democratic ideal, an economic theory of regulation by the market, or a bourgeois ideology whose function was to dissimulate class relations. In all cases, the implicit assumption is that the term "liberalism" refers to a collection of coherent and historically stable political or economic meanings.

Yet the English case, which often is taken as exemplary in this regard, cannot be generalized. The history of English liberalism is, to be sure, relatively unified; liberal political philosophy and the theory of the market economy developed in concert in that country. Whatever their differences, John Locke, David Hume, Adam Smith, and John Stuart Mill are all intelligibly placed in the same intellectual field. The coherence results in large part from the institutional context inherited from the seventeenth century: the achievements of 1688 are the common soil of their thought—whence the undeniable unity of the object of "liberal thought" in England. It evolved more or less smoothly from the eighteenth to the nineteenth century against the permanent background of an unchanging representation of the rule of law. The problem of the relationship between democracy and liberalism is never posed in England in radical terms, as the progressive process of the extension of the vote—symbolized by the reforms of 1832, 1867, and 1884–1885—proves. The figures of the individual and the citizen were never considered there as factually contradictory. This "equilibrium," however, has to be put in its proper place: it is an exception in European history. It is impossible, then, to extrapolate from it and to speak of a modern liberal philosophy either in general or as a single doctrine. The French case is especially striking in this regard. Montesquieu, Benjamin Constant, Say, Guizot, Tocqueville, Frédéric Bastiat, and Lucien Prévost-Paradol, to take some of the more significant landmarks, do not fit in a continuous route on a coherent map, except at the price of assigning to them too vaguely defined a notion of freedom.

The point is not simply that the distinction between economic and political liberalism is fundamental in France while it makes little sense in England. The principal factor in this difference is historical: it originated from the disruption that the fact of the French Revolution introduced into political reflection. Hence the rupture in France, absent in England, between the philosophes of the Enlightenment and the political thinkers of the nineteenth century. At the beginning of the nineteenth century, the crucial question that all of the French liberal authors were attempting to resolve was that of the relation between liberalism and democracy; the disaster of the Terror of 1793 had shown to what extent they were in conflict. The men of 1814 knew that they could not rest content with pursuing the intellectual trajectory of their forebears, whether Montesquieu or Rousseau or anyone else.

In two wonderful pages of his *Memoirs*, Guizot well summarized the problem that provided the point of departure of political reflection in his era: "Philosophy boasted that it would find the solution to politics," he wrote,

and that institutions, laws, and public powers would be nothing but the creations and servants of scientific reason. An insane arrogance. . . . Reversals and disappointments did not wait long before giving the Revolution its harsh lessons, but up until 1815 the Revolution hardly encountered, amongst the commentators on its ill-fortune, anyone except implacable enemies or disabused accomplices, the ones eager for vengeance, and the others for repose, and none of them knew what it meant to oppose revolutionary principles, except to champion retrograde reaction in the one case, or the skepticism of fatigue in the other. "The Revolution was nothing but error and crime," the ones said, "and the Old Regime should not have fallen to it." "The Revolution sinned only through excess," the others said, "for its principles were good, but it pushed them too far." The Doctrinaires rejected both of these assertions; and they defended themselves at once against the return to the maxims of the Old Regime and against commitment, however theoretical or partial, to revolutionary principles. In frankly accepting the new French society as our whole history, and not simply 1789, had created it, they took it on themselves to found their government on the basis of reason, but reason conceived wholly differently than in the theories in the name of which the old society had been brought down, or the incoherent maxims that were offered in the name of its reconstruction. Called by turns to the attack on and the defense of the Revolution, they placed themselves, boldly and from the beginning, in an intellectual sphere, opposing principles to principles, appealing not simply to experience, but also to reason, affirming right instead of relying simply on interest, and asking France not to confess that it had done only wrong, nor to declare itself powerless to do good, but rather to leave behind the chaos in which she had plunged herself and to raise her head once more towards the sky to find the light again. . . . It was to this blend of philosophical elevation and political moderation, to this rational respect for right and circumstances, to these doctrines at once new and conservative, antirevolutionary without being retrograde, and modest at their core even if often lofty in their expression, that the Doctrinaires owed their importance and their name. . . . The Doctrinaires responded to a true and deep need, however obscurely felt, in French minds; they kept at heart both intellectual honor and the good ordering of society; their ideas were the ones that regenerated and closed the Revolution at the same time.[4]

The long citation vividly indicates the objectives of the French liberal generation born with the century. It imposed on itself a triple task: ending the French Revolution, constructing a stable representative government, and establishing a regime founded on reason and guaranteeing liberties. Its quandary was in fact to find for France a way that would permit it to stop oscillating between despotism and anarchy in a double refusal of the Old Regime and the Terror alike. It was a matter not simply of constituting liberalism as a doctrine that would protect the rights of the individual, but rather of making it a *culture of government*. From this came the tirelessly repeated critique of the notions of divine right, on the one hand, and of popular sovereignty, on the other. Their common goal was to theorize the constitution of the social bond without reliance on contract and without returning to an organic representation of the social. The notion of *the sovereignty of reason* is intelligible only in this perspective.

Indeed, the theory of the sovereignty of reason formed the heart of this indissociably intellectual and practical enterprise. *Le Globe* noted in 1826 that it was "the theory of the century."[5] "I do not believe," Guizot wrote, "either in divine right or in popular sovereignty, as they are almost always understood. I see in them only usurpations of power. I believe, rather, in the sovereignty of reason, justice, and law. There is the legitimate sovereign for which the world is looking; for reason, truth, and justice are nowhere complete and infallible. No man, no assembly of men, possesses them or can possess them without gaps and limits."[6] No absolute power can be legitimate, and there is no rightful sovereignty on earth: these are the terms in which Guizot thinks about the problem of sovereignty. Like Benjamin Constant, he refuses to look at the problem solely as a difficulty about those who hold power; rather, he tries to understand the status of power in itself.[7] But in contrast to Constant, he does not at all ground this denial of worldly sovereignty on the principle of the inviolability of the rights of the individual, but rather begins with the assumption of the fallibility of all human power, to the extent that it is always different from reason.[8] His liberalism hence does not proceed from the autonomy and liberty of individuals. In a sense, he only sketches the room for uncertainty and error inherent in all power from the point of view of what truth and justice would dictate.

The "reason" to which Guizot refers is thus a transcendent reason, to which individuals could never wholly accede. It is not the utilitarian reason of a Destutt de Tracy, who defined good and evil, justice and injustice, according to what conforms to human nature and is likely to assure its happiness. Victor Cousin made himself the theorist of this impersonal and absolute conception of reason, and violently criticized the utilitarian approach. Man, for Cousin, can never claim to have discovered the truth. The *cogito* cannot lead to reason, since the moment man says "I think" he is commited to a particular opinion or feeling, a *vote* in some sense. The criterion of the truth is neither in opinion nor in the verification of men: it is in reason alone, in its essence and primitive purity, in absolute reason received only by the self and lost when it is presented as a personal and private reason. The Doctrinaire theory of reason, therefore, is poles apart from Kantian reason, which grounds itself in the autonomy of the will.

Taking this logic to its conclusion, Guizot did not stop with criticizing the principle of political sovereignty, for there is no possibility, either, of personal sovereignty in his eyes. "It is not true," he writes, "that man is the absolute master of himself, that his will is his legitimate sovereign, that at any moment, for any reason, anyone has power over him if only he has consented." If the will is not the legitimate sovereign of man, it is because it is not from the will that he receives such moral laws as he may acknowledge: "He receives them from someplace higher. They come to him from a sphere superior to that of liberty, a sphere in which liberty does not rule, where debate is no longer about what man wants or does not want, but rather distinguishes between truth and falsehood, justice or injustice, conformity to reason or departure from it."[9] The limitation of power, which cannot be equated with reason, thus has for its corollary the reduction of the rights of the will. "Instead of raising all individual wills to the position of sovereigns and of rivals in sovereignty," Guizot concludes, "they should everywhere proscribe absolute power, instead of affording it an asylum in each individual will, and allow to every man the right, which he does in fact possess, of refusing obedience to any law that is not a divine law, instead of attributing to him the right, which he does not actually possess, of obeying nothing but his own will."[10] Such is the essence of the Doctrinaires' theory of the sovereignty of reason. It is liberal insofar as it denounces all forms of despotism and denies to any power whatsoever the right to proclaim itself truly sovereign. But it concedes nothing to the intrinsic rights of the individual.

For the invisible hand of the economists, the Doctrinaires thus substituted an "irresistible hand" of reason whose empire extends over the world. But how is this reason to be found *in* the world? How to reconcile the presence and absence of sovereign reason as a practical matter? The theory of the sovereignty of reason resolves this question by turning sociologically to a theory of *capacities*: no one can pretend to possess reason, but certain individuals turn out to be more capable than others of recognizing and following it. It is thanks to this sociology that Guizot surpassed the practical contradictions of the generally shared liberal premises. In this perspective, the object of the representative system changes its nature. It no longer involves a complex arithmetic of interest and wills. Rather, it is a matter of "gathering and concentrating all the reason that exists scattered in the world,"[11] of "extract[ing] whatever of reason, justice, or truth exists in society in order to apply it to the practical requirements of government."[12]

Guizot's originality, in fact, chiefly resides in the way he sociologically instrumentalized the concept of the sovereignty of reason. If no one can pretend to own reason, then it is impossible, he says, to escape the need for a theory of its *mediation*. It is here that the theme of capacities, which is at the heart of the Doctrinaires' problematic, is born. The Doctrinaires resolved in *a sociological mode* the problem posed by the combined presence and absence of reason. The contradiction between liberalism and democracy is immediately overcome too, in their eyes, by this solution. "What we call *representation*," Guizot writes, "is nothing else than a means to arrive at this result. It is not an arithmetical machine employed to collect and count individual wills, but a natural process by which public reason, which alone has a right to govern society, may be extracted from the bosom of society itself."[13]

The theory of limited suffrage based on property and capacity is rooted in this conception of representation. It is understood as an alternative to universal suffrage and not as the first step, prudentially limited, on the road toward it. In Guizot's system, the middle classes have thus consecrated for them a function that transcends their class, in the economic sense of the term: they are instituted as agents of the realization of the universal. (It is difficult at this point to avoid the temptation to see Guizot and Marx as actually quite close, since it is in the end through a sociology that they both hope to surpass the contradictions of history.) Guizot is in this sense something wholly different than a simple defender of the bourgeois order, even if his activity under the July Monarchy eventually narrowed until he objectively played this role. Rather, he incarnated—in an exemplary manner, for having taken it to its last conclusions—the question of the entire French liberal movement of the beginning of the nineteenth century.

Alexis de Tocqueville, of course, belonged to a later generation, and he assigned himself the task of safeguarding the future of liberalism in a world in which the rise of universal suffrage had come to seem irresistible. But his entire project is equally centered on the same problematic relationship between liberalism and democracy. More profound than Guizot in many respects, he nevertheless was less radical, for Tocqueville's exclusive solution is, in the end, to plead for a moderated love of democracy. It is in recognition of his radicalism that Guizot deserves special attention. If his responses today seem superannuated and even scandalous, the question to which he wanted to respond and out of which his reflection developed continues to be posed in today's world. One must read Guizot as a kind of *test*, caustic and salutary, and undertake to think about modern citizenship by accepting a lucid confrontation with his work.

CHAPTER 6

Political Rationalism and Democracy in France

In France, there is a way of thinking about freedom that often impedes its realization. To understand it fully, one can begin with what appears to be a foundational contradiction in French political culture: the encounter between political rationalism and popular sovereignty.

France's Enlightenment heritage is not comparable to English liberalism. In France, the struggle against arbitrary rule and the protection of liberties took place through tribute to rational government and not by the establishment of representative procedures. The French Revolution's great contribution, for its part, was to affirm, earlier than anywhere else, the principle of popular sovereignty. A cult of reason on the one side and tribute to the will on the other—the fundamental contradiction of French political culture—lies in this duality. In order to retrace briefly the ways in which this tension manifested itself during the Revolution and in the nineteenth century, it is first necessary to emphasize that law and freedom do not have the same meaning in France as they do in England. To understand why, one must begin by recalling that there are two ways of conceptualizing freedom and the limitation of power: by establishing a network of opposing checks (the balance of powers) and by subordinating power to the rule of law. In England, representative government became the historical means for articulating these two conceptions, a process that made them inseparable. But the French case shows that there is another way to think about protective rule: the erection of a "good" power, a rational power, one grounded in science. Defined in this perspective, the rule-bound state presupposes neither representative government nor even the rule of law in the classic liberal sense; it is in no way tied to the notion of constitutional checks and balances.

French-Style Political Rationalism

In most countries, the expansion of voting rights was historically correlated with the progress of representative government. The history of universal suffrage, in other words, was inscribed in a history of the expansion and extension of freedoms. In seventeenth-century England, for example, the struggle against absolutism came to be expressed as a demand to improve the procedures of political representation. Nothing of the sort occurred in eighteenth-century France. It was primarily in the name of an imperative for rationalization that the case against absolute monarchy was built.

The work of the physiocrats in the middle of the eighteenth century reveals in remarkable fashion the nature and foundations of political rationalism, the political sentiment that the Baron Turgot and the Marquis de Condorcet would later incarnate. To see why, one must look beyond their strictly economic theory. For the physiocrat François Quesnay and his disciples, men do not have to invent anything to be free: they have only to observe the laws of nature and conform to them. "Legislation," wrote G.-F. Le Trosne, another physiocrat, in *De L'ordre social*, "is written in tender letters in the great book of nature."[1] Politics is, accordingly, an art of observation and a science of deduction; it creates nothing original and institutes nothing novel. In his *Maximes*, Quesnay puts it thus:

> Men and their governments do not at all make their laws, indeed they cannot do so. They recognize laws as conso-

nant with the supreme reason that governs the universe and then declare them; they *bring* them into society. . . . It is for this reason that the words are *legislator* (bearer of the law) and *legislation* (bodies of transmitted law) and that no one has ever dared to use the word *legisfactor*—lawmaker.[2]

The book that most brilliantly expresses this physiocratic vision of the political is Le Mercier de la Rivière's *L'Ordre naturel et essentiel des sociétés politiques*, published in 1767. Le Mercier de la Rivière did not have the intellectual fecundity of a Quesnay, but it is he who best succeeded in expressing the essence of French-style political rationalism. A barrister at the parlement of Paris, then *Intendant* (regional governor) of the Antilles, he is wholly representative of the cadre of enlightened administrators who, after 1750, ushered in state modernization.[3]

Legislative power, Le Mercier explains, cannot be defined as the power to invent laws. "Making bad laws," he writes, "is a misfortune, an accident of mankind, and in no way a *right*, a prerogative of authority. . . . Legislative power is not the power to make obviously bad laws for no good reason."[4] Freedom consists, in other words, in conformity to nature, while oppression comes only from a wayward human will. This vision of the relationship between freedom and law rests on an epistemology centered on the notion of *evidence*. The point is fundamental. It is in fact the source accounting for the originality of French-style liberalism, as a political rationalism radically different from English-style liberalism.

For the physiocrats, evidence constitutes the guarantee of freedom. Evidence, in effect, expresses generality, beyond all strife, equivocation, indeterminacy, and particularity. "When men have the misfortune of being deprived of evidence," writes Le Mercier,

opinion in the strict sense becomes the principle of all moral authorities: then we can no longer know any authority, nor count on any. In this perforce disorderly state, the idea of establishing checks to prevent the arbitrary abuses of the sovereign power is obviously fanciful: the opposite of arbitrariness is evidence; and it is only the irresistible force of evidence that can counter that of arbitrariness and opinion.[5]

On this point, the physiocrats are disciples of Nicolas de Malebranche, the seventeenth-century rationalist.[6] They read and meditated upon *De la recherche de la vérité* and relied on its author to disqualify will and opinion.

The overall strategy is a convenient way to displace or avoid the problem of the self-institution of the social. In the light of evidence, necessity and volition are in fact fused. "Evidence must be the very principle of authority because it is the principle of the union of wills," Le Mercier says.[7] It is equivalent to the principle of unanimity, the form of universal reason. It is a means of accessing truth and the general interest that in no way requires deliberation or experimentation. It is a means of immediacy (much like faith, its neighbor).[8] Later Diderot would give enthusiastic approval to this philosophy of liberty. "Montesquieu, before anyone else, diagnosed the illness; [evidence] prescribes the cure," he wrote.[9]

French-style liberalism found a unique and very particular way, then, of yoking the cult of the law to the praise of the rationalizing state, the notion of the rule of law with that of administrative power. Echoing the physiocrats' political theory, the Italian Cesare Beccaria would later extend this approach to the field of legal theory, thereby returning to the pioneering reflections of the Abbé de Saint-Pierre. For Beccaria, too, the law has two inseparable functions: it is a way of guaranteeing liberty (by enacting a general rule, it reduces the possibility of arbitrariness) and an instrument for the construction of the state.[10] In this perspective, the advent of the rational state is a condition of freedom: the law, the state, and general rules will overlap.

In the second half of the eighteenth century, this political rationalism did not only count as a doctrine; it also found a place and a means of implementation in the actual transformations of the administrative apparatus. Indeed, after 1750, the old world of notables began to recede as bureaucrats became more important, signaling a decisive turn in the evolution of the administration toward a modern form of organization. Enlightened despotism and French-style liberalism found an ambiguous meeting-ground in such a process of the rationalization of the state apparatus, leaving empty the intellectual space occupied by English liberalism.

If, in France, political rationalism prevailed over traditional, English-style liberalism (that of representative and intermediary bodies, of mixed government and pluralism), one may not, however, conclude that this latter way of opposing despotism completely disappeared. In fact, there remained a strong aristocratic liberalism in the second half of the eighteenth century. The Marquis de Voyer d'Argenson is an excellent example of it. In his *Considérations sur le gouvernement ancien et présent de la France* (1764), he could still write, for instance, that "the venality of offices is the great obstacle to the designs of despotism . . . The progress of the aristocracy must always be taken as a sure sign of the weakness of despotism, and the progress of democracy as an important result of its vigor."[11] Certain contemporary historians, Denis Richet most especially, have insisted upon the importance of aristocratic liberalism.[12] Though Voltaire and many others disparaged the parlements for their conservatism and their pretension to speak in the name of the nation, it is certainly true that their suppression in 1771 by René Nicolas de Maupeou stirred up a veritable campaign of indignation among elites. Even the Baron d'Holbach, one of the most virulent adversaries of privileged orders, thought that, at least in the absence of other forms of representation, they were "the ever-needed buffer between supreme Authority and the liberty of the subjects."[13] Nevertheless, such qualifications should not mask what really mattered: the unmistakable emergence and progression of political rationalism. It is on this basis that one must interpret the latent hostility to Montesquieu, whom many reproached as relying on "gothic" principles for fighting absolutism.[14] It also offers the premises for analyzing the relationship between the French Enlightenment and England or America.

If the fruits of the English regime—tolerance and liberty—were unanimously appreciated, the principles on which they rested enjoyed no such approbation. It is important not to misunderstand the Anglophilia of the Enlightenment: it was political rather than philosophical, as Voltaire's *Lettres anglaises* attest.[15] In the same vein, Enlightenment thinkers supported American colonial emancipation, even as they immediately distanced themselves from the American constitutional endeavor, criticizing it as excessively influenced by the spirit of English common law and the balance of powers. Thus, in his notorious letter to Dr. Richard Price of March 22, 1778, Turgot criticized his correspondent for remaining captive to the "mistaken foundations of a very outmoded and very vulgar politics."[16]

The opposition between French-style rationalism and English liberalism achieved its classic formulation somewhat later, in the notes added in 1789 by Condorcet and Pierre-Samuel Dupont de Nemours to the French translation of Richard Livingston's *Observations on the Government*.[17] The two French philosophers clearly lay out, in this material, the basis for their hostility to English-style parliamentarism. The existence of Parliament, they argue, in no way guarantees the protection of individuals. "What is wrong with arbitrary government," they insist, "is not who controls it, but the arbitrariness itself."[18] In fact, they contend, the Parliament can make damaging resolutions as easily as any absolute monarchy can. Certainly, England has excellent laws, "but they are accidental. They do not depend on the British constitution."[19] In their eyes, legislative authority must be strictly limited. "Nations and philosophers alike still have very confused notions about *legislative authority*," they note.

"The authority to make all sorts of laws, even those that would be absurd and unjust, can be delegated to no one; for it does not even belong to the social body as a whole."[20]

These lines resume the basic arguments of Quesnay and Le Mercier de la Rivière. For them, the production of law comes down to two things really: the achievement of a good *declaration of rights*, on the one hand, and the promulgation of *regulations*, on the other. There is no room for a parliamentary space in this scheme. The declaration of rights is part of the institution of society, and it is drafted once and for all time. For their part, regulations are decreed by the government, and their conformity to the declaration of rights is guaranteed because freedom of the press allows discussion to occur without interference. In other words, there is nothing in between the acts of the government and the constitution. The legislative body's sole prerogative is to exercise certain governmental functions, such as setting the tax rate or declaring war and peace; but it cannot produce general rules. In this conception, the liberal principle of the protection of persons and goods in no way depends on the development of representative procedures; it is sufficiently rooted in the erection of an authority at once unique and rational.

Logically, in this scheme, public education plays a determinative role in the formation of enlightened public opinion. In France, from the mid-eighteenth century on, schooling was endowed with a mission that went far beyond the goal of providing useful knowledge, and a whole train of utopian projects came to be grafted upon it. For the Enlightenment, schooling, along with the freedom of the press, counted as the principal means of the diffusion of reason, which spreads through imitation. It is too often forgotten that the physiocrats wrote extensively on the importance of the state's task of public education. In his *Despotisme de la Chine*, Quesnay thus explained that "the capital object of a prosperous and durable government must be . . . the extensive study and continual general teaching of natural law," while the Abbé Baudeau made the teaching of economics the primary condition of progress.[21] Le Mercier de la Rivière also devoted an important work to the question: *De l'instruction publique ou considérations morales sur la nécessité, la nature et la source de cette instruction* (1775). "A government must be the principal teacher of its subjects," he notes in his introduction.[22] The properly civic dimension of public education is given special emphasis by Le Mercier de la Rivière. To create a real political body, he explains, it is necessary "to create and maintain a unified will, a unified direction, and a unified strength."[23] Whence the exigency for uniformity in the teaching methods and programs he recommends, one that markedly prefigured the large reform projects elaborated during the French Revolution.

There is scarcely room at all for representation in such a model. The idea of voting rights is completely foreign to this world. Discussions among the enlightened, where Reason germinates, suffice to produce the conditions of liberty. "What does this noun *representation* mean?" asked Jean-Baptiste Suard, for example. "What can representatives represent if not public opinion? Debates can arise and continue so long as this opinion is uncertain. . . . But nobody divides into parties to decide who wins a game of chess, nor to decide which of two solutions to the same geometry problem is correct."[24] Louis Sébastien Mercier also addressed this theme in *L'an 2440*. "The Estates-General that we have lost," he writes, "have been replaced by that crowd of citizens who speak, write, and deny to despotism the power to alter the free and ancient constitution of the French too much."[25]

In the eighteenth century, in sum, a French-style model of political rationalism developed in opposition to the English model protecting liberties by according political representation to the country's principal social forces and allowing them to check one another. But how, then, did France pass from this political rationalism to the French Revolution's song of the general will? How could the notion of the right to vote become an essential part of this framework? If a rupture occurred in France with the Enlightenment tradition, when and how did it take place? The understanding of this mutation motivates the following analysis of French democracy and citizenship.

The Foundations of French Democracy

In the autumn of 1789, everything conspired to make social unity the cardinal value. Men wanted to come together and destroy everything that had separated them.

The perception of the social bond altered completely in 1789. The brutal rejection of the universe of privilege completely redrew the boundaries of the social system. It was the privileged classes who were excluded and symbolized what is exterior to society. "It is an absolute fact that the privileged class look upon themselves as another species of beings," said Sieyès in his *Essay on Privileges.*[26] A few months later, in *What Is the Third Estate?*, he extended the argument by inverting it. "Anyone privileged is entitled to be represented only on the basis of his quality as a citizen," he writes. "But for him that quality has been destroyed. He is outside the civil order and an enemy of common legality."[27] The new social bond is thus defined by the exclusion of the aristocracy.[28]

Some writers even went so far as to group the privileged classes together with foreigners. In the words of Jean-Baptiste Salaville, to take one example:

> The Third Estate is the largest order, and it comprises the nation. It has nothing in common with the others. The others have broken the social compact, they are no longer citizens. It is the wish of the Third Estate that forms the law; sovereignty resides in it. The others have not even the right to vote. They must instead conform to the laws of the Third Estate, like foreigners, who, while sojourning in a land, must conform to its law.[29]

"Since they want to separate themselves from us, let us separate ourselves from them," in *La Sentinelle du peuple*'s summary.[30]

The Third Estate and the nation redefined themselves through the movement of this exclusion. In 1789, one might say, the exterior of society becomes interior, and vice versa. The privileged classes came to be understood in 1789 as the populace had been viewed earlier: as a being that was completely other, cast out into the shadows of nature, deprived of civil rights, expelled beyond the borders. The privileged absorbed and condensed all social exteriority, and the image of the internal enemy and that of the foreigner coincided in them.

In 1789, civil equality and "civic equality" [*égalité du civisme*] were superimposed.[31] The critique of the orders and the corporations, and the refusal to represent their interests, led to the exaltation of the abstract individual, liberated from all determinations, simple member of the social whole. The political sphere, under such conditions, is neither derived nor separated from the sphere of the social, which implies a distinct form of collective existence. Rather, the political sphere is thought to coincide with the social order and can absorb it entirely. One reason this is so is almost mechanical: the suppression of intermediary bodies led to an expansion of the public space, called to become the central site of social interaction. The dynamic of events joined together with institutional logic.

More profoundly, the political and the social were caused to coincide as soon as the specificities, the differences, and the singularities that structure society were denied. In this way, the civic bond came to represent, in its abstraction, the archetype of the social bond. It is the pure representation of the social and incarnates its essence. In a few celebrated pages of *What Is the Third Estate?*, Sieyès demonstrated the implacable imperative of this process. "To sum up," he wrote, "it is a matter of principle that everything that falls outside the common attributes of citizenship cannot give rise to an entitlement to exercise political rights."[32] Sieyès had in mind, most immediately, the radical rejection of the notion of privilege. But his logic led him to base political rights on "common status," that is, simple belonging to the social body.

As a result, the individual as legal person and the individual as a citizen tended to become confused. If no strictly social variable, rooted in the heterogeneity of society, can be taken into account in this definition of the right to vote, then political rights are of the same basic nature as civil rights. They are no longer different in their essence (Burke grasped this point quite well in his analysis of the French Revolution). It is this development that made it so difficult in the period to grasp the distinction between the notions of active and passive citizenship. A distinction among rights-bearing citizens could not be established on the basis of the juridical specificity of each category of rights. A difference between political and civil rights could be secured only by establishing a difference between autonomous and dependent juridical subjects. The only distinction that allowed any abstraction from equality was that of the *nature* of real juridical subjects (age, sex, and so forth). The absence of political rights always had to be grounded, in one way or another, in the *partiality* of an individual's civil rights (as in the cases, at the time, of women, children, and the incompetent).

The propagation of citizenship occurred at the intersection of this equation of civil and political rights with the advent of the principle of collective sovereignty. Thanks to a double process of abstraction, each individual was made part of the sovereign power at the same time that the political sphere was identified with civil society. Political rights originated not in a doctrine of representation—insofar as the latter depends upon the recognition and the validation of the heterogeneous and diverse elements within society—but in the notion of participation in sovereignty. This is the great change. At the beginning of 1789, the question remained that of equality as belonging. For an almost mechanical reason, it quickly became confused with a new conception of equality as sovereignty, for the locus of sovereignty had been identified with the very being of the nation. It would remain so. Accordingly, the right to vote could no longer remain in a logic of representation. Therefore, it came to define a social status, that of the individual member of a people collectively taking the place of the king. French democracy, in other words, is not founded on a deconstruction of absolutism. On the contrary, it consists of its reappropriation.

The Revolutionary Equivocation

How to reconcile the concept of rational government with the affirmation of popular sovereignty? This is the central question of French political history since 1789. But it has never been clearly posed; the French have always avoided it. The way in which the notion of the general will has been understood suggests as much. The concept of the general will is in many ways the principal black box of the revolutionary process.

In the consecration of the general will, two registers are superimposed without wholly intermingling: that of the definition of the political subject, and that of the foundation of the social order. The first of these two senses is the easier one to grasp. The affirmation of the sovereignty of the general will results in the first instance from the awesome transfer of sovereignty of 1789, in which the nation appropriated the attributes of royal authority for itself, at the same time that the principle of the political equality of individuals made the right of suffrage the symbol of social inclusion. One can speak, in this regard, of the veritable "coronation" of the general will, which comes to seem almost a *technical condition* for the reconstruction of the political order. The figure of the absolute monarch could not be erased without transferring his power directly to the nation; the simple concept of the limitation of sovereignty, in the English style, seemed outmoded and insufficient.

Indeed, the strength of absolutism was such in the eyes of the men of 1789 that they did not consider a simple redefinition of the boundaries of royal authority possible. In their eyes, only an operation of total confiscation and reappropriation would make it possible for it to be reduced. The concepts of national sovereignty and the general will, which are connected, can therefore be understood in a liberal sense: their function is to make radical anti-absolutism feasible. Article 6 of the *Declaration of the Rights of Man and Citizen* is written precisely in this liberal perspective. In affirming that the law is the expression of the general will, the members of the Constituent Assembly meant, first and foremost, that the law can no longer emanate from the particular will of the monarch. But did they not, in exchange, erect the people as a new sovereign subject?

The moment is wholly ambiguous: in 1789, no one yet dreamed of founding an authority entrusted to the people. The *nation* was the sovereign subject, as Article 3 of the *Declaration* states ("The nation is essentially the source of all sovereignty, nor shall any body of men or any individual exercise authority not expressly derived from it"). As the figure of society as a whole, the nation cannot be reduced to any of its component parts, at the same time that it designates an empty space of power. Irreducibly unified, impossible to decompose into smaller elements, the nation, for the members of the Constituent Assembly, was thus sovereign only as an abstract totality—that is, beyond the reach of human power, inappropriable by any person or faction whatsoever. The new philosophy of law expressed in 1789 derived from these conditions by which royal authority was transmitted to the nation; the general will is, first and foremost, the nation's will. The advent of a new central political subject thus marked an obvious rupture with respect to absolutism, but it is more a political than sociological break. In summary, the sacralization of the general will did not necessarily imply popular power. The equivocation is fundamental and foundational.

If the ambiguity of the concept of the general will made it possible to mask the contradiction between the governance of reason and the sovereignty of the people, the forms through which citizenship was expressed led to precisely the same result. In setting up a two-tiered voting system, the men of 1789 allowed the universalist civic principle to border on the most elitist practices. Fundamentally, the right to vote belonged to practically all adult males. Of these, the only ones who were not kept from the ballot box were dependent individuals, considered then as nonautonomous (beggars, domestics, the homeless). The nineteenth-century republicans would refer to it as quasi-universal suffrage. However, the only choice the entire populace made is the electors at the upper tier, and the election of deputies occurred only at this latter level. At the base, more than four million individuals had the right to vote, but they decided almost nothing of importance. Their right to vote remained, first and foremost, the sign of belonging. Furthermore, they were not even termed the electors, even if only at an initial tier, that they were; juridically, they were merely "members of a primary assembly."[33] Only a small number were actually labeled voters: a mere 40,000 men directly elected the deputies. The technical dissociation of the two tiers of the voting system, then, allowed it to play two different functions at once: on the one hand, social affirmation of belonging to the nation (the moment of the sovereignty of the people, tied to the first tier) and, on the other hand, the maintenance of an elitist decision-making process (the moment of rational government, tied to the second level).

The French Equation

The distinctive quality of the revolutionary period is to have to a great extent dissociated the register of citizenship from that of the exercise of popular power. The symbolism of belonging on the one hand, then, and the organization of power, on the other. This duality principally took the form of an equivocacy during the Revolution, one in the notion of the general will, on one side, and one linked to the very modalities of the exercise of the right to vote, on the other.

The first organized form that the relationship between the governance of reason and the sovereignty of the people would take was Bonapartism. In Bonapartism, there is indeed a simultaneous affirmation of the sovereignty of the people and a preeminence of rational administration. The figure of the emperor allows the link between these two moments to be made. Bonapartism is both a populism and a rationalism. It not only represents a political experiment in French history, a caesarist experiment; much more profoundly, it amounts to a specific way of resolving and managing the contradiction between popular sovereignty and rational government. Bonapartism, it has to be said, is a fundamental political model of French democratic organization. This is why it would remain a recurring reference, reincarnated or reappropriated in various diverse ways, from the democratic caesarism of the Second Empire to the liberal caesarism in the Fifth Republic.

The history of the nineteenth century was also that of a search for alternatives to this Bonapartist model. But until the foundation of the Third Republic at least, it is striking that France was capable only of oscillating between these two poles. On the one hand, it paid tribute to meritocratic rights as outlined by François Guizot and liberal Doctrinaires; on the other, it paid tribute to utopian democracy, as in 1848 for example. The meritocratic system as defined by Guizot in the end is nothing more than the extension of the theme of rational government through sociological means. Those called "the meritorious" (*les capacitaires*) are those who have the intellectual ability to direct the country. The restriction of voting rights, as organized during the Restoration and the July Monarchy—vote by qualification—corresponds to this meritocratic system.[34] The Revolution of 1848 represents, on the other side, the triumph of democracy, one defined as a kind of fused expression of popular unity and sovereignty. But in this case, it is clear that the Republic takes a shape much more like a religion than like a regime. The dominant symbols of 1848 are those of fraternity and fusion of different classes. The issue is not one of organizing mass democracy, even with the institution of the regime of universal male suffrage on March 5, 1848; rather, it is the affirmation of the power of the nation.

Utopian democracy on the one hand, meritocratic liberalism on the other hand: French political culture long oscillated between these two poles. The oscillation in many ways reflected the opposition between rational government and popular sovereignty. It seems to me that this opposition makes it possible to provide a fuller explanation of the chaotic character of French history, the fact that French democracy was simultaneously precocious and delayed. Unlike English gradualism, in which the progress of liberty and democracy can be analyzed as cumulative and sedimentary, French history seemed to be forced to shift among beginning anew, groping for synthesis, and dreaming of generous utopias.

How could France finally achieve a kind of equilibrium? What kind of compromise could resolve the fundamental contradiction that I have tried to present? The formula of a modernized Bonapartism, in the foundation of the Gaullist Fifth Republic? It is certainly one part of the answer. But the achievement of equilibrium is not to be understood simply by analyzing supposed continuities between Napoleon and Charles de Gaulle. For wholly beyond such continuities, the problem had also been reconstructed in the meantime. The reconstruction of the French equation has been based primarily, it seems to me, on a dissociation of different registers.

In fact, the forms of social history, administrative history, and political culture have largely been uncoupled from one another in French democracy. From the perspective of administrative history, rational government did indeed win out. Authority residing in technocracy (with a consequent difficulty in defining a genuinely autonomous executive power and high value placed on the formation of elites and high functionaries): the contemporary French technocratic model is indeed, on this point, the heir of the system envisioned by Turgot and Malesherbes.

If one reflects on social history, however, it is easy to see democracy's role in driving it. But it must be emphasized that democracy is understood in France much more as a social form than as a political model. Democracy as a social formula, that is, democracy implying a system beyond which there is nothing else to demand—the system, then, that would bring to an end all contestations and all quarrels. It is what liberals of the 1870s marvelously termed "the power of the last word." Democracy is the necessary form of civil peace.

In the optic of cultural forms, finally, it would appear that the education of democracy has proved a major axis of French political culture. In France, obligatory schooling did not simply reflect a need for technical training that a developed country requires. Above all, it followed from the goal of forming rational men and citizens. The state came to be conceived as a pedagogue, as society's teacher. Its educational activities were expected to bridge the gap between democracy and rationality. In the theme of educating democracy, it is clearly the resolution of the contradiction between the democratic spontaneity of the masses and the rationality of the elites that is in play.

In French history, in summary, there occurred a permanent superimposition of these three registers: the register of democracy as a social form, the register of technocracy as rational power, and the register of educational activity as the condition under which the general will can become, finally, rational.

PART IV

Civil Society

CHAPTER 7

The Market, Liberalism, and Anti-liberalism

The end of the twentieth century saw the market economy celebrated and vituperated by turns. Around 1980, it triumphed; after two centuries of suspicions and denunciations, it was finally recognized as an unsurpassable mechanism for the regulation of complex systems. The very meaning of the socialist project came to be completely upset, notably after the twilight of communism finally retired the principles of the command economy and collective ownership of the means of production. But then, in the late 1990s, the tensions born of globalization and a financial and monetary crisis nourished a diffuse movement of opinion against neoliberalism, suspected once more of causing all evils. A vast debate over the conditions of mastering and governing the international economy resurfaced precisely among those who too quickly prophesied that modernity had entered into a new, stable and radiant economic future.

A short-term history of the final years of the twentieth century could limit itself to describing these developments and oscillations as if they were meaningful only if related to factual illusions or ideological dogmas. It could also leave the impression that it was all really just a matter of an almost technical controversy over the most effective forms of economic regulation. But it is not hard to see that the stakes and the problems are actually much deeper. It is, more profoundly, a whole model of society and its relationship to political will that have been under debate. If the market is seductive and worrisome by turns, it is in fact because more than a simple mechanism of management and regulation is at stake. The market appears as the agent of a far vaster ambition to organize civil society through decentralization and anonymity, presenting itself as the implicit competitor of the democratic project of artificially constituting the political realm.

Market Society

To clarify the great debate of the present, therefore, one must explore the long history of this notion of the market in its largest possible dimensions. For it suffices to plunge just a little into the economic literature of eighteenth century to see that it is not simply "technical." Instead, it is rooted in a deeper implicit debate about the regulation of society and politics in their totality. The study of intellectual history whose results I summarize here confirms this intuition. The birth of economic liberalism occurred not simply as a theory—or an ideology—accompanying the development of the forces of production and the empowerment of the bourgeoisie as a dominant class. It did not simply defend or translate a prior emancipation of economic activity from morality either. It has to be understood, first of all, as a response to problems left unresolved by the political theorists of the social contract; it is in this perspective that one must try to understand the concept of the market as it arose in the eighteenth century. It has an essentially sociological or political meaning and is opposed to that of the contractualist philosophy; it is therefore no "technical" concept (defining a mode of regulating economic activity through a system of competitive pricing). The affirmation of economic liberalism is the sign of a more profound aspiration for a civil society immediate to itself—one that would be entirely self-regulated. This perspective, apolitical in a strong sense, makes *market society* the archetype of a new representation of the social: it will be the market and not the contract, economics and not politics, that will be the true regulator of society. And not simply the economy.

To this extent, the concept of the market has to be placed in the intellectual history of modernity as a whole. Modern political thought, beginning in the seventeenth century, has been centered on the notion of the social contract: it is this concept that is understood to furnish the very foundation of society. The great problem of political philosophy has been to conceptualize the autonomous institution of society, without reference to any external guarantee (notably one of religious derivation). But all of the theories of the social contract, from Hobbes to Rousseau, ran up against several theoretical difficulties that proved quite weighty. Two are especially important. The first related to the fact that if social contract theories grounded the principle of social peace, they did not allow the problem of war and peace among nations to be treated. While the social contract presents the formation of society as a bargain in which everyone wins—gaining security and civil peace—the relations among nations continue to be understood as a zero-sum game (in which no one can win without others losing). The second difficulty is that the notion of the social pact, centered on explaining the institution of society, is not directed at the problem of its regulation.

The representation of civil society as a market would furnish a response to these two difficulties left behind by the representation of society as a political body. The theory of exchange makes it possible to believe that, in contrast to military relationships, economic relationships among nations can transcend the zero-sum game. Further, it makes possible the treatment of the institution and the regulation of society at the same time and in a coherent manner: in civil society, need and interest govern by themselves the relations among men. The formation of this representation of society as a market occurred most prominently in the Scottish Enlightenment, especially in Adam Smith's thought. The essential consequence of such a conception consisted in a global refusal of the political. It is no longer politics that should govern society but the market instead. The latter is thus not the limited technical instrument that organizes economic activity, but has a much more radical sociological and political meaning. Reread from this perspective, Adam Smith is not so much the founding father of modern economics as the theorist of the withering away of politics. He is not an economist who does philosophy, but a philosopher who becomes an economist as a continuation of his philosophy. For this reason, Smith is the anti-Rousseau *par excellence*.

The praise of the commercial society that one finds in numerous authors of the eighteenth century has to be understood from this starting point. It does not represent a strictly mercantile perspective and the Industrial Revolution had in any case produced no real effects up to this point. The concept of the market really counted at the time as a kind of alternative *political model*. To all formal and hierarchical figures of authority and subordination, the market opposes the possibility of a kind of organization and direction that largely dispenses with all forms of authority: it makes its adjustments automatically, and allows for transfer and redistribution to occur without needing the will of individuals in general and of elites in particular to play any role. The expanded meaning of "commerce" in the eighteenth century testifies to this generalization. The term came to cover everything that gives coherence to the social bond independently of all forms of power and authority. It was frequent to oppose, in just this sense, the sweetness of commerce (*le doux commerce*) to the harshness of power relations. Montesquieu was among the first to develop this great liberal topos in *The Spirit of the Laws* (1748): commerce softens manners and encourages peace. For him, the rise of the market society portended a genuine transition of humanity. The era of dominating authorities was to be succeeded, it was hoped, by one of neutral mechanisms (beginning with exchange), and the period of the confrontation of great powers would disappear and give way to an era of the cooperation of commercial nations.

Thomas Paine would take this notion to its last conclusions when he proposed that the goal of revolutions was to accelerate this shift by replacing governments founded on violence with societies founded on the natural harmony of interests. Was this vision of the economy a utopia? Today we are naturally inclined to venture such a diagnosis, since the contrast of the putative virtues of *le doux commerce* compared to the vices of evil politics can seem naïve. But one should not forget that the publicists of the eighteenth century lived in a precapitalist world. The market, one could say, remained for them a brand new idea, with almost all of its tests before it. Is such still the case? I do not mean to respond to this question with a value judgment. For it is much more interesting to try to understand what was at work, what perhaps continues to be at work, in the attraction of this model of society as a market.

What explains an intellectual phenomenon that is genuinely close to seduction? The answer has been a major characteristic of modern society for three centuries: the aspiration to discover a way of dedramatizing the confrontation of individuals, to drain their relations of passion, to minimize the hidden violence of power relations. The market says it responds to these problems. It attempts to substitute the power of an invisible hand, neutral by nature since it is not personalized. It brings about an abstract model of social regulation: objective "laws" govern the transactions among men so that no relations of force or subordination need intervene. It is the equivalent of a kind of "hidden god." In his book *Free to Choose*, Milton Friedman explains in precisely this manner why the market is *politically* superior to all other forms of social organization: "Adam Smith's flash of genius was that the prices that emerged from voluntary transactions between buyers and sellers—for short, in a free market—could coordinate the activity of millions of people, each seeking his own interest, in such a way as to make everyone better off," he writes. "The price system is the mechanism that fulfills this task without central direction, *without requiring people to speak to one another or to like one another. . . .* Economic order can emerge as the *unintended* consequence of the actions of many people, each seeking his own interest. The price system works so well, so efficiently, that we are *not aware of it* most of the time."[1]

In other words, the notion of the market fulfills a certain ideal of the autonomy of individuals by depersonalizing the social relation. The market figures as the archetype of an anti-hierarchical system of organization and of a model of direction in which no intention intervenes.[2] Professional procedures and mechanisms are substituted for will-driven interventions. This displacement, which continues in contemporary society, also explains the emergence of a new relation to the notion of social change. In a purely procedural universe, one that is depersonalized and juridified, there is no room left for ancient revolutions, since there is no superintending authority to dismiss or to replace. There may not even be room, perhaps, for genuine revolts, as a certain passivity in the face of unemployment suggests. How to rise up, one might think, against what apparently results from neutral procedures and purely objective mechanisms? This is one of the major qualities that make it possible for our societies to be called liberal ones. One is very far, in summary, from simple and basic technical considerations for the regulation of modern economies. It is for this reason that I have labeled this phenomenon *utopian capitalism*, to designate what seems indissociably a temptation and an illusion.

One must, therefore, return to Adam Smith's work, in order to follow the genesis and spread of this utopia of the market as a principle of social organization. Then one must chart its development, principally in the nineteenth century. For the picture of the self-regulated society would leave behind its original economic framework—the victorious world of capitalism obviously no longer able to be mistaken for the world of harmonious commerce—and transform into all of the grand visions of the withering away of politics and of the substitution of the reign of men with the administration of things. It is this sense that Marx is

Smith's natural heir. The liberal economic utopia of the eighteenth century and the socialist political utopia of the nineteenth century paradoxically are part of the same representation of society founded on the ideal of the abolition of politics. In spite of their obvious divergences, liberalism and socialism correspond to the same moment of maturation and examination of modern options. In this manner, it will be clear, intellectual history does not content itself with making sense of the past and the source of our vision of the world: it also informs our perspective on the present. For the aspiration for a self-regulating civil society, which the notion of the market has borne with it since the eighteenth century, has never ended its presence in the background of our economic and political thinking.

The Triple Utopia of Liberalism

This sketch, admittedly rapid, allows the problem of contemporary attitudes toward liberalism to be faced on a new basis. It is often marked by what appears to be a contradiction, or at least a tension, between a "political liberalism" grounded in the recognition of rights and the maintenance of pluralism, generally viewed positively, and an "economic liberalism" much more frequently held in suspicion. The way in which I have just proposed to think about liberalism allows the contrast to be framed in a different way. The market and the rule of law in effect participate in the same refusal: that of accepting a certain kind of institution of authority on individuals. In each domain, the same principle holds: that of individual autonomy, rooted in a denial of all absolute sovereignties. If there is a common plank that allows one to speak of liberalism in the singular, it is indeed this principle. There is thus no *foundational* difference between the philosophy of the rights of man, which drives political liberalism, and the belief found in economic liberalism in the organizing character of economic *laws* and *constraints* that order the market. In both cases, the presumption is that there is no great master of men and things, and no personal power of subjection is allowed to exist between individuals. The central site of power is called to remain empty by the refusal of all personal subordination and all collusion among men to restore unchosen obligations. "Representative government and the market," Pierre Manent justly writes, "belong to one another and respond to one another. The individual does not win his liberty and emancipate himself from personalized rulers except by dividing his allegiance between these two impersonal authorities. In neither register does he obey anyone's orders: the results of market allocation are not chosen by anyone, and the laws of the state are general laws that make no exceptions for anyone, and in any case thanks to political representation each person, along with everyone else, is their co-author."[3]

The liberalism that arose in Europe beginning in the seventeenth century thus marks a new step in the relationship between the individual and authority. It furthered the process of political secularization and the affirmation of the preeminence of the individual that had been at work since the fourteenth century. It characterized a culture, in this sense, far more than it represented a specialized doctrine. Liberalism accompanied the entry of modern societies into a new era of representing the social bond, one grounded in utility and equality rather than the outmoded representation of society as a preexisting totality. Against the Rousseauean universe of the social contract, it is the expression of a criticism and subordination of the will. Liberalism, indissociably economic and political, made the *depersonalization of the world* the condition of progress and liberty. In his *Political Essays*, Hume, the greatest liberal thinker of the eighteenth century, takes this sentiment so far that he can praise *habit* and *custom*. So that order can avoid grounding itself in the dependence of individuals vis-à-vis political or religious power, he explained, it is necessary for the conduct of society to be regulable by what is most impersonal, and least appropriable or manipulable by any party: tradition. The intellectual history of liberalism finds the unity of its object in this search for an alternative to inherited relations of power and dependence.

Still more generally, an unprecedented relationship to morality arose along with the principle of the sovereign autonomy of the individual considered complete master and possessor of himself. A single culture is therefore to be found at work in both the "economic liberalism" that appeals to the market, a "political liberalism" that appeals to the rights of man, and a "moral liberalism" that makes man the sole judge of his own actions. In separating power from opinion, state from society, the private from the public, individual morality from the rules of social life, and sin from crime, these "three liberalisms" contributed to redefining the forms of the social bond. It is this fact that allows one to speak of liberalism in the singular. Among Locke's *Letters on Toleration*, Smith's *Wealth of Nations*, Montesquieu's *Spirit of the Laws*, and Benjamin Constant's *Principles of Politics*, there is thus a single project of emancipation at work. In these different books, a common task is shouldered.

This attempt at a new perspective, then, allows liberalism to be conceived in the singular and the difficulty in which one finds oneself confronted by a diversity of great texts from different fields to be surmounted. The proliferation and occasionally contradictory character of this literature, all called "liberal," is an irritant only if one begins by thinking that it is a matter of understanding liberalism as a *doctrine*, that is, a coherent if differentiated body of judgments and analyses. For it is clear that there is no doctrinal unity to liberalism. But if it is not a doctrine, *liberalism is a culture*. From this comes both its unity and contradictions. Liberalism is the culture at work in the modern world that since the beginning of the seventeenth century has been attempting to win emancipation from both royal and religious authority. (Hence liberalism's essential connection to the Reformation, which lies beyond the scope of these reflections.) Its unity is that of a *problematic field*, a work to accomplish, a sum of aspirations.

When placed in this general framework, the utopia of market society appears inseparable from two other liberal utopias. The first is that of a reign of law that might serve as a replacement for the political order of conflict and negotiation. It amounts to the other face of the *utopia of regulation* that also underpins the modern concept of the market. The second utopia is an *anthropological utopia*: that of a moral and social world made up of pure individuals, absolutely autonomous and sovereign masters of themselves. What one could dub *absolute liberalism* should logically include this figure of a tripartite utopia. Of course, it is not difficult to acknowledge that it only rarely appeared in this form, even if the Scottish philosophers of the eighteenth century and, especially, John Stuart Mill in the nineteenth century approached it. The disciplinary specialization of different works goes a long way toward explaining the rarity of the advocacy of this "complete" liberalism, including market society, a regime of rights, and the radical individual. But there is also an intellectual difficulty. It flows from the fact that the utopian character of liberalism can be concealed if it is presented piece by piece (the market reduced to a technical mechanism, the regime of rights to a practical means of guaranteeing pluralism and protecting the individual). But it emerges with full clarity when seen whole.

Liberalism and Its Enemies

This approach to liberal utopia also helps make sense of the paradoxes of modern anti-liberalism. The most remarkable fact in this regard is that "radical" anti-liberals—those who reject market society, the reign of basic rights, and moral liberalism—have almost entirely ceased to exist. Only among traditionalist thinkers, like Louis de Bonald, or else in the totalitarianism of the twentieth century, is such a complete anti-liberalism made manifest in coherent and explicit form. Fascism and communism, for example, had in common the simultaneous rejection of the anthropological foundation of liberalism as well as the ways of constituting and regulating the society that were linked to it.[4] The situation has now considerably changed. Anti-liberalism has become much more composite, dissociating the three liberal utopias from one another in order to accept part and reject part of the original triad. One can thus distinguish three principal anti-liberal formations active in the present. *Moral anti-liberalism* often coexists with a frank acceptance of market society and a cautious attitude toward rights; the "moral majority" in the United States, like the conservative right in Europe, illustrates this position. *Economic anti-liberalism* joins in a good number of cases with a militant moral liberalism under the banner of human rights; more and more, such is the position of the new extreme left or of the radical left in France. *Juridical anti-liberalism* characterizes, finally, republican milieux worried that the rise of judges and other independent authorities menaces popular sovereignty; often associated with a critical attitude toward the market economy, this approach leaves room, however, for contrasting approaches to moral liberalism.

These three configurations constitute only ideal types, of course, and multiple composite arrangements are to be found in reality. But they at least aid in reflecting on the contradictory nature of contemporary anti-liberalism, which almost always shares in at least one aspect of modern liberal culture. In fact, as a result liberalism and anti-liberalism turn out be always blended together. This variety also helps explain the polysemy of the adjective "liberal," which means in the United States what Europeans would consider "left-wing" positions while the same word has right-wing connotations in Europe.[5] How to make sense of this strange confusion? Consider the following hypothesis: the contradictions of anti-liberalism suggest a critique of liberal utopia and a recognition of the irreversibility of the modern world that this utopia represents. The duality therefore is other than a simple incoherence.[6] With due allowance for different sensibilities, it reflects a similar judgment. It also relates, in each of the anti-liberal configurations, to the expression of a counter-utopia: the utopia of a structuring human nature for

moral anti-liberalism; the utopia of an organizing and rationalizing voluntarism for economic anti-liberalism; the utopia of the
clearly reigning general will for juridical anti-liberalism. These
three counter-utopias are not all of the same nature. The first
could be called archaic. It expresses a reaction in the strong sense
of the term, a refusal of modernity and a celebration of an older
and putatively coherent age in which the community was prior
to the individual. It rests also on the belief in the impossibility of
the radical self-engendering of the individual. The other two
forms of anti-liberalism are more political. They relate to the
ideal of a society deliberately and voluntaristically instituted and
governed. As a result, they participate in what could be called the
democratic utopia (precisely that utopia that the utopia of the
market was intended to replace).

Understood in this fashion, anti-liberalism contributes to a
double tension. One is an anthropological tension between the
old and the new, between the community and the individual. The
other is a tension between the two rival utopias of modernity,
the sacralization of the will on the one hand and the wish for impersonal regulation on the other. None of these contradictions
can be ignored for anyone who wants to understand human
emancipation, for each utopia is permanently destined to criticism from its opposite. One thing, however, seems impossible:
advocating a plausible vision of the world rooted in a selective
anti-liberalism. For it is after all modernity in all of its facets that
one must try to grasp, as much in criticizing society as in considering its reform. That is, in the end, why parting ways with
utopian liberalism cannot limit itself to targeting the market as a
system of regulation. The challenge is more severe. It is a matter
of imagining political society in its double difference both from
the state and from civil society. The objective is first to free up
and to particularize the political field rather than to dissolve it; to
realize that democracy cannot develop except beginning with the
recognition of the irreducibility of social conflict and division.
Democracy need not involve the utopia of a unified people and a

general will that it is simply a straightforward matter of recognizing and activating; instead, it has to be imagined as a combat that will never have finished with its difficulties or even with the search for its object, rather than as a transitory reality that will pass into something else. It is a matter, in a word, of coming back to the political. In this vision, it is also necessary to get beyond the utopia of the market, but not at the price of substituting for it an impossible communitarian ideal; the way ahead is through a *reinstitution of individuals*. Only on these conditions will we stop being the orphans of lost illusions, restored to continuing a struggle day after day for a present that will not simply be waiting or preparing for a great dream ahead.

CHAPTER 8

Marx and Civil Society

The Liberal Horizon of Marx's Thought

It is well known that Karl Marx's thought originated in a critique of Hegel. Marx's reversal of Hegel has generally been understood as an inversion intended to place Hegel "on his feet" (as Marx put it). But, at least in the dominant Marxist approaches, the relation between Hegel and Marx has constantly been reduced to a simple opposition between idealism and materialism. It is of course not false to think of the relationship as an inversion. But the full meaning of this inversion only comes into view when one places it in the context of Hegel's relation to British political economy. In such a framework, Marx's *Aufhebung* of Hegel has to be understood as a return to liberalism. *Marx brings Adam Smith to bear on Hegel.* His whole reading of *The Philosophy of Right* testifies to this liberal critique of Hegel's thought. If he does not explicitly present it in this manner, it is only because he treats Smith and Hegel as if they were unrelated. He reads Hegel as a pure philosopher and Smith as a pure economist. Nevertheless, it is significant that in his *Contribution to the Critique of the "Philosophy of Right,"* Marx concentrates only on Hegel's chapters on the state, as if this finale of Hegelian political philosophy were not the product of a reflection on civil society. In the same way, Marx is interested only in *The Wealth of Nations,* and visibly shows little interest in *The Theory of Moral Sentiments.*[1] He thereby masks both the philosophical origins of political economy in Smith and the economic origins of philosophy in Hegel. One can defend him only by noting that some of Hegel's more fundamental texts (like the Jena *Realphilosophie* of 1803), in which his engagement with British political economy is clearer, were not yet known in Marx's time.

If Marx criticizes Adam Smith, it is only on economic matters. One is almost tempted to say that his critique is simply "technical," as the lengthy arguments of *Theories of Surplus Value* suggest. It is possible, then, for him to "go beyond" Smith economically, thanks notably to the invention of the concept of surplus value, all the while remaining implicitly on the ground of the same political theory. This association becomes even clearer as soon as one compares his critique of Hegel with the theories of William Godwin, for example, whose chief achievement was to transpose and continue Smith's philosophy in the political realm.[2] Marx's entire project is in fact shot through with two essential political themes that are equally central to what I have called utopian liberalism: the extinction of politics and the critique of the rights of man. For this reason, Marx's thought takes on a new meaning when he is placed in this perspective.

The basic critique that Marx addresses to Hegel is to have theorized the distinction between civil society and the state and to have been able to overcome it only through a truly "formalistic state." For Marx, the division between civil society and the state, which is to be found in the distinction between citizen and bourgeois (i.e., man, in Hegel's problematic), is the expression of a broken society. For the state represents only an abstract and exterior universal, because it has to be separate from the community. It is thus an illusion and a contradiction, Marx says, to think of realizing the unity of society in political life. Only civil society can be the locus of this unity. He writes, in this sense, in *The Holy Family*: "*Interest* . . . hold[s] the members of bourgeois society together; *civil*, not *political* life is their *real* tie. . . . Only *political superstition* still imagines today that civil life must be held together by the state, whereas in reality, on the contrary, the state is held together by civil life" (CW, 4:120).[3] All of Marx's *Contribution to the Critique of Hegel's "Philosophy of Right"* is founded on a similar rehabilitation of civil society against the state. And if Marx offers a radical criticism of bourgeois society, it is insofar as it is not a genuinely realized civil society, as we will soon see.

It is in this sense that he stands Hegel on his feet: in rejoining the liberal vision of the self-sufficiency of civil society. All of Marx's political philosophy is grounded in this representation. Like Godwin, he conceives of democracy, in his *Critique of Hegel's "Philosophy of Right,"* as a social state and not as a form of political government. "In true democracy, the *political state* is annihilated" (MER, 21). It starts from man in order to view the state as man objectivized rather than, as in Hegel's thought, starting from the state in order to view man as the state subjectivized. For Marx, real democracy is nothing other than "the actual element which gives to itself its *rational form* in the state organism *as a whole*" (CW, 3:116). It is conflated with the natural movement of a true civil society. That is why "the abolition of the bureaucracy is only possible by the general interest *actually* . . . becoming the particular interest" (MER, 25). In his eyes, politics can involve alienation and subordination only when it is understood as a separation. In this regard, he does not fear showing a certain admiration for the Middle Ages in which "property, trade, society, and man are *political*" and "every private sphere has a political character or is a political sphere too" (MER, 22). "When the structure of civil society was still political and the political state was civil society, this *separation*, this *doubling* of the significance of the estates, was not present. They did not *signify one thing* in civil society and *something else* in the political world. They acquired no *significance* in the political world but *signified themselves*" (CW, 3:82). It is wholly logical, then, that he could define the Middle Ages as "*the democracy of unfreedom*" (MER, 22). True democracy is nothing other for Marx than the reabsorption of the political into the social, and the realization of a society immediate to itself.

It is from this perspective that one must understand Marx's critique of Hegel's conception of a constitution as a "system of mediation." Representative democracy in his eyes, whether it is social states or undifferentiated and equal citizens that are represented, is a contradiction in terms. The representation of civil society is its separation or division. In his assumption that the *common interest* cannot be represented, he returns to Rousseau, for whom the *common will* cannot be represented. On this point his critique of Hegel is practically a reprise of Smith: "The transition of the particular interest into the general is likewise not a conscious law of the state, but is mediated by accident, proceeds *against* consciousness, and Hegel wants everywhere in the state the realization of free will!" (CW, 3: 56). It turns out to be the theory of the invisible hand and the natural harmony of interests that serves as the instrument of his criticism of the Hegelian theory of the realization of the universal will in the state. But if democracy as a form of representative government is unacceptable, it could nonetheless lead to real democracy through a process of the *universalization* of elections. Universal suffrage, once liberated from all the restrictions in which it is imprisoned, anticipates from the very interior of the political sphere as a separate domain the importance of that sphere's dissolution: it points to the coincidence of civil and political society. "In this situation, the significance of the *legislative power* as *representative* power completely disappears. The legislative power is representation here in the sense in which *every* function is representative. . . . He is here representative not because of something else which represents but because of what he *is* and *does*" (CW, 3: 119).

At the limit, then, universal suffrage points toward the suppression of politics; *it is identified with the market.* The text is remarkably illuminating. It shows in a limpid way the liberal horizon of Marx's thinking that sees in the realization of market society the figure of real democracy. To say that everyone is my representative to the extent that his function fulfills a social need is in effect to make the distribution of social tasks the sufficient foundation of the social bond: it is to understand the market as the principle of social organization. It is in this sense that *one can understand Marx's reversal of Hegel as a return to Smith*: it is the negation of Hegel's negation of Smith.

In this perspective, Marx's goal is to theorize the withering away of politics. The question of the withering of the state is, in fact, only secondary in his view, and is simply a consequence. But he does not confuse the question of politics with that of government. He wholly believes, on the contrary, that the withering away of the state, the expression of social division (which for him means class division), allows governmental functions to remain. But they are no longer really political functions, and are transformed into "simple administrative tasks." One discovers in this optimism the liberal theme of *political simplicity*: politics becomes simple because its only purpose is *administration*, and is no longer, in this sense, really political. It is this fact that allows one to understand that the withering away of the state in Marx's thought, as only the form that a deeper extinction the political takes, is not contradicted by the survival of simple functions of social administration.

At the same time, the modern state is criticized as a political form expressing the division of society into classes (this is the theme of the extinction of the political) and as a complicated bureaucratic apparatus (this is the theme of political simplicity). These two themes are only superficially joined together by Marx, who offers a rather fragile connection between the development of bureaucratic parasitism and the bourgeoisie's interest in occupying well-paid administrative posts.[4] But beyond this question of the withering away of the state, it seems to me essential to emphasize that Marx does not simply denounce the class-based state and the bureaucratic state, for it is equally the state as *rule of law* that he puts in his sights. Like Godwin and most of the utilitarians of the end of the eighteenth century, Marx in fact criticizes the very concept of the rights of man.

For Marx, to speak of the rights of man is to collude in the renunciation of the universal. In his eyes, the whole theme of the rights of man comes down in the end to a repetition and consolidation of the separation of state and civil society and the mutilation of man and citizen. He regards the Declaration of the Rights of Man and Citizen of 1791 as the fulfilled expression of this separation, which he analyzes at length in his 1843 response to Bruno Bauer's *On the Jewish Question*. The rights of man add up to the attempt to pose the liberty of each person without harming anyone else; in this sense, "liberty as a right of man is not founded upon the relations between man and man, but rather upon the separation of man from man. It is the right of such separation. The right of the *circumscribed* individual, withdrawn into himself" (MER, 42). They are thus simply the complement of political abstraction. To defend the rights of man is therefore nothing more than defending "emancipated slavery" (CW, 4:122). It confuses the emancipation of humanity with their transformation into bourgeois, since bourgeois society is precisely the expression of the division between worker and citizen; it is to make the reduction of civil society to *bourgeois* civil society more palatable, a reduction that requires the corollary of the creation of a separate political society.

In contrast, in a true civil society (we will see in a moment what Marx understands in this regard), "individual man, in his everyday life, in his work, and in his relationships, . . . has recognized and organized his own powers as *social* powers so that he no longer separates this social power from himself as *political* power" (MER, 46). That is why he can say in *The Holy Family* that the modern state and bourgeois society are what the rights of man imply. The rights of man are to modern society what slavery was to the ancient world. The struggle for the rights of man is thus an illusory one. "None of the supposed rights of man," he writes in *On the Jewish Question,* "go beyond the egoistic man, man as he is, as a member of bourgeois society; that is, an individual separated from the community, withdrawn into himself, wholly preoccupied with his private interest and acting in accordance with his private caprice" (MER, 43). One recognizes in these lines an approach still quite close to Godwin's, with the difference that unlike Godwin (who is ambiguous on the point), Marx refuses to take bourgeois society as a true figure of civil society. In his *Contribution to the Critique of the Hegel's "Philosophy of Right,"* however, Marx uses terms quite close to Godwin's when he makes the principle of a government of reason the condition of the true abolition of the sphere of law. "The will of a people can no more escape the laws of reason than can the will of an individual. . . . The legislature does not make the law, *it only discovers and formulates it*" (CW, 3: 58, emphasis added). The extinction of the political and the withering away of law are thus as logically entailed in Marx as they were in Godwin.

The classic Marxist distinction between formal rights and real rights has to be understood in this way. It is not a matter of opposing true and complete rights to limited and contradictory ones, rights for all men to rights that are useful principally to the bourgeoisie (freedom of enterprise for instance). Marx shows, on the contrary, that one cannot select among rights. The demand for "real" rights actually means the suppression of the rights of man *tout court.* True emancipation is inseparable from the extinction of law. This conception is not simply that of "the young Marx," since it is to be found throughout his works. His *Critique of the Gotha Program* (1875) is especially significant in this regard. Marx shows there at length that law, which only exists among *equals,* is bourgeois law in its very principle. It is commercial society, governed by the system of exchange value, that is in reality "the system of equality and freedom" (CW, 28: 180), since exchange always poses value against value.[5] In this context, the law of equals actually means unequal reward for unequal labor. Marx goes into detail on this point so that he can show

German socialists that their demand for an "equal share of the product," far from going beyond the bourgeois logic, is wholly enmeshed in it. He does not disagree that this step is necessary in a period of transition, since from capitalism's perfection will necessarily follow socialism's rise; but he concedes this point only on condition that everyone is clear that the struggle for equality is a bourgeois campaign. For Marx, of course, it is necessary to go beyond and surpass this cramped bourgeois horizon in a later communist phase of history, an event that will realize the genuinely new principle "from each according to his abilities to each according to his needs."

It is on the basis of this theory of the extinction of the political and the withering away of law that the whole of Marxist philosophy is erected. It is in this sense that politicized liberalism of Godwin's type amounts to its unsurpassable horizon. It is hardly possible, if this view is correct, to make distinctions among Marx's works. For it is in all of them that one finds this philosophy, which is "strategically introduced" simply depending on whether the texts are devoted to pure theory or practical intervention. But in all cases, even if he develops arguments that appear contradictory, Marx remains faithful to this liberal foundation. When he substitutes the practical necessity of the proletariat's seizure of political power for the theory of society's "real movement" his objective remains the same: that of the withering away of the political sphere. At best he simply places a moment of reinforcement of the political (with the dictatorship of the proletariat and the ratification of the state) before the final moment of the withering away of the political. No wonder his epigones, Lenin first of all, erected the dialectic, reduced to the possibility of affirming contradictory things, into the great principle justifying all of their shifts in tactics!

If one had to locate a break in Marx's thought, it is not between the works of his youth and those of his so-called maturity, but rather within those of his youth.[6] The sole and fundamental break in Marx's thought can therefore only be found at the very beginning of the 1840s. For it is in this period that Marx passed from a conception of democracy founded on the rights of man to a conception of the extinction of the political. It was between his 1842 article on "Lumber Theft," in which he demands an enlargement of rights for the poor,[7] and his *Contribution to the Critique of Hegel's "Philosophy of Right"* that the rupture took place, if there is a need to posit one at all.

Marx's Individualism

All of modern philosophy can be understood as a philosophy of the subject. It came about through contrast to the traditional organic conception of society that understood it as a whole of which each individual counted as a part without autonomy. To this extent the distinction between holism and individualism captures quite well the distinction between traditional and modern societies, as the latter progressively distinguished themselves beginning in the seventeenth century. What is the relation of Marx to this distinction? The response to this question is decisive because it provides the key for the analysis of Marx's relation to modernity, at least if one accepts, as a first approximation, the pertinence of the distinction between holism and individualism. In the conventional wisdom, most Marxists and anti-Marxists are agreed, probably without difficulty, that Marx is no individualist, certainly not in the common meaning of the term, that his thought is on the contrary directed at the object of society as a whole or the collective as the point of analysis. I agree with Louis Dumont and Michel Henry that such a view is a complete mistake.[8]

All of Marx's philosophy can in fact be understood as an attempt *to deepen modern individualism*. His critique of capitalism and bourgeois society takes on all of its meaning only when placed in this perspective. He shows in *Capital*, in fact at length, how capitalism's specificity is in making society, considered globally and abstractly, progress even as it makes men regress individually. "Indeed," he writes, "it is only by dint of the most extravagant waste of individual development that the development of the human race is at all safeguarded and advanced" (CW, 37: 92). *Capital* swells with examples illustrating this contradiction; Marx never stops gathering precise references to relations and citing reports on the workers' condition that illustrate the contrast between the overall wealth of society and the penury of the majority of those who constitute it. Michel Henry has justly written, accordingly, that *Capital* is the memorial and martyrology of the individuals of his time. The concept of the class struggle itself has no meaning except in the framework of an individualist representation of society. In a traditional society, in contrast, it would have no meaning. Social differences are understood in that case as part of a globally organic representation, one impossible to overturn, of social orders that are distinct but complementary; each individual can search for more just treatment, but never dream of emancipating himself from the place to which he is assigned. The class struggle, however, implies the possibility of a disruption of assigned places, and presupposes the possibility of classlessness, an undifferentiated and fluid society. The class struggle is unthinkable outside of the representation of society as a market.

Nevertheless, Marx does not accept the concept of the individual as it appears in eighteenth-century philosophy. Just as he repudiates the Hegelian idea of a universal *will*, he devotes long pages to the critique of Max Stirner's *The Ego and His Own*, which exalts the role of the individual will. Marx's individualism occurs as part of a critical movement in which one can distinguish three stages.

1. In a first stage, Marx denounces the fiction of the isolated individual on which a large number of social contract theories were grounded, theories according to which (as in Rousseau's thought) naturally independent individuals freely decide to join

together to form a society. On this point, he wholly parallels Hume's analyses or the histories of the Scottish school, which upended existing conceptions of the institution of society in showing that it was need rather than an abstract desire for society that brought men together. Marx shows at length in *The Holy Family* that this atomistic representation of man is nonsense. It is worth citing him at length:

> The egoistic individual in civil society may in his non-sensuous imagination and lifeless abstraction inflate himself into an *atom*, i.e. into an unrelated, self-sufficient, wantless, *absolutely full*, blessed being. Unblessed *sensuous reality* does not bother about his imagination, each of his senses compels him to believe in the existence of the world and of individuals outside him. . . . Every activity and property of his being, every one of his vital urges, becomes a *need*, a *necessity*, which his *self-seeking* transforms into seeing for other things and human beings outside him. (CW, 4:120)

It is thus the economic logic of interest, rather than the state, that creates the social bond. That is why "they are *atoms* only in *imagination* in the *heaven* of their fancy" (CW, 4:121).

2. In a second stage, Marx shows how this *representation* of the individual is simply a historical product of specific circumstances. "This individual [is] the product on the one side of the dissolution of the feudal forms of society, on the other side of the new forces of production developed since the 16th century" (*Grundrisse*, in MER, 222). The isolated individual, *Homo economicus*, free of any determination, has never existed from Marx's point of view, and "only in the eighteenth century, in bourgeois society, do the various forms of social connectedness confront the individual as a mere means towards his private purposes, as external necessity" (MER, 223). For Marx, it has always been a matter "from the beginning of individuals producing in society." The conception of the individual as it arises in the eigh-

teenth century is thus simply a *historical representation*; it is simply an ideology that makes appear as an eternal truth what is in fact the product of a specific mode of social existence.

Marx's argument on this point is, however, not completely coherent. If this representation of the individual appears only in the eighteenth century, with bourgeois society, how then to explain that the fundamentals of the representation of the individual at the basis of all social contract theory have existed since the end of the sixteenth century? To resolve this contradiction, Marx is logically constrained to answer that they are "anticipations of bourgeois society" (MER, 11). But he thereby obscures the process of emancipation of politics from religion (which began in the thirteenth century) and the process of the autonomization of the economy from politics (effectively achieved in the eighteenth century). Capitalism, bourgeois society, and modern society are all the same thing for him. While the "Robinsonades" were only the effect in the economic realm of the modern political representation of the individual, Marx implicitly considers them to be the foundation of this representation.[9] But there are no Robinsonades in Smith. When he speaks of the isolated fisherman and hunter, it is only with an illustrative goal, and these abstractions are constructed for a pedagogical end, to facilitate the reader's understanding of certain arguments. It is a methodological shorthand, and not a philosophical position. For Smith, in fact, it is exchange that comes first, and it is thanks to it that one must understand the origins of the division of labor. Not the reverse. Without exchange, fishermen would have to do their own hunting.

In spite of these contradictions, it is still possible to understand the sense of Marx's critique: it is not the notion of the individual in itself that he rejects, but only the abstraction of *Homo economicus* as it developed in the eighteenth century. In fact, he denounces this abstraction only in order to give back to the individual its complete meaning. The paradox of bourgeois society resides in the fact that the recognition of the individual occurs in the very movement that produces his alienation. It is the category of interest, then, that Marx most wants to challenge.

3. In a third stage, Marx therefore proceeds to a radical critique of the concept of interest on which the bourgeois representation of the individual is based. For him, interest is simply the result of a separation between the individual and life: "Under the guise of interest the reflecting bourgeois always inserts a third thing between himself and his mode of action" (*The German Ideology*, CW, 5: 213). It is a destructive mediation, and erects the individual only at the price of making him a stranger to himself. The category of interest, in fact, leads to the reduction of the diversity of needs and aspirations. As he will argue at length in *Capital* and in the *Grundrisse*, the individual's work is condemned to take on "the abstract form of generality," possible to apprehend only through reference to a general equivalent. Bourgeois society thus amounts to an obstacle to the universality of needs, in making them all homogenous and equivalent. Wealth is hence understood in a limited way if it is understood only in these terms: this is the whole meaning of the distinction Marx draws between use and exchange value. In reducing the individual to his economic interests, social activity is "petrified," transformed into an objective power that then dominates individuals and over which they have no control. Property itself reinforces this alienation. Far from enlarging the existence of the individual, it only accentuates his interior division: it forces everyone to be bourgeois, as individuals whose existence is restricted to the sphere of interests alone (cf. *The German Ideology*, CW, 5: 228–32). That is why the sole revolutionary objective can be to abolish rather than enlarge property.

The critique of interest therefore amounts to a critique of commercial society in which relations of individuals are fixed in things. Social life is reduced to "relations of exchange become the basis of all other relations," relations between persons presenting themselves in inverted form as a social relationship between things. All of these elements of Marx's analysis are sufficiently well known and are unnecessary to review at length. It is useful to emphasize, however, that Marx did not consider it possible to surpass this state of things, thanks to a generalization of the concept of interest. The point is not, he thinks, to substitute common for private interest. Agnes Heller has helpfully shown that the concept of class interest is not found in Marx's thought.[10] The general interest cannot be simply the sum of egoistic interests. To rely on the category of interest, even that of general or class interest, is necessarily for Marx to remain inside the capitalist world. The notion of interest therefore has to be suppressed, rather than enlarged, so that it is no longer the basis of individual or social action.

Marx's project, all things considered, is very clearly devoted to the enlargement and transcendence of the traditional representation of the individual. He turns out to be the theorist of a kind of *integral individualism*, founded on the search for a development of the ensemble of potentialities and possibilities that each individual richly possesses. But he does not understand these potentials as having an independent existence, for society in his view is the condition of individuality: man is "not merely a gregarious animal, but one that can individuate itself only in the midst of society" (*Grundrisse*, in MER, 223). It is a conception that is, in the end, quite close to Adam Smith's, since for the latter it is the propensity to exchange that grounds the division of labor and hence the ability to exist at once as a singular being and as one indispensable to others. Marx's conception is absolutely not essentialist; it is relational: "The human essence is no abstraction inherent in each single individual. In its reality it is the ensemble of social relations" (*Theses on Feuerbach*, MER, 145).

The full realization of the individual requires a society with fully realized and transparent interaction. Society has to involve pure commerce between individuals without the intermediation of merchandise. It is worth dwelling on this point. For it is significant that Marx often uses the words *Verkehr* and *Verkehrs-*

form [exchange and form of exchange] in order to describe social relations. These terms have in German a very clear commercial meaning. It is striking that Marx used them, as if he were himself wholly immersed in the commercial representation of society, as if commerce were the archetype of all communication (one should recall the double meaning—economic and social—of the word commerce since the eighteenth century).[11] His perspective is in the end that of the realization of a genuine civil society, a *menschliche Gesellschaft* that will no longer be simply a *bürgerliche Gesellschaft*.[12] Bourgeois society is simply a caricature, a travesty of civil society understood as pure commerce among men. It is in communism that man will realize himself individually and socially at once; communism is in fact nothing other than "the complete return of man to himself as a *social* (i.e., human) being" (*Economic and Philosophical Manuscripts of 1844*, MER, 84), and the condition of "the free development and movement of individuals" (*The German Ideology*, MER, 198).

The Extinction of the Economy

If communism is to surpass bourgeois society, the mediation of interest in the social relationships on which it is based must be suppressed. Only on this condition can the relation between men be transformed into pure commerce. *In this sense communism implies the extinction of the economy.* The point is often neglected in the analysis of Marx's thought. But it is essential, for it is one of the keystones of his whole system. Marx does not hope simply to control or reorient the economy, so that it will fulfill needs and no longer simply allow profit. His philosophical analysis is far more radical: he rejects the very principle of market exchange. Indeed, it is the economic sphere *as such* that to his mind is the source of the alienation of individuals. He explicitly assimilates capitalism to market society and, even further, to the economy *tout court*.[13]

The ensemble of Marx's work is incomprehensible absent this assimilation, which constitutes the logical connection that unites his philosophy with his critique of bourgeois economy. This is the reason that communism is supposed to be equivalent to a society of abundance. It is only in such a society that the economy is abolished, because there is no more scarcity. If not, he writes in *The German Ideology*, "*want* is merely made general, and with *destitution* the struggle for necessities and all the old filthy business would necessarily be reproduced" (MER, 161). In *Capital*, he returns several times to this central thread: it is only beyond production that the spread of human riches will begin. The world of complete wealth radically contrasts with the world of limited wealth (the economy). This belief is fundamental for Marx and is there as of his first writings. It is at once the product of his analysis of alienation, which remains imprisoned in the liberal representation of the economy, and the result of his fascination for capitalism. It is worth dwelling on these two points in turn.

1. As of the moment that he defines alienation as separation, Marx is led to criticize *all* forms of the separation of the individual from himself. This is the meaning of the critique of the political insofar as it is based on the distinction between man and citizen. It was only logical that Marx should have been led to restate this critique on economic terrain, too. The divorce between man and producer can be surmounted thanks only to a radical critique of political economy, *for the very fact that it is a separate and autonomous branch of knowledge*, a separation that is only a reflection in the realm of theory of what really happens in society (as the Marxist theory of ideology would dictate). Communism is at once the extinction of politics and of the economy. It is only on condition of this double extinction that "universal relations" among the human race can be established. The divorce between man and producer, which is given in the contradiction of the present historical stage between productive forces and social relations, can be surpassed only if the productive forces become

pure praxis, wholly identifiable with human activity in its wealth and diversity. Productive forces and social relations would overlap exactly: "Only at this stage does self-activity coincide with material life. . . . The transformation of labor into self-activity corresponds to the transformation of the earlier limited intercourse into the intercourse of individuals as such" (*German Ideology,* MER, 192).

The suppression of separation as alienation takes place through an interior universalization of society by each individual; the activity of each individual takes on a universal bearing, and there is no more "separate sphere of activity." It is "possible for me to do one thing today and another tomorrow, to hunt in the morning, fish in the afternoon, rear cattle in the evening, criticize after dinner, just as I have a mind, without ever becoming hunter, fisherman, shepherd or critic" (*German Ideology,* MER, 160). In such conditions exchange becomes simply free; it is no longer based on necessity and dependence and is converted to gift and generosity. Individuals no longer exchange merchandise but share their realized individuality. In fact, human labor, which is the measure of value, is only an interchangeable value for the individual whose labor it is. It is only in the individual that qualitatively different acts of labor could be the same thing since they then become simply this individual himself. Market exchange, in contrast, is based on the acceptance of the separation of the individual with himself, since it necessarily transforms his own particularity into an abstract and commensurable generality (measured by labor hours).

It is for this reason, no doubt, that Marx speaks so often of the development of art in communist society: art represents the incommensurable *par excellence,* what can only be given or received but never exchanged in the strict sense of the term, i.e. reduced to an abstract and interchangeable quantity of work. To this extent, communism is indissociable from the extinction of the economy, and the word henceforth reverts to its original meaning of saving. The economy no longer exists as a *sphere* of separate activity, but becomes nothing but individual and collective *action* with a view toward saving up the product of work hours in order to expand free time. Economy changes its meaning, becoming the means of the development of individuality for whom the material conditions of life are now transparent: Economized time "can be considered as the production of fixed capital, this fixed capital *being man himself*" (*Grundrisse*, in CW, 29: 97). Free time now becomes the true measure of wealth, in place of labor hours, since free time is not exchangeable.

For this reason, it seems absurd to speak of a communist political economy. Economics as the science of limited wealth simply disappears along with its object. In *its economic action*, society has no need now for anything other than *simple* methods for administering social production. It will suffice to know how to count in order to economize work. It is in fact a return to political arithmetic, though Marx would have said social arithmetic.[14] Political simplicity and economic simplicity will suffice to govern communistic societies. Because they become immediately accessible to themselves, such societies have no need to generate knowledge about their own practices. Lenin in politics and Trotsky in economics had adopted this premise sufficiently to be surprised at the brutal resistance that the facts put up against this idyllic vision of a simple society!

Upon discovering this conception of the extinction of the economy, one might wonder if Marx's relationship with his object of study—capitalism—is its source. For he ends up making classical political economy the theoretical apparatus exactly appropriate to the real nature of capitalist society. The manner in which he attacks Friedrich List's *National System of Political Economy* (1841) is particularly illuminating in this regard.[15] List reproached the classical economists for having conceived of the human race as a great international and cosmopolitan community in which there might reign an integrated harmony of individual interest. He responded with a theory of national economy prizing productive forces and criticized the theory of exchange value. In effect, List targeted the *representation* in classical economics of international economic life, suggesting that it ignored the concrete impact of various political conflicts. Marx ferociously takes him to task on this very point. "It can never occur to him that the political economists have only given this social state of affairs a corresponding theoretical expression.... Nowhere does he criticize real society, but like a true German, he criticizes the theoretical expression of this society and reproaches it for expressing the real thing and not an imaginary notion of the real thing" (*Critique of National Economy*, CW, 4: 276–77). Marx is the prisoner of his own theory of ideology. In taking the theoretical presentation of political economy as if it were the truth of the capitalist system, he excludes the possibility that it might be a *false or inexact representation*. He finishes, then, by mistaking this depiction for reality.

Marx's critique of certain French socialists fits in the same context. He attacks them for having tried to show that socialism amounted to the realization of the bourgeois ideas of the French revolution. For Marx, such an attempt is vain, involving as it did "the superfluous task of changing the ideal expression itself back into reality, whereas it is in fact merely the photographic image of this reality" (CW, 28:180). He believes, in contrast, that the system of exchange value, i.e., capitalism, is "the system of equality and freedom" (CW, 28:180). Following this critique, Marx proceeds to reproach the American economist Henry Carey for calling on the state to reestablish the harmony of economic interest; for Marx, after all, it is the intervention of the state in the economy from the outside that is the cause of the disruption of "natural harmony" (CW, 28:7). Marx thus turns out to be a dogged partisan of the most hallowed liberal representations of society. He does not share them, of course, but he presupposes that they are accurate. And his whole theory and his critique of alienation incorporates the simplifications and the illusions of this starting point. His radical critique of bourgeois society is thus in large part a critique of bourgeois society's liberal self-representation, which leads him to situate the conditions for the transcendence of this society in a highly abstract realm. The communist hope for the extinction of the economy thus can be understood in this sense as the effect of the incorporation of the illusions of economic liberalism into Marxism's heart.

2. But Marx is not only a prisoner of his own general theory of ideology. He is simultaneously the captive of liberal representations of the economy and fascinated by the capitalism developing before his eyes. He is the witness, at once horrified and admiring, of the capitalist revolution transforming the face of the world. It seems to me that this aspect of Marx's thought is not emphasized often enough, but it plays an essential function in pushing his analyses toward their radicalism. Marx considers the power of capitalism to be irresistible, and its further development is ineluctable. One could cite many pages of *Capital* or other writings that testify to this sentiment, one combining violent repulsion with ambiguous attraction. The brutality of his denunciation of the limitations of worker action is one sign, as if he sometimes felt that capitalism historically deserved its victory. He sees in such action ineffective skirmishes, entirely incapable of taming the redoubtable power of capital, even unintentionally reinforcing it. (His *Value, Price, and Profit* [1865] is an example.) Capital cannot be surpassed except through and on condition of its absolute triumph: this profound conviction is everywhere evident in Marx's thought.

He can only regard communism, therefore, as the conclusion of the historical process of which capitalism is the motor: the impoverishment of the mass of humanity will progress in tandem with a development of productive forces permitting complete abundance. Marx finally and explicitly sees the possibility of the abolition of capitalism as depending on its complete economic success. Thanks to this condition, he can contemplate the achievement of communism and the simultaneous extinction of the economy as a sphere of activity. If capitalism fails to play its historical role, if it does not bring humanity to the gates of abundance, nothing will. Capitalism will become impossible. Marx is wholly consistent on this point. Since the economy is determining, it can only be either all or nothing. It is impossible, in his perspective, to subordinate the economy to politics, as Hegel suggested (in any case, such subordination would simply replace one form of alienation by another); but it is also impossible to reduce the importance of economics in society, as Godwin recommended. In summary, Marx's critique of alienation and his fascination before capitalism's power converge to encourage him to think of communism as the extinction of the economy.

From the Natural Harmony of Interests to the Natural Harmony of Men

The movement of Marx's thought goes through two stages. First, he returns to the liberal economic representation of society in order to criticize politics as a useless and alienating mediation. This representation is in his eyes, in fact, the exact translation of the reality of bourgeois society. Second, he offers a philosophical critique of bourgeois society as such, and not simply its representation, through denouncing the alienation that the mediation of economic interest engenders. He follows through logically to see communism as the double extinction of politics and the economy, i.e., as a society that is no longer separated and in which no exterior mediation orders the relations among men. It turns out that bourgeois society surpasses political mediation by itself and communism, finally achieving abundance, allows for the suppression of economic mediation.

As a result, Marx defends a conception of the *natural harmony of men* that transcends the bourgeois limits of the natural harmony of interests. The latter is in effect a representation that corresponds only to a historically determined and temporary reality, even if it represented progress in its time. Marx says of utilitarianism, for example, that it is "a historically justified philosophical illusion" (*German Ideology*, CW, 5: 410). Marx in the end followed a path that is exactly the opposite of the one followed by Smith. The great turning-point of *The Theory of Moral Sentiments* consisted in its passage from harmony through sympathy—which Smith came to consider precarious—to harmony through interests. For Smith, interest or utility amounts to a guarantee of harmony, the concrete terrain on which the social bond can continue to be forged even if no reciprocal benevolence among men is assumed. In his critique of bourgeois society and the mediation of interest, Marx does nothing else than return to the classical theories of the eighteenth century of sympathy and the natural harmony of men. He does not surpass Smith except at the price of a veritable regression; this regression in a sense compounds the regression operated by Smith and modernity as a whole in relation to Machiavelli's thought.[16]

This is why Marx feels comfortable with all of the "materialists" of the eighteenth century, not hesitating to describe Bernard Mandeville as "typical of the socialist tendencies of materialism" (*The Holy Family*, in CW, 4:131). This "materialism" is for Marx the true naturalism. And one should recall that, in the *Economic and Philosophical Manuscripts of 1844*, he defined communism precisely as realized naturalism. For Marx, it is the fault of bourgeois society that the individual is corrupted, for having reduced him to living in society only through the manifestation of his economic interest. In another context than bourgeois society, however, the arithmetic of the passions could produce spontaneous harmony, and would no longer need the crutch of interest in order to produce it. Marx considers himself, accordingly, Helvétius's heir. He implicitly thinks of the natural functioning of society in the terms Helvétius believed society worked in general.[17] Communism thus becomes the place in which the most classic philosophy of the eighteenth century is realized. He returns even to La Rochefoucauld. Marx in fact lays out this genealogy quite expressly in *The Holy Family*: "There is no need for any great penetration to see from the teaching of materialism on the original goodness and equal intellectual endowment of men, the omnipotence of experience, habit and education, and the influence of the environment on man, the great significance of industry, the justification of enjoyment, etc., how necessarily materialism is connected with communism and socialism" (CW, 4: 130). While Smith conceived of the economy as the realization of the philosophy of the eighteenth century, Marx believed this realization would take place through the economy's suppression, which is to say he thinks of it in itself.

How to make sense of what one is forced to call a regression? It seems to me that it had two sorts of causes. Marx first of all began from a very simplified vision of the movement of modernity. He does not distinguish the moment of the emancipation of politics from religion from the movement of the emancipation of the economic in relation to the political. But it is clear that the birth of political economy is unintelligible unless one places it back in this double movement of modernity confronted by the wholesale redefinition of the institution and regulation of the social. For Marx, the question of emancipation from religion amounts to modernity, all by itself. Communism is nothing other than integral atheism. It is religion that expresses most fundamentally all of man's alienations. He writes, quite significantly, in *Capital*: "The religious reflex of the real world can . . . only then finally vanish, when the practical conditions of everyday life offer to man none but perfectly intelligible and reasonable relations with regard to his fellow-men and to nature" (MER, 327). Society produces evil effect only to the extent that it remains alienated, religion being the symbol of alienation understood as separation. Marx thus fully consummates the modern illusion of social transparency, Smith's liberalism having in some sense compensated for his political idealism thanks to a certain economic cynicism. It is Marx's critique of religion that masks from him the reality of division, fundamental and internal to man and society; it allowed him to mistake this division as purely historical and exterior. He remained, on this point too, the prisoner of his theory of ideology. Since, *a priori*, religion can be suppressed and surpassed, the division and alienation of man for which religion stands can be too. His whole "utopia" depends logically on this hypothesis of the possibility of transcending religion; he never poses the question of whether, in his terms, religion expresses a genuine distress that is man's ontological fate. He only conceives it as historical and transitory.

It is thanks to this last point, however, that one could analyze the second cause of what I have called Marx's regression. It is his conception of history that turns out to be problematic: he over- and underestimates the significance of history at once. He overestimates it insofar as it seems to him the forum in which the true nature of man can be idealized, in allowing social division to be cast as a historical product. History is then overloaded with the task of explaining everything lacking in transparency in human life, in individual man and in the relations among men. But in parallel, Marx is logically constrained to end history with the appearance of communism since it is the agent that brings transparency about. History thus exists only as the history of alienation: and it thus has to pass, itself, into history.

But there is a last conundrum, a central one in Marx's thought: that of the relation between the future communist society understood as achieved transparency—an association of realized freedom among men—and earlier historical forms of communal life. I have already noted that Marx often appealed to the latter in order to criticize bourgeois society, going so far as to depict the Middle Ages as "the democracy of unfreedom." In *Capital*, he insists at length that in medieval society social relations appear as what they are, relations between persons, with the natural form of work existing in its particularity and not, as in commercial society, as an abstract generality. "Those ancient social organisms of production are, as compared with bourgeois society, extremely simple and transparent. But they are founded . . . on the immature development of man individually" (MER, 327). Does this

mean that communism is simply the old social organisms plus
the maturation and generalization of individuality?

Marx is, in fact, not far from this position. It is the reason he
interested himself in the Russian peasant commune, in which he
thought immediate association took place, and in the same spirit
he could make admiring reference to the rustic and patriarchal
industry of a family of peasants who provide for themselves. The
famous drafts of his letter to Vera Zasulich are especially interesting from this point of view. He suggests that the peasant commune is the point of departure of Russian social regeneration,
but that it can be preserved only through revolution, since it conflicts with the ambient capitalism of its day that will never stop
eroding it otherwise: "To save the Russian commune, a Russian
revolution is needed" (CW, 24:357). In fact there runs through
Marx's works a subterranean nostalgia for *Gemeinschaft*; and it
is this term, actually, that he uses to describe communist society
as a community both immediate and transparent to itself. In a
significant passage, Marx vilifies Henry Sumner Maine, author
of the famous *Ancient Law* (1861), for distinguishing between
community and society and claiming that the transition from the
status of the one to the contract of the other represented immense social progress. Marx sees in this distinction nothing
more than an apology for capitalism (CW, 24:359).

As Louis Dumont has well shown in *From Mandeville to
Marx*, communism looks to be the reappropriation of primitive
or medieval communitarianism within the framework of the
widespread generalization of the modern individual, liberated
from the limitations even of bourgeois society. But this thesis
begs a question. For how really to reconcile the principle of community and the principle of individuality which are contradictory
by definition? Marx did not possess the theoretical materials to
respond to this question, since his conception of capitalist development led him, going against the grain of his heartfelt nostalgia,
to insist on the *continuity* of the development of society's productive forces (capitalism germinating as of the development of

cities and the renaissance of commerce). And it even led him to obscure the elements of cultural break in the origins of modernity in order to insist on this continuity even more. So once again it is a failure to understand the movement of modernity that turns out to be the culprit, and it led him not to grasp the nature of the contradiction he developed, longing for an unavailable communal past through a radicalized individualism in the future.

But it seems to me that one must go further. In defining communism as the immediate and transparent society, Marx ended up conceiving of a wholly abstract society, in which each individual is an aspect of universality, and society is structured only by a pure commerce among men. Communism, taking the revival of liberalism to its last consequences, ends up imagining the possibility of a social bond relying on nothing other than the "sweetness of sympathy," in Smith's expression, expelling all political or economic mediation from the relations among men.[18] Marx perceived this difficulty and addressed it explicitly in the *Grundrisse*, as if he became conscious, if only for a moment, of the utopian character of the vision of a society without mediation. "*Mediation has, of course, to take place,*" he writes.

> In the first case [i.e., commercial society (PR)], which starts from the independent production of individuals—however much these independent productions may be determined and modified *post festum* by their interrelations—the mediation takes place through the exchange of commodities, through exchange value, money, which are all expressions of one and the same relationship. In the second case [i.e., communist society (PR)], the *presupposition itself is mediated*; i.e., a communal production, community as the basis of production, is assumed. The labor of the individual is taken from the outset as social labor. (*Grundrisse*, CW, 28:108, first emphasis added)

The text is decisive. It is the presupposition of society as a totality that grounds the possibility of the social bond. Put differently, the abolition of political or economic mediation is redeemed by the identification of all individuals as part of one fused body. Communism as a purified market, as a society of pure commerce among men, fulfills the liberal utopia, if at the price of the contradiction of a total social organism. The partial alienations are replaced by a single and unique but global alienation: man is forced into a universality to be realized only through a power external to him, and even more difficult to identify since it presents itself as if it were nothing other than himself. Totalitarianism is therefore the last word of the utopia of social transparency.

PART V

The Future
of Democracy

CHAPTER 9

From the Past to the Future of Democracy

The Decline of the Will?

How to understand the turning point of the 1990s, which strangely saw the disenchantment with the life of democracies grow at the very moment that the fall of communism seemed to vindicate their supremacy? Did it follow simply from a tacit concession to the ideological trends of the time? From an unreflective submission to the consequences of European integration—unreflective because they were so imperceptible for so long? From a discreet abdication of politics before the new potency of the world economy? The blindness of men and the passivity of governments certainly had a role in this historical reversal, which different observers will judge each according to his own criteria. Every situation is made up, in part, of missed opportunities and unmastered events. But clearly these factors do not explain everything. One cannot rest content in framing this problem in the simple terms of a kind of political physics, gauging the relationship of the "positive" force of the will in its opposition to the "negative" factor of a putative abdication. What is at work goes much farther and involves the very essence of the political, and the meaning of democracy as well. What can politics accomplish? What does it mean to will change in politics? These are the two radical questions that are actually posed. To understand the apparent decline of a democracy based on the will requires an interrogation of the foundations of modern politics. For if something collapsed, it is first of all a certain historic conception of politics as a "science of the will."[1] This conception, directly derived from a theological-political understanding of power, arose inseparable from a presupposed image of society as *a single thing*, but one *ungraspable by itself*. This is the necessary point of departure for coming to terms with the political disarray with which this century has opened.

To begin at the beginning, then: the history of modern politics is without doubt bound up with the exaltation of the will.[2] Machiavelli made a break, for the first time, with the ancient order in showing that politics is not really pursued through virtuous action or the set-up of political regimes according to the plan of natural law. For him, politics is the singular art of erecting the city as an autonomous power, of constituting it as a sovereign actor in its own story. Simultaneously, the prince is no longer an ordinary master who is simply supposed to guide or supervise activity so that it is in conformity with the prerequisites of morality and justice. Instead, he becomes the historic agent of the work of incarnating a collective will, permitting the city to exist at all and through time. Two and a half centuries later, Rousseau amplified this break, calling for the end of the distinction between prince and people. In *The Social Contract*, democracy is the regime defined by the fact that it is uniquely founded on the human will. The problem is that this sacralization of the general will was by no means innocent of ambiguity. In fact, both the principle of an emancipation and the affirmation of a desire to substitute for all prior powers were combined in it. From this fact very quickly followed a challenge to political voluntarism, which indicted it for nourishing a pride that would lead men to the abyss. From Louis de Bonald to José Maria Donoso Cortes, a whole line of traditionalist thinkers painted an image, a prejudicial one to be sure, of what they called "democratic madness." Meditating on the avatars of the French Revolution, liberal thinkers, for their part, called during the same period for a more modest politics that would take its distance from too ambitious an exercise of the will.

The sacralization of the will and "hatred of the will" were, as a result, locked in opposition, and the reaction of the traditionalists and the hesitation of the liberals combined to stimulate awareness of the dangers and fragilities of the Rousseauean program.[3] The caution was not without foundation. Many of the ordeals of the nineteenth century and—even more—of the twentieth century proceeded from the attempt to artificially construct a meaning and a magnified form for a collective power that hardly existed by itself. But fortunately, political voluntarism did not always manifest itself in its hubristic form. It also existed more modestly and peaceably in the workaday functions of public activity and reform, constituting a kind of unsurpassable factual horizon of modern politics. The desire to make history, and to lift natural burdens and inherited encumbrances, always informed the positive utopia of men and women to create a world more habitable for everyone. Even more so since each individual, taken separately, had discovered as a result of his emancipation that he felt less sure of himself. The age of democracy as sacralization of collective will and the age of psychoanalysis as recognition of the lack of self-mastery are for this reason easily linked.[4] As a result, the modern political project likewise had an anthropological dimension. Politics could seem dedicated to make up for the weakness of individuals through the erection of a redemptive social power.

The route this project followed did not, as everyone knows, resemble a tranquil avenue. Its exits always remained attractive. Similarly, a sense of disappointment kept recurring, born of the realization that social reality would not bend so easily to fit the agenda of the will. It was from this disenchantment that followed the permanent temptation to surmount the timidity of actors and the resistance of facts by calling for the advent of exceptional circumstances, which alone might be able to give capacity and palpable energy back to a failing or hampered will. Only on condition of the ordeal of a limit situation, some apparently believed, could politics regain its substance and visibility. Alas, the martial celebration of a decisionism that burst the limits of the boredom of deliberation came to be seen—if no doubt differently on left and right—as the royal road to the will's restoration.[5] In an identical direction, blind faith in technology has often been affirmed, in hopes of mobilizing and revolutionizing a world that human action has proven too slow to change.[6]

Hence the sacralization of the will has always been both a problem and a solution. The relationship to political will could not be simple, a fact for which the evidence of its immediate functioning provides banal testimony. It has always needed to be staged for its meaning to appear legibly; hence the dramaturgical function often attributed to political rhetoric in a democracy. Decisions have to be made theatrical in order for them to be converted into meaningful and effective acts. Democracy is, accordingly, simultaneously the exercise of the will and the religion of it. Whence the importance of actions or productions that can sometimes make it appear clearly and distinctly in public. Such is the case, in France, of the secular politics of *"grand travaux"* (great public works projects). Monuments and prestigious public buildings are there in order to testify before everyone's eyes to the materiality of the public power. They provide a striking proof that a head of state's "Make it so" can have visible and durable consequences. The political philosophy of the will, which is at the heart of the democratic imaginary, transformed as a result and over time into a genuine *religion of will,* with its catechism, priests, rites, sacraments, and—sometimes—miracles.

It is this whole system that so brutally imploded at the end of the twentieth century. Multiple factors—political, sociological, even symbolic—combined to precipitate this result. The first, and probably the most important, proceeded from the transformations that affected the different forms of economic and social regulation. The classical vision of the exercise of political will presupposed a strong state, alone capable of taking charge of a dispersed society, one without any coherence of its own. Unable to pretend to institute society, except in rare circumstances, political action freely confounded regulation with the exercise of will. This trend occurred quite palpably in France in which an institution like the Plan was, for at least the thirty years following 1945, relied upon to project the orientation of the country, with all of its diverse units and domains, in an organized way. More than elsewhere, the idea of the will was fused in France with that of regulation. But the conditions for effective regulation were completely undermined in the last quarter of the twentieth century.

Is the "deregulation" that accompanied the globalization of the economy therefore the great culprit in the story of the decline of political will? One cannot rest content with understanding the process in these terms alone. If it makes sense of the relative decline of certain actors, such as the state, it leaves out the multiplication of decisionmakers and individual participants. Put otherwise, the growth of the self-organizing capacity of civil society stands out as the truly remarkable phenomenon. A complex system of interests and wills substituted for the former ideal type of *the* political will, a model that presupposed a unified agent. What results is a much more disseminated and differentiated type of economic and social regulation. The regulations did not disappear, but they lost their comprehensive scope and, above all, their legibility. Society has not stopped "willing," but it has come to express its wishes in muted tones, even pretending at times that its implicit choices, for some of which it may not feel much pride, were imposed upon it by nameless forces.[7] Civil society indeed has a "politics," but a discreet and silent one, the result of a multitude of deliberations in low voices and discreet choices that are never openly tallied. There is no way to make the adjustments of the market theatrical and no dramaturgy of decentralized transactions![8] The feeling of the erasure of the political thus corresponds to a real problem, at the same time as it rests on the confusion of regulation with a simple exercise of the will.

Society has, in consequence and in parallel, become more complex. This process also led to the loss of evidence of the notion of collective will. The stigmatization of a confiscated sovereignty made sense when the unity of society and the clarity of a common desire went together; the theme of social unanimity runs though the radical visions of democracy from the eighteenth to the twentieth century.[9] But it is no longer the same when "the people" are impossible to locate, no longer having the form of an evidently coherent totality. The principle of a strong and visible will dissipates when the subject that was supposed to give rise to it has been eclipsed. Behind the theme of the decline of the will hides the difficulty of making accurate enough reckonings to give strength back to the social bond. The "lack of will" does not refer so much to a weakness of character of the leaders as to a blindness of society about itself. It corresponds to a *social state* in which the meaning of collective obligation has been obscured. Its invocation is at the same time a means of attempting to exorcise the indolence and passivity of citizens who refuse to lucidly consider the effects of their behavior on society as a whole.

But it is not only the changes affecting the mode of regulation and the forms of community that have shattered the notion of political will. There is also a new and more disabused relationship to the earlier religion of the will itself. The staging of the political realm has becoming less rousing at a time when reference to "external constraints" has become one of the obligatory fixtures of political discourse. In the age of inexpensive government, when lower taxation becomes the generalized order to the day, the modesty that results, even when it is of a sincerely reformist brand, is not the stuff that excites the citizenry. Society's will and its leadership gave way together. For their part, the social sciences ended up adding to the disenchantment. In dissecting the mechanism of unintended consequences, sociology, for example, made a weighty contribution to abbreviating the reign of political will, in emphasizing its lack of practical effect. The sublime and powerful exterior of the will was seriously tarnished by the documentation of the actual mechanisms of collective decisionmaking, haphazard and creaky as they are. All of these factors contributed to the desacralization of politics.

This disenchantment has been felt everywhere. But it produced especially palpable effects in France, for reasons that were structural and political. First, the state there played a historically more central role, pretending to incarnate a strong collective exigency. The restructuring of its forms of intervention, beginning in the 1980s, was felt for this reason in an especially acute manner, creating a stronger impression of an abdication and a departure. The political factors also mattered. At the same time as the regulatory Keynesian state faded away, Gaullism saw its historic identity dissipate. It was not only a party political page that turned. For Gaullism in effect incarnated a very particular *political style*, centered precisely on permanent dramatization. The heir of both the political culture of resistance and dissidence and a military culture of action and decision, Gaullism, for a long time, could symbolize a politics of the will, and not just for its partisans.[10] The General's own theatrical manner only made this perception more obvious. The unraveling of Gaullism symbolically exacerbated the democratic disenchantment in French politics. The decline of the Communist Party and the collapse of the Soviet Union furthered this perception, as much in suppressing the image of a grand finale to history that would compensate for all of its burdens as in dedramatizing the terms of political contest, inscribed up to that point in ordinary cycles of alteration. The political scene, from then on, ceased to be the site of the frontal and vital collision of principles and wills, allowing the adversaries the belief that important things were at stake, requiring their own self-affirmation as well as an attitude of resistance toward the enemy.

Exposed in these terms, the history of this "decline of the will" suggests that it is above all a *metaphysics of the will* that disappeared at the end of the twentieth century. It is now quite simply impossible to continue to regard democracy in the theologico-political mode that had implicitly been its own for so long. It is not certain that "all significant concepts of the modern theory of the state are secularized theological concepts," as Carl Schmitt maintained.[11] But the thesis holds for the concept of the general will. *The Social Contract* well understood the new power of men as a secularized form of divine power, called, like God, to create a people.[12] And it supposed that the will could not take shape unless society made up a unified body, a personifiable totality. It is this last representation that has now found itself practically nullified. Originally bound up with the idea of the set-up and staging of society by an all-powerful creative will, does the sovereignty of the people now make no more sense? Certainly not. But it is now necessary to conceptualize it in a radically desacralized manner, in a break with the prior demiurgic imaginary with which the democratic project initially arose. It is not a matter of renouncing the hope of making the history of humanity or, at least, of mastering it. But it is to propose entry into an *ordinary age of the political*, in ceasing to believe that it takes on meaning only in the sound and fury of exceptional circumstances or that it exists only as the fleeting creation of a mighty idiom. The task is to imagine an age, both ordinary and desacralized, that forsakes impossible restorations, perverse nostalgias, and implicit abdications.

The Illusions

The path of a democracy that is both ordinary and exigent at once is far from easy to find. It requires first a compilation of the illusions and temptations that can endanger it. And the first temptation, and the most widespread today, is simply to give up on the notion of popular sovereignty. Numerous, in fact, are those who believe that democracies must henceforth content themselves with a minimalist and negative definition. A whole crowd of figures, from fine thinkers to hurried ideologues, repeat without imagination the theses of Karl Popper or Joseph Schumpeter, declaring the perspective of a self-governing society obsolete for good. The triple reign of the market, of the rights of man, and of opinion counts for them as a sufficient ideal, capable as it is of keeping at bay the specter of a sovereignty that might fall into an implacable tyranny. New frontiers, distant ones like the right of humanitarian intervention or the reorganization of the forms of cooperation among nations, or closer ones like the development of local solidarities, might continue to mobilize energy within this framework. So the triumph of negative democracy does not necessarily mean the end of history. But, for certain, it does imply the end of a very long cycle of inherited representations of the political. The problem is that most of these authors, yesterday called "empirical theorists" of democracy and today imprecisely labeled "liberals," too rapidly conflate the justified denunciation of "social constructivism" with the illegitimacy of any positive collective project—joining, as a result, the position of Friedrich Hayek, who thought he saw no intermediate position between the spontaneous order of the market and totalitarian dictatorship.[13] Nor do these authors distinguish enough between the "metaphysics of the general will," whose exhaustion I have just chronicled, and democracy defined as the attempt to institute an ensemble of individuals in a community. This is the topic of the rest of these reflections. Against the overly cautious vision of a definitively disenchanted democracy, it is indeed necessary to find a new emphasis on and centrality for the political function.[14] On condition, to be sure, that it is rethought and reformulated from the ground up.

As a precondition for this task, however, one must begin with the rejection of proposals that offer themselves for the restoration of collective will. They are seductive at first glance, but turn out be illusory and misleading. Two main cases of such illusions, in fact, can be distinguished, which are in turn opposed to one another: the *sovereigntist* illusion and the *globalist* illusion. The first hopes to restore meaning and power to political life through stigmatizing the "abandonment of sovereignty." But it does so by presupposing that the question of sovereignty is to be posed solely at the level of the state and in international relations. The defense of the nation and the reconquest of sovereignty of the people are understood, in this analysis, as strictly equivalent. The champions of this approach write as if the question of popular sovereignty were uniquely "external" and "institutional." When they stigmatize the supposed abdication of leaders, they believe the only remedy is a reenchantment of the will. Hence, in France, the permanent pull of a nostalgia for the Resistance, combining the cult of General de Gaulle with that of the author of *Strange Defeat* (Marc Bloch), improbably associating Joan of Arc, the soldiers of the Year II, Napoleon, and Clemenceau. It is believed that a moral posture is enough to solve constitutional problems and to fulfill philosophical needs. In this perspective, sovereignty is understood only as a effort of making the everyday heroic, always as if only exceptional circumstances could allow democracy to be thought.[15]

Lacking such circumstances, imaginary battles and resistance on paper are conjured up and simulated. The basic problem of this sovereigntist approach is that it presupposes the resolution of the question of the workable forms of popular sovereignty. It conceives sovereignty as already fixed, given, and known, something that needs only to be reestablished, by reversing the decisions that led to its inadvertent or malicious dissipation (whether the culprits are to be found in Brussels or on the Conseil constitutionnel). But this is to suppose that the determination of the procedures of representative government had not been entangled in any of the debates of which the history of democracy has been made. It is also to presume that the people constitutes, in the form of the nation, a self-evident subject, naturally united in a bloc without fissures. Restorative only at the price of fantasy, then, the sovereigntist perspective marginalizes the two problems that make up the democratic difficulty: those of determining its political forms and its sociological makeup.

The globalist illusion is the mirror image of the sovereignist one. It intimates, too, that there is nothing new to say or think as to the content of the democratic idea, the only problem residing in the gap between the inherited dimensions of institutions and the new space of issues to master. The project is thus to *transpose* the procedures of representative government to the European or global level. Multiple versions of the project have been formulated to create, in this spirit, a planetary citizenship and world democracy: the invention of a second chamber at the United Nations in which NGOs, businesses, and unions meet to discuss the stakes of the forms of globalization; the erection of forums in which "world opinion" on important topics could be expressed, which might allow for the emergence of planet governance; and so forth.[16] These different suggestions share in common a failure to discuss the foundations and the functioning of opinion-driven democracy or representative government.

But it is just these questions that one must face and confront now. Not with the pretense of giving a "solution" to the aporias that have constituted democracy as a problem. But at least there is reason to attempt to indicate what could become the lines of a program of thought and action that would redefine the democratic imperative in the age of a wholly emancipated civil society. The full presentation of these elements is the subject of a future work. I will limit myself here, therefore, to a summary presentation of some of the main themes, exploring in order the paths of a new, complex sovereignty, the pluralization of the temporalities of politics, and, finally, the perspective of a generalized emancipation.

Complex Sovereignty

The traditional conceptualization of popular sovereignty, as I have already insisted, involves a monistic vision of the political. One could label it, indeed, a *polarized sovereignty*, in two respects. It presupposes first of all that the vote is the sole principle of the coalescence of this sovereignty: the expression of the general will is apprehended in the framework of a zero-sum game among the different powers. The growth of the role of an unelected authority is thus perforce seen as an attack on the power of the ballot box. Sovereignty comes to be understood in a manner analogous to independence (for which the development of interdependence is automatically seen as a loss). And then a "sociological" polarization joins this "mechanical" polarization, since a monistic vision of the sovereignty of the people implies their unity. Divisions, therefore, are felt as a social pathology or a historical residue, and unanimity is understood as the usual and desirable face of society. Caesarism exacerbated this polarization that republicanism also presupposed in a slightly less flagrant manner. The exhaustion of the old metaphysics of the will has, however, sounded the death-knell of this conception. All the same, this event does not mean that the idea of an active sovereignty of the people is immediately robbed of all content, destined to a necessary decline. The key is to learn to conceive it in a pluralist and not monist manner.

Popular sovereignty, it has to be recalled, expressed itself *in practice* in a pluralistic manner througout the nineteenth and twentieth centuries, in noninstitutional forms like opinion and demonstrations (even if one must acknowledge in the same breath that republican political culture had trouble recognizing them). But it has never been *theorized* in this way. Except, perhaps, during the French Revolution, when certain publicists sought in 1791 to find forms of political expression in between direct democracy and representative procedures, or when Condorcet prepared in 1793 the first constitutional project.[17] A figure like Adrien Lezay-Marnézia could also ask, in the same spirit, for the "pluralization of the sources" of social power to make it more effective.[18] It is necessary now to take these forgotten intuitions as a point of departure in order to make them systematic.

The perspective of a complex sovereignty has to be won as much in terms of form as as in terms of procedures. The plurality of forms is the most simple and most obvious. It corresponds to the fact that the vote is only one of the modes in which preferences and wills are expressed. Whether for an individual or a collectivity, however, there are many other outlets to have a voice, to formulate opinions, to exert power, to announce a judgment, to maintain supervision, to manifest agreement or opposition— to participate, in a word, in public life. A sort of "social citizenship" has now coalesced, alongside the political citizenship formally associated with with electoral ritual.[19] Evidently, not the same kind of sanctions and obligations reign in these two registers, but they have, as a matter of fact, become complementary; and they are integrated into the same economy of the political, as many works of sociology and political science have emphasized. The "influence" exerted by citizens, to invoke the phenomenon in the most general sense, is, clearly and by general agreement, the result of all of these diverse modes of intervention. But the pluralization of sovereignty does not manifest itself only in this register. It can also take the form of an *expansion of the levels of sovereignty*.

The representatives of the people are of course, in the first instance, those who have been elected. But they are not the only representatives. Those who speak, act, and judge "in the name of the people" can also be considered representatives. One thinks not only of the case of judges, whether in a regular or constitutional judiciary;[20] but also, by extension, of the multiple authorities of regulation. Representativity is thus an ability that can have two origins: functional or procedural.[21] *Functional representativity* is the kind that is allowed and recognized by the texts that organize public life, whether laws or, above all, the Constitution, while procedural representation is that immediately derived from the electoral body. The monist vision of the political wanted for a long time to avoid recognizing anything but procedural representativity, that deriving from its electoral anointing. There followed all of the expectable consequences (notably the resistance to judicial review). But the perspective of complex sovereignty breaks with this approach, in making the recognition of a representative pluralism the key of a type of government both more faithful and more attentive to the general will. Is taking into account the functional dimension of the representative process a grievous attack against popular sovereignty, with unelected powers arrogating powers that would limit those of the representatives immediately selected through the ballot box? One cannot reason in these terms, since it is also the people themselves, in the constitutional case, or else their direct representative, who put these functions in place (the representativity of a constitutional judge is not, indeed, necessarily more indirect than that of a senator elected at one remove from the popular will and in fact chosen by his political party).

The two forms of representativity are thus complementary, even if they are always *in fine* in a hierarchy and a pecking order, with electoral legitimation constituting the keystone of the edifice of representation. The diversification of representatives is even, in this case, the condition of a more effective submission of representative government to the citizens. Édouard Laboulaye illuminatingly says on this count that a constitution has to be understood as "the guarantee chosen by the people against those who run their lives, so that they will not abuse the mandate conferred on them."[22] The expansion of sovereignty contributes, to this extent, to increasing it rather than to diminishing it. All this leads, indeed quite rapidly, to a complete transformation of the terms of debate on the relation between direct democracy and representative government. As a result of the expansion of representation, they form a situation in which the whole is more than the parts, rather than a zero-sum game. One can even go so far as to say that the closest equivalent to direct democracy is, from this perspective, a system of *generalized representation*. The different representative powers and functions end up in this case controlling and checking one another with as much efficacy as any people perpetually monitoring their government. A system in which all powers are simultaneously watching and watched [*réflectivité en abîme*] results in a political scene that resembles a hall of mirrors. A notable consequence of this conception is that the idea of the referendum, so often abusively presented as the major potential instrument of democratic progress, is resituated and put in its place.[23]

The relationship of liberalism and democracy can also be understood in a new way thanks to this perspective. In a complex sovereignty, the multiplication of functional authorities—often labeled "liberal" in the sense that they limit the omnipotence of the elected powers—is a positive means of enlarging the influence of society in the political process. The situation is thus precisely the opposite of what takes place under the model of illiberal democracy, in which a more consequential sovereignty of the people ends up implying the restriction of certain public liberties (in a manner that realized a better polarization of the political). Democracy can, on the contrary, be wholly and completely liberal thanks to the affirmation of complex sovereignty. Democracy and caution, or democracy and reason, can in this way stop being antithetical.[24] The progress of democracy must involve, therefore, a certain desacralization of electoral life,[25] even if the latter remains, in the end, its unconditional guarantee, its alpha and omega, always playing the role of periodic relegitimation, as well as assuring the proper hierarchy of the different kinds of power and representation.

Complex sovereignty owes its justification to the fact that it is a political form that allows a more trustworthy expression of the popular will, precisely because it is expanded functionally *and* materially. But it also corresponds to the "unlocalizable" character of the people. Far from forming a bloc, whose unanimity would reveal the secret of its content, the people remains a power that no one can possess or pretend to incarnate by oneself. The people is at once the central and absent subject of the political process; it always exceeds the approximations that are given of its identity. At the moment of an election, it exists in an instantaneous and evanescent form. It only materializes approximately. Since it is always complex, incomplete, and renewed, the people can only be known by a kind of representation at once expanded and refracted. It is the reverse of what the liberal theorists of the 1830s, who believed that this sociological respect for differentiation called for a limitation of popular sovereignty, affirmed.[26] In response, it is necessary to emphasize that the recognition of the complexity of the people should lead to the growth of its means of expression. Understood in these terms, democracy is a political form incomplete by definition; it always remains an approximation of itself that only a complexification of sovereignty can make less imperfect.

If the future of democracy proceeds down this route, it is the problem of resymbolization that becomes the decisive challenge. The history of popular sovereignty certainly suggests the importance of the various mechanisms for making power theatrical. How to stage the new complex sovereignty and how to celebrate a people now absent? The solution is not, of course, to revive or reinvent the old metaphysics of the will. The symbolization of politics will not be a florid transfiguration and enchantment of reality, but the enterprise of perpetually recalling a task to be carried out: the constitution of an unlocalizable people in a living political community.

The Plural Temporalities of the Political

An expansion of the forms and subject of sovereignty, then. But there is more. The relationship of democracy and time also has to be rethought. And it has to be said that political theory has remained indifferent before this subject. The duration of institutions and the rhythm of democracy have never, in fact, been understood as decisive questions. The temporalities of the political are usually understood as simple technical constraints. They are at best made part of an elementary physics and chemistry of power. It has been emphasized, for instance, that too long a representative term will exacerbate the distance between representative and represented; or, to take an opposite example, that too short a term in the executive reduces the governability of the system. Time is understood as a purely mechanical variable, worsening or reducing the everyday contradictions and tensions of democracy. The central question is always implicitly in this case that of the relationship between direct government and the representative system. But that vision is too restrictive. The utopia of an *immediate democracy* can play just as decisive a role as that of direct democracy. An analysis of this idea, therefore, provides an interesting basis for beginning the attempt to elaborate a theory of the relation of democracy to time.

Begin with Ernest Renan's formula: "Direct government," he notes, "is the situation in which the general will would be nothing other than the caprice of each moment."[27] The author of *La Réforme intellectuelle et morale* emphasizes what could be considered a *logical limit* of a certain conception of the reign of popular sovereignty. If democracy is the regime of that sovereignty, then it follows that fidelity to the exercise of the general will has to be constant. Ideally, then, this will would have to be formed and assessed all the time. But the problem is that such permanence, such immediacy, would paradoxically lead to its destruction: it would end by dissolving itself through its segmentation, existing only in perpetual variation. The bar to an immediate democracy is not just a mechanical one, owing to the impossibility of its practical organization. It is philosophical. If the general will cannot be a "caprice of each moment," in Renan's vivid formulation, it is because the will is *substantively* elaborated in time. The relationship between immediate democracy and representative government is therefore not the same as that between direct democracy and representative government. The impossibility of direct democracy is due far more to practical constraints, even if that is far from its only difficulty.[28]

The examination of this logical paradox of immediacy suggests that democracy takes on meaning and form only as a *construction in history*. One cannot therefore rest content with a procedural definition (the mechanisms of decision and legitimation) or with an essentialist approach (taking into account the "social quality" of power and the representatives) to the democratic regime. Democracy is a function of time. This discovery *a contrario*, derived from the fact of immediate democracy's logical impossibility, is corroborated sociologically. The people, as a collective political subject, is in effect itself a figure of time. Its content *is* a history. Democracy is thus not only the system that allows a collective to govern itself, but is also a regime under which a communal identity is constructed. To this extent, memory is a key variable of democracy. It articulates the temporalities of the will, joins liberty and identity, and allows distinction between the positive recognition of tradition and a negative imprisonment in it.[29]

These remarks lead to the realization that the technical possibility of "teledemocracy," in the age of the internet, does not bring with it any kind of solution to the constitutive aporias of modern politics. The ideas of the electronic town meeting or televoting were all the rage in the 1990s, suggesting as they did the imminent entry into an age in which citizens would permanently run their affairs.[30] Some commentators did not hesitate to celebrate a world in which the force of the citizens in politics would become just as permanent and omnipresent as that of consumers in the economy.[31] What invalidates this conception is not simply that it underestimates its implications for the deliberative moment of politics, but also and more profoundly that it obscures the historical dimension of democracy.[32] The same main criticism can be directed as well against all of the attempts to see media and polling as ways of invigorating democracy more effectively than the political system in supposing that they allow the citizenry to manifest their feelings continuously, in contrast to the ballot boxes in which they deposit their views only at fairly distant intervals. Such procedures are suspicious not simply because of their likely informality or technical unreliability, but, most problematically, in the presumption that immediacy is the most desirable quality of popular voice.

Against the grain of these approaches, I insist on the necessary pluralization of the temporalities of democracy. The construction of a history as well as the difficulties of the present in effect demand the articulation of very different relations to social time. Time-consciousness needs to be vigilant in the case of memory, lengthy in constitutionalism, variable for diverse institutions, and short in opinion-formation; and all these have in turn to be mutually adjusted and harmonized. No doubt, political life is made up of the inevitable collision of these various temporalities. And such collisions, it bears remembering, are explicitly anticipated by institutions. The ordinary rhythms of democracy are enmeshed in one another, crossing one another constantly, since the lengths of different terms of office are various, just as the dates of different elections do not always coincide. Midterm elections can always end up disrupting the expected calendar, and the principle of dissolution of a chamber (what Georges Burdeau called "one of the officious forms of direct democracy") also leads to the disturbance of temporalities and a resynchronization of the expression of popular sovereignty. But the pluralization of democracy's temporalities that I have just evoked goes beyond even this institutional framework: it unites the different facets of the will, making sure that no one of them comes to eclipse the others.

This vision, it has to be emphasized, is not simply a revival of certain nineteenth-century authors, like Renan, Alfred Fouillée, or Maurice Barrès, who offered the prospect, each in his own way, of a people that could not take on unity except transgenerationally. One can recall, for instance, Barrès's formula defining the nation as "the possession of an immemorial cemetery and the will to value this indivisible heritage." For such authors, taking account of time meant above all the limitation of the present will, as part of a larger theory of debt to the past.[33] Leaving Fouillée aside, who saw this reality as the generative matrix for intergenerational agreement, this perspective generally bespoke conservative or reactionary commitments. It was a matter of making a kind of sovereignty of the dead weigh on the living, thereby empowering tradition.

The recognition of the plurality of democracy's temporalities, in contrast, is pursued here to extend and to expand civic participation. The degradation—or even the denial—of democracy typically follows from a refusal of this complexity. The aim of conservatives who would like to see tradition triumph once and for all, the trap of an illiberal democracy dissatisfied with the life of institutions, the media-driven attention to the momentary whims of the public, the revolutionary celebration of a single moment of foundation—all of these represent in effect still narrow appreciations of democratic time that deny or mutilate it. This observation, however, actually allows one a framework for understanding the meaning of conflicts among militants, journalists, representatives, executives, intellectuals, or judges. Each of these figures of the political scene implicitly inhabits the role of guardian of one among other democratic temporalities, thanks to the very fact of the particularity of function of each. *Guardians of the temporalities of the political*: the recognition that the different mentioned actors are this too helps expand the inherited understanding of the life and development of democracies. The expansion of its forms and the conjunction of its different temporalities converge at this point, together allowing the new perspective of a *plural democracy*.[34]

The perspective affords another new consideration of the relation of law and democracy, judicial and legislative power. Instead of thinking of them as antagonistic or, at best, coexisting forces happily outfitted for mutual containment, it is possible to place them in a single framework. Constitutional law relates to a longer timeframe of democracy, while the decisions of the executive or the lawmaking of the legislature inhabit shorter cycles. Absent this approach, the relation to the past, even the recent past, always risks seeming (as Rousseau put it) like "chains in which one wraps oneself for the future." The very existence of a constitution can seem like an atrocious limitation of the general will.[35] Then only the "caprice of the moment" will count as democratically admissible. It is against the grain of this whole way of reasoning that it is necessary to give a temporal breadth to the project of constructing a democracy, and to link it to the development of the rule of law. One can, from this point of view, consider law as the sovereign will's memory, as Victor Hugo once saw it: "Law shines in the eternal, where universal suffrage acts in the moment. Law reigns where universal suffrage governs."[36] It is exactly in this sense that one must think. The development of liberties and the furtherance of participatory democracy can then be pursued in concert.

Generalized Emancipation

The pluralization of the *forms* and the *temporalities* of democracy has to be continued by a reconsideration of the *fields* of the political. The central problem of modern times resides, in this regard, in the conflict-ridden relationship between the two imperatives of personal independence and social power. Liberalism and democracy, to refer to this binary distinction again, have in fact appeared for two centuries as twins, often separated or even antagonistic, but twins because they represented the two aspects of the same modern program of emancipation. On the one hand, the collectivity's empowerment. The goal of democracy is in this sense to substitute a principle of self-institution of the social for all the old powers imposed from outside. On the other hand, the affirmation of a principle of the personal autonomy of individuals. The liberal objective is to protect each person against outside authorities, whatever form they may take. Locke and Rousseau incarnated these two moments and two faces of modern emancipation. The problem is that these twins, quite rapidly, were revealed to be rivals. Democracy sometimes could appear as vulnerable to a tyranny of majorities, just as the objective of radically protecting individuals could seem to empty the idea of a collective project of meaning, the idea of a society of individuals undermining any notion of political community. The political history of the nineteenth and twentieth centuries has very largely derived from this contradiction. Such an insight allows, for example, understanding why French history oscillated between moments of *illiberal democracy* (like Bonapartism) and *undemocratic liberalism* (the Restoration and the July Monarchy, for instance). An equilibrium finally discovered between the models resulted from a prudential bricolage, but it has been one fated to perpetual instability—as the spectacular rise of illiberal democracies at the end of the twentieth century testifies.[37]

This foundational tension can be reconsidered today, and for reasons that are anthropological, sociological, and political at once. The anthropological reasons stem from the new relationship between self and others that has slowly arisen. The modern individual became *at once* more autonomous and more wedded to a dynamic of social interaction, light years from the old atomistic perspective that was implicitly the basis of early liberal individualism.[38] This does not mean that the individual has become more absorbed into the collectivity, transformed into this "mass" that the pioneers of the social sciences feared a century ago. Rather, it is more a consequence of the fact that the modes of production of identity have become more complex and differentiated, no longer resting on a logic of similarity and on a mechanically inclusive sense of belonging; they now imply the deployment of a process in which recognition and differentiation are linked. Some part of modern individualism involved the distancing of the social, but much has brought it back: or so one might schematically summarize the matter. The perception of "the social" has, in parallel, also been modified. It is now conceived less as the agglomeration of particular existences, distributed in clearly distinct and stable groups, than as the complex system of figures drawn by homologies of trajectories and communities of situations, forming a tangle of relations as multiple as they are variable. *It gathers together histories and experiences*, and not simply essential characteristics. The constitution of the political world and the construction of the self have thus become at the same time much more confounded with one another; the conquest of autonomy and the affirmation of social power combine; the development of rights and the advancement of democracy are now bound up together.

The different registers of emancipation have, in this way, come to be decompartmentalized. This transition, in fact, started to be perceived as of the aftermath of May 1968, notably in France where the theme of *autogestion* linked individual liberation and political change in unprecedented respects. At the same time that it participated in the mutation—at once cognitive, cultural, organizational, and political—of the 1970s, the idea of *autogestion* accompanied the entry in a world in which emancipation could no longer be thought of except in a way indissociably individual *and* social. Care of the self and political combat demanded the ending of their antagonism, leading to a fundamental reevaluation of the older horizon of militancy. In an admittedly confused way, the wave of *autogestion* contributed to the introduction into the era of a new understanding of the democratic imperative, implying both its de-institutionalization and its enlargement. That it later subsided did not imply that this turning point was false. There resulted above all a process of the purification of this theme, which dissipated and renewed it at once, stripping away the still archaic language in which it was originally expressed (in "leftist" accents which were utopian both for better and for worse).[39]

If the age of *autogestion* could thus come to seem, in consequence, to have passed, the era of a new democratic exigency has endured. The life of democracy could no longer limit itself to the moment of the vote nor, more generally, to the political sphere alone. As a result, it authentically completed the vision of those who gave democracy a social definition in the nineteenth century—by radicalizing it. The earlier antagonism between the two approaches to democracy, political and civil, was for such reasons almost completely transcended. The rise in prominence, during the 1980s, of the notion of citizenship later testified to the same fact. The need for its enlargement—people started to speak of "new economic citizenship" or "social citizenship"—little by little substituted for the exclusive project of extending democratic procedures.[40] It is under the banner of the triumph of law that this new approach to the democratic idea finally become generalized. By the end of the road, democracy imperceptibly had ceased to be a simple political method; it became a moral and social norm.

This new perception of the democratic imperative allows, in this way, a new consideration of the variety of forms that human emancipation can take. The goal of democracy is not to deploy power, but to lead to a process of generalized emancipation, linking and bringing into coherence personal experiences and social situations. The notion of sovereignty will keep a useful meaning, from this point of view, only if it is also conceived as an enhancement of liberties and opportunities, and that far from portending closure it provides openings.[41]

The interpenetration of different forms of emancipation leads, indeed, to a reformulation of the very object of politics. The point is no longer simply to put the people in power; more radically, it is to institute the people in a coherent collectivity. The central political concept is no longer will but justice. There is a transition from a voluntarist democracy to a *constructive democracy*, whose goal is to organize a common life through the regulation and distribution of rights and goods among men and women. The discussion of norms of justice and their application is at its heart.[42] The approach, clearly, runs against the stream of all those sovereigntist proposals in which the people exists as an immediately coherent datum, with a self-evident identity, determined sufficiently in its confrontations with the "outside." It sees popular sovereignty as a problem to be resolved rather than a solution to call into service. A far cry, then, from the common fantasy according to which the people preexists democracy in the form of an idealized totality—a fantasy that does not cease to nourish itself on the dangerous exaltation of exclusivist homogeneity. The rejection of the stranger becomes in this case the way in which the terms of social debt are obscured. It is as if the nation could proceed from a simple opposition to others, not founded itself on reciprocal obligations constituting a space of redistribution to realize. Against the grain of this artificial and perverse vision of social unity, the goal ought, in contrast, to be to organize the social bond in a positive and legible way, with all of the differences it involves.

The republican idea responded to this imperative in the nineteenth century. But the terms of the enterprise have since changed. To produce the nation today, it no longer suffices to refer to such general juridical principles as separation of church and state, the rule of law, or equality of opportunity. These principles have to take on the flesh of economic, social, and fiscal realities. Beyond the key question of multiculturalism, the organization of the coexistence of different beings requires talking about the welfare state and the politics of redistribution, continuing to draw the dividing line between acceptable differences and illegitimate inequalities. The people in a democracy is always a fragile people, ever incomplete and never a fused bloc. Instead of magnifying an unlocalizable unity, it is a matter, on the contrary, of ever making clear the tensions of life together, to allow the attempt to overcome them. Far from calling for a hypothetical "return of the will" of a powerful state that would tower above men and transcend their differences, it is necessary today to begin with a frank acknowledgment of the realities of society that produce the interactions of civil society. Beyond even the analysis and potential criticism of the dysfunctionality of the workings of the market, there is the ensemble of "civil society failures" that it is now a matter of recognizing in order to address.[43] This approach, I note, leads to blending the redistributive perspectives that originally belonged to socialism with democracy's preoccupation with institutionalizing society. It gives back a lost unity to visions of political progress.

But the democratic imperative is not limited to this enterprise. Now added to this last task is the insistence on universal-izing the human project of emancipation. Democracy tends in fact to spill over its originally national framework and inspire a conceptualization of emancipation and justice on the larger scale of the globe as a whole. The pluralized forms of the political already require, by themselves, posing in new terms the question of the democratic field. If electoral mechanisms remain basically national (with some exceptions like elections to the European Parliament), the public sphere for its part has been globalized to some extent, also allowing forms of surveillance and control without any precedent. The space of emancipation is therefore, in ways that are parallel and responsive, enlarged too. The no doubt difficult formation of international norms in the field of human rights testifies to this fact. The movement has been launched, a cause as impossible to stop now as the conquest of universal suffrage was in the nineteenth century. It will probably not take the same course, however. The globalization of democracy will likely give birth only to a partial "democracy," limited to the guarantee of certain rights, very different from the adoption of common electoral procedures, and even then often restricted to purely regulatory tasks. This extraordinary expansion of our field of vision and commitments should not lead us astray. It is one thing to create a field of consciousness and another to institute a polity. It is also one thing to notice the growing internationalization of regulatory mechanisms, another to envisage the creation of a supranational sovereignty. The sovereignty of regulation is not that of institution.[44] It is for this reason that the democratic idea is not ready to break the bonds that unified it at the level of the nation. Not at all. And this for a very simple reason: the nation always remains an object to be constructed, it is still to be realized, at the crossroads of the inheritance of memory, the elaborated norms of judgment, and the requirements of a generalized emancipation. The "open" nation, which one could contrast with the closed nation of sovereigntism, thus has before it a future that remains to be sketched.

Nothing makes it impossible *a priori* that nations could die one day, or transform themselves. But it is important to see that this is not the question of the present. Quite far from the possibility of dreaming of a transcendence of nations from above, we are rather faced today with the risk of their disintegration from below. At the same time as elements of law and forms of regulation are internationalizing, solidarities are partially withering. The multiplication of secessionist movements in the world suggests as much. Instead of simply following from the need of cultures to turn on themselves and celebrate their positive identities, these movements often represent the waning of hitherto accepted norms of solidarity. Rather than giving in to costly redistribution, some would rather limit the dimensions of their nation-states to more homogeneous bodies. The temptations in Europe today are strong: the Flemish and Walloons no longer wish to forge a common welfare state in Belgium, the former complaining that they support the latter; a growing number of northern Italians call for a political separation from the southerners, whom they deem too poor; the Czechs and the Slovaks have already bade farewell to each another for such reasons.

There is no longer any economic argument to oppose to these movements. Great nation-states could be socially costly, but they were necessary in order to generate sufficiently large markets. The nineteenth century saw the rise to power of great nations in part for this reason, and not simply out of military imperatives. It was thought that they would be better off large than small because they would benefit from a large internal market and, therefore, from a stronger economy. German and Italian unity was forged on this model, and before them the United States was and remains the best example of the point. Sheltered by a militant protectionism, the United States in fact permitted its businesses to benefit from amazing economies of scale, allowing the country to become the giant of the history of capitalism. A large market, a strong federal state charged with protecting it and to welding it together with the same currency (which nonetheless took some time, as in Europe, to be fully institutionalized): efforts at national unity in the nineteenth century were founded on this example, as are those powering the drive to European unity today.

This vision has run out of steam. Economic power, territorial size, and demographic mass can be uncoupled from one another. Globalization allows small nations to easily gain access to larger markets. The success of tiny city-states like Hong Kong and Singapore shows that the existence of a large internal market is no longer the condition of wealth and growth. Economic theory today even stresses that small nations "cost" less than large ones: the larger a nation-state, the more serious the heterogeneity of its population. And in that case, the costs of redistribution for managing difference will be correspondingly important. Conversely, the smaller and more homogeneous the nation, the lower the expenditures of its welfare state.[45] The economic benefits of large size once entered an equilibrium with corresponding social costs. But such is much less the case today, which makes sense, in some part at least, of the vast wave of political secessions occurring in the world. Behind cultural or political nationalism, apparently alone responsible for the trend, an impoverished approach to solidarity is silently decisive.

At the same time as frontiers and minds open, the meaning of what is possible to join and share is on the wane. Our societies have therefore become morally schizophrenic, allowing the comfortable coexistence of sincere compassion before the misery of the world and ferocious defense of self-interest. The withering of the properly civic space is its cause: solidarity is not strongly structured enough by it. The feeling of solidarity has difficulty even expressing itself coherently; it "floats," so to speak, between the very far and the very near. The development of the "humanitarian" at the same time as there occurred a growing flight from fiscal and social responsibilities is a symptom of the malady. More visibly each day, two conceptions of solidarity confront each other in our societies: the *solidarity of humanity*, on the one hand, and the *solidarity of citizenship*, on the other. The first testifies to a new and enlarged awareness, one without frontiers, of the responsibilities of people to one another. But this extension of conscience is related to a minimal duty of solidarity: if possible, keep people from suffering death by hunger or genocide. This duty corresponds, according to a typical United Nations estimate, to a financial obligation that a sum on the order of one percent of the world's wealth would satisfy. The solidarity of citizenship is much more demanding. It implies the realization of a certain equality of opportunity as well as a basic (if still quite relative) proximity of standards of living. In industrialized countries, this obligation translates to a figure that oscillates between 35 and 50 percent of national wealth. The philosophical difference between the two conceptions is thus related to a considerable material difference. The great temptation today, everywhere at work, is to see the more exigent solidarity of citizenship wane in favor of a solidarity of humanity both less taxing economically and more spectacular in its mediatized consequences. The feeling of solidarity is globalized, but its content is minimized: such is the hidden, and silent, moral face of globalization.

For this reason, a renewed and exigent vision of the nation has a future. Its mission is to realize on a small scale what the world cannot manage on the large scale. It is in the nation that the general and the particular can be synthesized in a positive way. Between the near and the far, it is a stepping-stone, and allows forms of experimentation with universalistic content and potentially universal consequences to be tried. The debate over globalization and reflections on solidarity thus converge to put the question of democracy in its national forum back at the heart of our societies. Far from disappearing into the void left behind by the increased experience of individuality and the accelerating rise of the global scene, the idea of popular sovereignty has a long future ahead of it. But it will have no meaning unless it is put back in the irremediably complex movement of forms and temporalities through which the nature of a life in common will have to be discovered.

The Transformation of Democracy and the Future of Europe

The utility of Europe in an ever more globalized economy and an increasingly unstable world is self-evident but problematic. In reality, Europe is a project that has yet to find a political form adequate to its ambitions and to the expectations of the citizens of its various member states. For this reason, it has become commonplace, in the last ten years, to denounce the deficit in legitimacy that is supposed to characterize the functioning of European institutions and to call for their "democratization." Hesitation and impatience have combined, in this atmosphere, to increase the number of skeptics at precisely the moment that the extraordinary revolution involved in the institution of a common currency took place.

One cannot simply brush aside these fears, anxieties, and objections of the skeptics, as if an imperious historical necessity allowed one to save oneself the trouble of introspection and reflection. But at the same time, one must understand that the fear and impatience characterize a more general stage in the life of our societies. The feeling of powerlessness among citizens and ever more difficulty in believing that the world is intentionally governed—that is, apprehension before a decline of the political—are not simply features of the project of European construction. They are part of much larger mutations relating both to the process of globalization beyond Europe and to transformations internal to each individual society. The same observation applies to the fears, so often expressed, that the increasing power of the media is progressively falsifying democracy and that the growing presence of legal and market forces, along with the multiplication at all levels of unelected regulatory authorities, has insidiously undermined the sovereignty of the people.

1. The Four Mutations of Modern Democracies

The so-called democratic deficit in Europe is, in fact, only one symptom among others of an inner transformation in the history of democracy. Independent of European construction, the life and forms of democracy are being revolutionized. One can even say that, in large part, the notion of a "democratic deficit" in Europe is the *consequence* of the phenomenon rather than its cause. The problem is posed in just the same way when facing the disruptions following from the globalization of the economy. Economists have usefully advanced our understanding of the question by emphasizing that the difficulties attributed to globalization have been primarily due to a third industrial revolution, that the problems are caused by the emergence of a new mode of production rather than by a simple geographical extension of the old system. Similarly, European construction does not simply raise the question of the extension of democracy to the European level. Rather, it implicates the future of the very life of modern democracy. I therefore consider the potential forms of Europe in the making by clarifying the terms in which the contemporary transformation of democracy may be understood. These contemporary mutations of democracy are taking place at four levels. The first of these is a differentiation of the political; the second, a "pluralization" of the agents of the political; the third, a dissemination of the political; the fourth, finally, an increasing secularization of the political.

The Two Functions of the Political

The differentiation of the political, first of all, is occurring thanks to the growing distinction between two essential functions: institution and regulation. In Jean-Jacques Rousseau's language, one would say that the two great functions are sovereignty and government; in the older language of the seventeenth century, politics and justice. In the modern nation-state, these two functions of institution and regulation have been superimposed on one another. Today, regulation has largely overflowed the field of the nation-state, whether one considers the growing role of law, the new prominence of the market, or the more important place taken up by supra- or inter-state authorities (the World Trade Organization is an obvious example).

In the meantime, the function of social institution, which remains the heart of democratic life, has been weakened by the crisis in the welfare state (for democracy does not simply consist in establishing a community of sentiment but also constitutes a community of redistribution). Today, the growing differentiation of the functions of the political is a result of the fact that the two functions no longer overlap, and that, at the very moment of this uncoupling, democratic life, essentially linked to the work of institution, suddenly finds itself atrophied. Furthermore, this differentiation between the regulatory and the institutional functions occurs very largely at the level of agents, where it is identical with the difference between civil society and the nation. Civil society is the space of regulation, while the nation is the space of institution. So it is also the emancipation and rising power of civil society that produces the current feeling of a decline in the political. These remarks, as a matter of fact, point to the continued importance of the debate about the relationship between "the liberty of the ancients" and the "liberty of the moderns" that has been repeated again and again over two centuries.[1] But the differentiation of the political does not just push these two great functions further apart. It also affects the transformation of the way in which democratic sovereignty is exercised.

Historically, democratic sovereignty was built up around the electoral procedure as the central mechanism of legitimation and control. But at the same time history makes clear that the life of democracy has never been reducible to the electoral moment alone. Albert Hirschman has explained very cogently that it is necessary to view the relationship to institutions in the larger framework of a complex economy of forms of adhesion or suspicion, and suggests a distinction between the three modalities of social expression: *exit, voice,* and *loyalty.*[2] Analyzed within this framework, the classical democratic moment could be considered as the moment of loyalty. The introduction of universal suffrage, for a period, led democracies to identify citizen intervention with this procedure of legitimation. But *voice*—protest, critique, the expression of opinions—or *exit*—that is to say, defection—are also modalities of participation. And they play an ever greater role in a society that is doubly opened up by the expansion of the public sphere and of new possibilities of interaction. The differentiation of the political today, then, follows from the fact that more and more modes of representation, types of supervision, procedures of monitoring, and manners of the expression of preferences are becoming available and distinguishing themselves from one another. Paradoxically, democracy thus seems to be diluted precisely because the possibilities of relating to institutions and one another are multiplying.

The juridification of politics has to be analyzed in this way, too. The possible mechanisms for guaranteeing political responsibility have been extended. People now demand in the courtroom what they could not always get through the ballot box. There is a modification of the terms in which what one might call a "democracy of allegation" elaborates its forms and its institutions. None of this is really new. In France, since the time of the Revolution, men like Jacques-Pierre Brissot or the Marquis de Condorcet have conceptualized the exercise of sovereignty not simply as the exercise of suffrage but also as popular monitoring or control by opinion. Today, however, a moment has been reached at which the double differentiation of the functions and forms of the exercise of sovereignty implies an alteration of the institutions themselves. Up to now, this difference in functions and procedures in the exercise of sovereignty could accommodate itself to existing institutions. But no longer.

From the Particular to the General

The second great transformation through which our democracies are living can be characterized as the "pluralization" of the agents of the political. The classic agent of the political is the citizen. The citizen is the person who represents the *general* interest of society. The man of needs is the man of *particularity*, unlike the citizen representing generality. This vision of the citizen lies at the heart of the classic definitions as forged by Rousseau as well as the Abbé Sieyès. Generality can lead to a representation of society as a unified will because it is based on the possibility of abstracting from particular men.

One of the most important transformations in our societies resides in the fact that the "mode of production" of generality has been transformed. Traditional regimes of generality were conceived in a unitary and aggregative sense, compatible with Rousseau's thought, while present-day generality more often has to be understood as rooted in the partial parallelism of singularities. The narrative identities of today, for example, differ from the classical social identities of "position," and allow at best only a rapprochement of trajectories. Contemporary generality proceeds by means of successive approximations and can no longer derive from a unified view of society. From now on, generality means that the category "people" cannot exist immediately in its universality as a globally representable phenomenon, but is intelligible only as the result of the aggregation and the overlapping of particularities. What makes it most possible to approach generality, Sieyès said, is to distinguish more and more what separates the abstract citizen from the concrete man of needs. Today, then, one might say that what allows for generality is not separating and taking distance from the man of needs, but the survey of all the ways his needs might overlap with those of other men. It is in this direction, or so it seems, that one can grasp the deep meaning of multiculturalism in today's society. It does not merely stem from some denial of generality simply in order to further particularity; it also corresponds to an unprecedented recomposition of particularities and, thus, the kind of generality that they permit.

This new connection between particularity and generality means that nobody owns the people: the people is simply a function of its different figurations over time, the succession of its inevitably partial representations. The people are at once a function of time and of experience. This formulation is markedly different, quite obviously, from the one Rousseau could give of the people and the general will. This transformation of the availability of generality in different societies likewise corresponds to a differentiation of the forms of representation. Alongside a basically procedural representation (that is to say, representation through the electoral mechanisms), there are new forms of representation developing today. Some of these could be called functional (arising, for example, in procedures of expertise, since representation is a process of knowledge and not just a mechanism of delegation). Others could even be called moral (as when charities are considered representative of a problem, or a population is imagined in a similar way thanks to the very fact of their concern with it). This diffraction of representation has the consequence of multiplying the agents of the political and changing our vision of the separation between civil and political society. Civil society, in its multiplicity, becomes one of the possible faces of political society; it is not simply the site of private life or the locus of particularity. Large consequences follow, in fact, for the demands of this civil society on the political order, as well as at the level of a certain number of European institutions.

Which Emancipation?

The third development characterizing present-day democracies is the dissemination of the political; emancipatory purposes are becoming more undifferentiated. What is the definition of emancipation in the modern world? It is a twofold one: emancipation can mean individual autonomy or it can mean collective power. John Locke gave the definition of emancipation as autonomy. The purpose of emancipation in this perspective is the construction of an individual ever more independent of others. But the other, Rousseauean, vision of emancipation is to make everyone stronger through their participation in the collective. The history of modernity has unfolded as a process of competition and permanent conflict between these two approaches. The tension between emancipation as individual autonomy and emancipation as collective power is equivalent quite simply to the breach between liberalism and democracy (the one representing the moment of personal autonomy, the other expressing the moment of group empowerment). It is redoubled in the distinction between law and politics (with law the key vector of emancipation interpreted as the assurance of autonomy, and politics the key vector of emancipation understood as the empowerment of society). Today, however, a unification of the registers of emancipation is taking place. Individual and collective emancipation, autonomy and social power, increasingly overlap, one might say. There is now one sole register of mastery that runs from personal self-respect through the sovereignty of the people. A porous language and porous practices of mastery in the world are united, so that neither individual nor social empowerment is thinkable apart from the other.

At the same time, however, as the dissemination of the political implies a growing lack of differentiation between the tools of personal and social emancipation, domestic and foreign policy also increasingly overlap without distinction. Today, the very term "foreign policy" no longer carries the meaning it had just two decades ago, in the untroubled possibility it allowed for contrast with national politics. It once presupposed the specificity of forms, purposes, and methods as well as of a difference in field. In each of these aspects, the differentiation between national and foreign is less perceptible. There is a general economy of sovereignty that features a *continuum* in areas like protection, integrity, and identity. Security problems, for example, are more and more inextricably domestic and foreign (while Hobbes's entire theoretical problematic was founded on this latter distinction). But the contrast between domestic and foreign politics did not simply depend on a difference of purposes between the two realms; it also involved one of method. While national politics could be understood as a space of publicity and deliberation, foreign politics was defined by the reign of secrecy and decisionism. The national and foreign worlds were also very strongly dissociated from one another, too, in the ways that they constructed authority, allowed intervention, and countenanced debate. But now these differences and boundaries have vanished.

The Meaning of Political Will

The fourth great transformation perceptible in our democracies is the growing secularization of the political, reflecting that fact that we are living through the end of a democracy based on the will. The superseded democracy of the will presupposed that social life could be acted out and transformed from a central point. The very history of political theory has followed, in a sense, the transformations of the perception of this "theater of the will." Political theory, for example, has recently begun to emphasize the distinction between ordinary and extraordinary politics, making clear that if the first sometimes seemed to be relegated to everyday housekeeping, the theatrical dimension of the will could sometimes return in the heat of exceptional circum-stances.[3] Whether such extraordinary times were those of foundings or refoundings, or whether they were full-fledged revolutions, they were once perceived as essential moments of reinvigoration that allowed politics to be relived as a theater of the will. The felt decline of politics, from this perspective, has to be placed in the perspective of such "cycles." But it also corre-sponds, more profoundly, to a "disenchantment of the will."

The very belief that there exists a "general will," the verita-ble *deus ex machina* of democracy, is cast into doubt today, and more and more people accept the reality, more modest and actu-ally more coherent, of the interior dynamics of society. It is bet-ter understood that the general will cannot be seen as a "gener-ality" that would be imposed on the life of individuals, and that it could have a real sense only if redefined as the "truth" of so-cial interactions. Such is the lesson of the social sciences, one spread to such an extent that it has forced the retreat of "magi-cal" visions of the political. The social sciences, in fact, make clear that the reality of the general will is to be found not in the at-tempt to declare or stage it, but rather as the product of compro-mises, choices made among rival options, and preferences of a complex civil society. (The role of politics in this perspective is to clarify them, to render them more explicit so that they can be modified).

It is impossible, then, to understand the contemporary world if one contents oneself with deploring the existence of a "deficit" of the will that simply continues to mount. Put otherwise, the growth of the self-organizing capacity of civil society stands out as the truly remarkable phenomenon. A complex system of in-terests and wills has substituted for the former ideal type of *the* political will, a model that presupposed a unified agent. What results is a much more disseminated and differentiated type of economic and social regulation. The regulation has not disap-peared, but it has lost its comprehensive scope and, above all, its legibility.

2. Europe and the Nations: A Poorly Constructed Debate

If I evoke these different aspects of the contemporary transformation of democracy, however rapidly, it is because they allow an understanding of the direction in which and conditions under which one can reasonably expect the construction of democracy in Europe to occur. One must note at the outset that it is not to be imagined as a kind of restoration, or as a transposition or a recombination of traditional forms of democracy.

It cannot occur, first, in the direction of a restoration: it is impossible to hope for the reconstruction, at the level of Europe as a whole, the forms of the will that seem to have deserted each of its member states. The former French prime minister Lionel Jospin remarked, not long before his 2002 defeat: "To be a socialist is to be a voluntarist." But does the impossibility of reanimating the theater of the will in each of the nations make plausible its restoration at another, European level? I am most skeptical on this point. The challenge, in fact, is to pass from a conception of the will as production of volition to a notion more like the production of legibility. The point is not to restore the old utopia (always an illusion) in a new framework. One must avoid, therefore, the hope for impossible restorations: there is no way to find anew at the European level the forms of sovereignty that have been painfully lost nearby. It is a matter, rather, in both realms, of substituting for a "metaphysical" with an instrumental conception of sovereignty.

If it is past time to reason about Europe from within a framework of "democratic restoration," however, it is equally impossible to think of Europe as the forum of "transposition." This is precisely the limitation of the notion of cosmopolitan democracy, whose champions propose to reproduce the forms of the nation-state and representative democracy at a higher level—even, for example, at the global level. This vision of a cosmopolitan democracy that has nourished a whole sector of the discussion in political thought for a decade, around works like those of

Jürgen Habermas or David Held, commit the capital mistake, in my opinion, of implicitly believing that the "dysfunction" of contemporary representative democracy is the fault simply of the framework of its exercise, and not of its very forms.[4]

Finally, what one could call "improbable recombinations" also seem to me to be blind alleys. I mean by this phrase all those who bet on the development of a new type of civil society that could finally substitute for the world of politics. On this front one finds the naïve representatives of NGOs—leftists who have re-invented themselves as humanitarians—and the executives of multinational corporations, all of whom commune together to-day in a touching defense of an international civil society. The utopias of the ones, alas, are hardly different from the hypocrisies of the others. And so there is to be found today a whole dubious apology of "governance," as the new name of a government that would suffice for everything, that could replace politics by widely disseminated techniques of management, leaving room for one sole actor on the scene: international society, uniting under the same banner the champions of the market and the prophets of law.

If the descriptions of the transformations of contemporary democracy that I offered as well as these words of caution about the contending supranational visions are of any use, it is because they lead to reflection on Europe in terms that will avoid the er-rors of simple transposition. A British historian, Larry Sieden-top, recently published an interesting work entitled *Democracy in Europe*. One of his chapters is entitled: "Where Are Our Madisons?"[5] And it is true that Europe has no Madison, and no Sieyès either. But the problem is that this author presupposed that Europe is today in the same situation American democracy faced two centuries ago. Yet it is not in such terms, in my opin-ion, that one should think. The term of federalism is illuminat-ing in this regard. Different federalized experiences have all been particular, and (unlike the state) there is no single "model" of federalism that political science could describe and that is simply waiting to be applied. The common call for a federalist perspective is therefore misleading, and says nothing precise: it simply indicates the existence of a problem to which no one yet possesses the solution.

The question to consider today is the extent to which Europe could play a role between nation and globalization. For the desiderata today are a restored nation and a regulated globalization. What can Europe accomplish in this regard? One must begin by observing that European construction is inseparable from a refoundation of nations *and* from a construction of international regulation. Europe cannot be the substitute for the undoing of nations and the impotence of globalization. In this sense, Europe is not a sort of "middle term" between these two defeats, paradoxically enacting their simultaneous resolution. Why not?

The first reason is that there is no European *demos* in the offing. What defines the nation is a community of redistribution, based on a "solidarity of citizenship." That solidarity differs greatly from a simple "solidarity of humanity," one aimed not at limiting inequality, but rather at guaranteeing that the peoples of the world are not made victims of hunger, war, or genocide. The latter involves a comparatively minimal debt. It is not the creation of a *life in common*, but simply the defense of *life as such*. If one places the solidarity of humanity and the solidarity of citizenship on a continuum, where, one might ask, do European institutions fall between them? In quantitative terms, the response is simple. Social redistribution by European institutions represents 1.27 percent of the gross European income. The implication is that the whole of the European machinery does not generate a solidarity of standards of living. Undoubtedly, it puts in place undeniable mechanisms of redistribution (notably in the agricultural realm). But they remain limited and are reduced rather than expanded by the dynamics of enlargement, as the perspective of the reform of agricultural policy illustrates very well. For this reason, the construction of Europe cannot substitute for the refoundation of nations. For the central question of the refoundation of nations is precisely that of the consolidation of the world's welfare states. Where the welfare state wanes, the nation itself vacillates. And one sees today that secessionist movements, where they are taking place in Europe, are very often grounded in the refusal to share a common welfare state. The most classical example is that of the tension between the Flemish and the Walloons, who no longer want a common social security plan. The refusal leads expectably to the destruction of the nation. It is for this same reason that there is no European *demos*. European construction does not allow Europe, then, to save itself the trouble of refounding its nations. At the same time, Europe cannot do without a more effective regulation of the international economy.

If one acknowledges that the double task today is the refoundation of nations and the organization of a better international economic regulation, what is the place that Europe could take up in the enterprise? It is one both simple and decisive. It amounts to the creation of a new space in which a limited but important experiment with universality can take form. Consider a debatable but potentially illuminating analogy. What was the supreme concept at the time that the horizon of empire, at the end of the Middle Ages, began to disappear? It was to create spaces that permitted limited experiments with the universal. It could no longer practically be lived out within Christianity, nor within the empire. It thus had to be "incarnated" in the then unprecedented and unique space of the nation-state.

The experience of the nation-state is that of a *universal in miniature*. It does not correspond simply to *a sharing by the similar* in the optic of "identity." I believe that in its own manner, the construction of Europe today must once again attempt to realize a certain form of universality in miniature, a universality of legal and economic regulation that global regulation cannot attain. This means, then, that if one takes seriously the differentiation of the functions of the political that I indicated before, European construction ought to be considered solely from the point of view of regulation and not from the point of view of the institution of the social. The question of institution remains that of nations (so long, in any case, as there is no European *demos*). In return, however, there is an essential historical task that such an exclusively regulatory project must face. Confronted with the constitution of new empires that demand a regression to archaic forms of domination or impoverished forms of cultural homogeneity, Europe's role could be to put into practice an alternative modality of new, if limited, universality.

The great question posed from this perspective is whether there will be other equivalents of Europe, understood in the sense just outlined, in tomorrow's world. European construction cannot be developed further without posing this question. The answer is decisive for contemplating European enlargement. It makes no sense, in a way, to pursue this course without first inquiring into the existence of other Europeanizing projects at work in the world. Indeed, the future of the whole world might turn out be the choice between Europe and empire! It is necessary, then, to theorize the possible multiplication of Europe—and if one does not do so, then one has not theorized Europe itself.

A Constitution or a Charter for Europe?

The last question to examine is whether Europe should have a constitution or a charter. I would like to show why the notion of a charter is different from that of a constitution, and to say why, in my opinion, a charter is the document that could provide the right framework for the continent.

A constitution's goal is to organize a *demos* in a closed space on the basis of a well-defined architecture of public powers. A charter, in contrast, aims at organizing diversity in an open space by affirming regulatory principles and envisaging regulatory institutions. The differences between them, then, are of two orders. The first is that the logic of a constitution involves the erection of institutions, while the logic of a charter is the expression of regulatory principles. What organizes a charter is law; what a constitution puts in place are public powers. But there is a second great difference, very palpable in the European case: a constitution defines a restricted space, a full space, while a charter can embrace an open field. For this reason, when the United Nations outlined its principles, it did so in the form of a charter and not a constitution. For similar reasons, there can be no constitution on the world level: it would be a contradiction in terms.

It is impossible to reflect on the forms of a future Europe without posing the question of its frontiers. I have tried to suggest as much already in imagining a multiplicity of such entities in the world. Nevertheless, the enlargement of its frontiers is evidently Europe's most immediate problem. It can happen only within the framework of a charter. Europe must become a political form under the guidance of an open charter and not through the imposition of a closed constitution. What consequences could such a choice have on the forms of life of the European democracies? For it is no simple matter to pass from an interrelation of governments to democratic institutions. The criticisms leveled at Europe today are, at bottom, criticisms that attack Europe's democratic deficit as a result of the intergovernmental nature of its procedures and institutions. Europe, it is charged, floats between the technocratic and the democratic. The destructive equivocation, it is often insisted, has to be left behind by "parliamentarizing" it (that is to say, by erecting a legislature chosen on a European basis, election of an executive figure, and so forth).

But it seems to me that things have to be approached differently, beginning from the functions and forms of sovereignty today, and not from institutions, if Europe's future is to be correctly defined. Europe has no chance of living up to the expectations of its citizens unless it becomes one of the laboratories of contemporary democracy—allowing itself to give new forms to deliberation, to representation, to regulation, to authority, to publicity. Rather than considering the development of "European representative government," it is necessary to ask how original forms of deliberation, representation, regulation, accountability, and publicity might develop in the European space.

Take the case of deliberation, for example. Is the problem simply that of how to modify the enumerated powers of the European Parliament? I do not think so. In any case, it is not the sole problem; there is also the need to find a kind of deliberation that can bring the societies themselves together. It is, in this regard, closely related to the development of a common European public realm. The effort Europe must undertake is to become a living public arena, and not to rationalize a conventional parliamentary space. In the same way, the questions of representation today imply the search for modalities for the intervention of civil society in the political process. And one should not forget that, for twenty years, the United Nations has organized the participation of NGOs at their large conferences (as is well known, a resolution of the Economic and Social Council institutionalized such participation).

If one wished to consider matters in Europe in this way today, an essential objective would be to transform the nature and function of the European Economic and Social Committee sited in Brussels (which, for the moment, is restricted to a consultative role). The EESC could become a space of representation and of the intervention of organized civil society. In the same fashion, if one looks at the modalities of the division of functions, is the goal that the European Commission will simply become more and more like an executive authority, in the classical sense of the term, or is it rather for it to become an agent of applying, coordinating, and arbitrating a whole ensemble of regulatory procedures? If one considers for example the agencies of the regulation of telecommunications, or else the role played by commissioners charged with international commercial negotiations, they ought to be understood—and to act—more as *strong agencies of regulations* rather than as parts of a weak government. Similarly, one of the great challenges for modern democracies is to remedy the weakness of publicity, to put an end to the rule of secrecy. Europe, in this domain too, could make itself a space of experimentation.

It is for all of these reasons that we must learn to think of European construction as the development of a new age of democracy and not simply the project reproducing, on a different scale, the inherited democracy whose sails have lost their wind, and left everyone today, wherever they are in the world, with the same problem.

Democracy in an Era of Distrust

The erosion of the trust of citizens in their leaders and in democratic institutions has been one of the most heavily studied phenomena in political science over the last twenty years. A series of famous works, in a national or comparative framework, have clearly established a diagnosis for the malady, and they are sufficiently well known to make it unnecessary to revisit them. It is simply useful to emphasize that eroding trust does not necessarily imply civic apathy, at least as precisely as one might be led to believe by those who consider the growth of electoral abstention the privileged indicator of the changing relationship of civil society to the political system. For the phenomenon of abstention in fact reflects a transformation of public life and not simply a decline of interest in it. One could even claim that the decline in electoral participation has often gone along with a more general development of civic activity. But how to understand such a turn of events? The brief answer is that we are moving bit by bit from a "polarized" political democracy to more disseminated forms of "civil democracy."

Voting is the most visible and institutionalized form of citizenship. It is the act that long has both crystallized and symbolized the concepts of political participation and civic equality. But this notion of participation is complex. For it blends three dimensions of interaction between the people and the political sphere: expression, implication, and intervention. *Expressive de-*

mocracy involves society's voice when it passes judgment on politicians and their actions or when it engages in more serious protest. *Implicative democracy* concerns the totality of the means by which citizens act in concert and join with one another in order to produce a common world. Finally, *interventionist democracy* implies all the forms of collective action on which the people might rely to achieve a desired result. Together, these three kinds of political activity make up democratic life.

What makes the vote special is that it allows these different modalities of civic existence (which correspond to different "moments" of public life) to factually coincide. Elections amount to the most condensed and potent form of civic engagement—and the most incontestable because they have been the most organized and visible. The history of democracy, for this reason, has for a long time simply been identified as a process of concentrating the political field of which the long struggle for universal suffrage has been both the means and the symbol. It is in this perspective that one must understand the contemporary transformations of democracy: if *electoral democracy* has undeniably eroded, the expressive, implicative, and interventionist aspects of democracy have been gaining strength. A number of clues confirm the suggestion. The scale of participation in associational activities and the massive support for a welter of advocacy groups contradict the idea of an individualist withdrawal from civic life. The notion of the advent of a new civic passivity, so often accepted unreflectively, therefore has to be revised.

With this important specification of what has been called "democracy's discontent" in mind, the difficulty of contemporary democratic disenchantment can be faced anew. The moral stigmatization of political leaders—the frequent denunciation of their lack of "political will" and of their excessive indifference toward the general interest—has been frequently invoked as the major cause of the resentment of citizens toward their representatives, with the notion of a "decline of the political" sometimes called upon to explain the results. In this way, a deficit of contemporary democracy, as it were, is often targeted, as if the moment simply called for denouncing an inability to live up to a given model or deploring a betrayed promise.

Instead, I would like to explore another approach to illuminate the difficulty. I propose that it is *the very structure* of the contemporary democracies that is at issue, rather than simply the malfunction of a workable model. More precisely, what has nourished the distrust of the citizens is paradoxically the *consequences* of diverse responses that have failed for more than a century to correct the insufficiencies and solve the problems of representative government. To put my thesis schematically, distrust is a constitutive rather than a recent feature of democratic life. It is almost coeval with the birth of universal suffrage. At the turn of the twentieth century, if not before, anxiety and disillusion about actually existing democracy made their rude appearance. The French and American cases are especially revealing, with populist antiparliamentarism and the Progressive movement both expressing the same sense of expectation and the same politics of refusal.

But how to analyze the phenomenon comprehensively? It seems to me that the best way to think about it is to stress that it has occurred thanks to the dissociation from each other of two traits that were confounded before, both in history and in the theory of representative and democratic governments: legitimacy and trust. Elections, it was thought, would combine the two—and this is the one of the main reasons why elections by vote were preferred to elections by lot. Elections do not simply allow for the division of labor and the discrimination of abilities between voters and leaders: the form of choice that they put into motion allows linking a procedure of selection with a *qualitative* relation (while lot allows the one without the other).

These two political traits once believed to coincide in the electoral result—legitimacy and trust—are not of the same nature, however. Legitimacy is a juridical quality, of a strictly procedural order; it is created perfectly and completely by elections. But trust is different and far more complex. It amounts to a kind of "invisible institution," in Kenneth Arrow's famous phrase. It fulfills at least three purposes. First, it *enlarges* the quality of legitimacy, in adding to the latter's strictly procedural character a moral dimension (integrity in the general sense) as well as a substantive dimension (interest in the common good). Trust also plays a temporalizing role: it allows for the presupposition of the *continuity in time* of this enlarged legitimacy after the electoral moment. Finally, it is an *institutional shortcut*, "internalizing" as a working premise a whole series of mechanisms of verification and ratification.

Indirect Democracy

It is the dissociation of legitimacy and trust, then, that has been the central problem of the history of democracy. This dissociation ought to be familiar, for it is the rule and not the exception. Hence, there is even a phrase—in French, *l'état de grâce*, and in English, political honeymoon—to express the reality that there is after each election a short and exceptional period during which the two qualities are not separated.

Responses to this situation have developed in two directions. First, proposals and experiments for reinforcing the basis of procedural legitimacy have abounded—whether by making recourse to the ballot box more frequent, developing the mechanisms of direct democracy, or even reinforcing the dependence of the representatives on voters (as with procedures for recall in certain American states). In all of these cases, the amelioration of electoral democracy has been the goal. But, in parallel, there has also been a whole congeries of efforts—through informal social movements but institutions too—*intended to compensate for the erosion of trust by institutionalizing distrust*. This trend has progressively defined the contours of what I propose calling *indirect democracy*. This indirect democracy amounts, together with the institutions of electoral democracy, to a whole. And yet it has never been understood as a political form in its own right. The different elements that compose it have, of course, been noticed, or even meticulously examined. But they have never been placed within an overall framework that makes sense of their deepest characteristics in a serious and coherent way.

Having devoted a whole series of works to the extended history of the first half of the democratic equation, the dynamics of electoral democracy on the basis of the French case, the new focus of my research is to come to grips with this other and indirect democracy. Indeed, it is thanks to the understanding of the difficulties posed by this indirect democracy that I believe it will become possible to propose a new interpretation of the democratic disenchantment of historical and contemporary life.

Three ensembles comprise the mechanisms of distrust characterizing indirect democracy: the exercise of mechanisms of oversight, the creation of independent institutions, and the formation of powers of rejection. It is worth hazarding a very brief evocation of each.

The mechanisms of *oversight*, first. They continue to play a growing role in the life of contemporary societies. By this expression, I mean the forms of constraint and the weight of pressure that civil society can bring to bear on political society (and not the reverse as in Michel Foucault's classic perspective, though this other dimension is always also there). These forms of testing the leaders are of two kinds: acts of denunciation and revelations of fact on the one hand and airing of evaluations, information, and counter-expertise, on the other. The muckrakers vividly illustrated the first function in the United States at the start of the twentieth century, but one must also mention, of course, the famous "committees of surveillance" during the French Revolution. The politics of suspicion or transparency have thus always allowed civil society to extend and complete its self-expression only begun at the ballot box. The worker's movement, for its part, memorably exemplified the exercise of the function of evaluation and counter-expertise when it developed in the middle of the nineteenth century important practices of social inquiry, amounting in a sense to a civil reappropriation of procedures previously restricted to parliamentary action.

These different mechanisms of denunciation or evaluation have a number of points in common. First, their effect is to test the *reputation* of a power. Reputation is a kind of "invisible institution" constituting one of the structuring elements of trust. This process of testing has four characteristics: it is permanent (while electoral democracy is intermittent); it is open to individuals, and not simply organizations, to enact; it enlarges and opens the field of intervention to society (already John Stuart Mill noted that while it is not possible to undertake everything, it is possible to check up on everything); and it allows a specific kind of intervention, forging a third way distinct at once from the regime of exit and from that of voice. One could add that this "democracy of oversight" is today in full expansion. The "new social movements," like the advocacy groups, are less and less organs of negotiation or even of representation; they devote themselves more and more to activities of oversight. For this reason, new modes of protest take place more and more often through the media.

Mistrust of government has also occurred along a second axis—the erection of independent institutions, ones shielded from the direct authority of executive power. One of the first historical examples of this kind of institution is the Interstate Commerce Commission (ICC) in the United States, which dates from 1887. It was the advertised goal of the legislative power in that case to exempt the regulation of the railroads from the authority of an executive suspected of close ties to business interests. This commission, it was frequently emphasized, aimed to keep the regulation of the given economic sector "out of politics." It also answered to a declared intent to promote the general interest and to protect the consumer, functioning in this regard as a sort of protective judge ("acting as the poor man's court," in the formula used at the time). Guaranteed true independence thanks to its bipartisan composition, the ICC thus brought the superiority of substantive legitimacy (one due to impartiality) to bear on the procedural and electoral legitimacy of the president.

The support of public opinion eventually led more or less everywhere in the world to the development of this kind of institution. Forms of the regulatory state have thus been erected to counteract a political sphere believed to be too influenced by interest groups. In the French case, it is the figure of a state "above parties" that arose to express mistrust of politicians. The path leading to the conferral of a *status* on the public function followed this course, ending in the notion that the "corporatism of the universal" that functionaries were supposed to incarnate would have more legitimacy than the "corrupted universalism" of the elected representatives. In this manner, citizens often chose in favor of their bureaucrats and against those victorious at their own ballot boxes.

This approach to the general interest, opposing what several authors have called an "output democracy" (judged by its consequences) to an "input democracy" (following from procedures), has played a trailblazing role to make *independence* a major criterion in politics. While electoral democracy maintains the dependence of politicians on voters, indirect democracy pursues the project of developing the independence of implemented policies from partisan logics. Without entering into the details of the question, one may nevertheless suggest that the same terms of thinking suit a number of other institutions like constitutional judiciaries or central banks. To evoke an image to anticipate the full presentation, one might cite an American author of the 1830s, John Rowan, who wrote: "The independence of the judiciary has been greatly misconceived. The true independence of the Judges consists in their dependence upon, and responsibility to, the people."[1] No doubt, to make sense of this "democracy of limitation" one would have to turn to the body of literature on the comparative legitimacy of different kinds of institutions, or even works of sociology or social psychology establishing a hierarchy of types of legitimacy.

The multiplication of the powers of sanction and rejection is the third form of structuring mistrust of indirect democracy. In *The Spirit of the Laws*, Montesquieu emphasized the distinction, central in his opinion, between the ability to act or judge and the ability to reject. He placed the accent on an asymmetry whose importance has continued to grow as citizens increasingly experienced the limitations of electoral democracy in achieving their objectives and their hopes. Realizing that they were little capable of constraining their governments from undertaking certain actions or making certain decisions, citizens turned to the path of multiplying the sanctions on power. And so there slowly grew up, in the shadow of a positive but uncertain democracy, what one might call a "negative democracy."

There is first of all a "technical" reason that explains this development. Acts of rejection produce results that are genuinely tangible and visible. To repeal legislation fully realizes the intention of the actor, while the measure of success of a campaign to bring about a specific policy is in all cases more subject to controversy and partiality. The will is always fulfilled completely in an act of rejection because it is driven in such a case to a univocal and clear decision that exhausts a given intention. The simple mandate or authorization, in contrast, possesses none of these qualities: the question of the fulfillment of the will remains open in this framework, since the future is uncertain in what it will bring and the actions of the empowered agent are undetermined. The tension at the heart of the democracy of mandate, in other words, is suppressed in the framework of negative democracy.

From a sociological point of view, it is obvious that negative coalitions are easier to organize than positive majorities. One might say that a growing difference is emerging between electoral and social majorities. Political majorities are in their essence aggregative; they are constituted by an arithmetical addition of votes. Each person can be the vehicle of a particular intention or a specific meaning. The voters deliberate as they please, often without ever attaining a precise conception of their rationale, the combination of adhesion, sanction, or prevention in their choice. The ballots mechanically reduce these complex expressions to simple and cumulative data. Their only tangible meaning is that they can be counted and added up. But what one could call social majorities are different. While political majorities produce overall legitimacy and exist over a legal timeframe, social majorities play the role of making specific actions possible. It is unthinkable, for example, to reform social security without a corresponding social majority. But most often, social majorities manifest themselves negatively, in the form of passive consent. And they are always in movement, constantly shifting, evolving in tandem with the issues.

These reactive social majorities are, generally speaking, quite heterogeneous. And it is for this reason that they are easily formed. They do not need to be coherent to play their role. They have a power all the more considerable, since in their field of conflict the intensity of their reactions often plays an essential role. In the street, in media outlets, or through symbolic expression, it is not simply a question of arithmetic. But true social majorities are difficult to create. They presuppose by nature either a passive consensus or a positive and deliberated agreement. They cannot, like electoral majorities or reactive coalitions, take root in equivocacy and ambiguity. They are therefore more fragile and volatile. Experience, in any case, proves that it is much easier for a politician to lose support thanks to clumsy statements than to gain it thanks to taking original stands.

For all these reasons, the veto has become the dominant form of political intervention in contemporary society.

The Mixed Regime of the Moderns

This sketch of the three modes of civic mistrust suggests that the indirect democracy that they constitute is indeed an original political form: they are not simply a matter of curious exceptions or aberrant developments. But it is surprising to observe that the diverse theories of representative government or of the democratic regime have remained confined for all intents and purposes to electoral and institutional democracy. I am therefore proposing an enlargement of the understanding of the political functioning of contemporary societies in offering this analysis of democracy's indirect modalities. The insight seems to me all the more important since it allows one to incorporate the most living and habitual phenomena of the life of democracies; it gets at the heart of what practically and emotionally links today's citizens to public life. This indirect democracy presents four great characteristics, which I outline below. They lay out a future program of research and the working hypotheses of a project (they can by no means, therefore, anticipate its finished results).

1. Indirect democracy is distinguished by its attraction to a judicial model of politics. Of course, this attraction takes place on different levels. One could first speak of a "functional" judicialization of politics thanks to the impulse to construct a more impartial state. The pole around which this movement organizes itself technically and legitimates itself socially is a juridical notion of judgment (impartiality) rather than a notion of will (the majority issuing from universal suffrage). But one could also think of the "moral" judicialization of politics. The forms of oversight and stigmatization that society enacts in indirect democracy lead the role of procedures for checking actors to be minimized and a markedly personal and penal responsibility to be deployed around political leaders more and more each day. "Scandals" play a central role, therefore. Finally, one might argue for a "political" judicialization, meaning that the function of opposition is framed more and more often in terms of indictment (on the model of the great English political trials of the seventeenth and eighteenth centuries), eclipsing a vision of politics as the rivalry among different programs. To summarize this triple judicialization of politics, one could say that the figure of the *citizen as voter* is today more and more overtaken by the image of the *citizen as juror*.

2. Indirect democracy can also be understood as the socialization and dissemination of legislative power. For it is striking to note that it is many of the principal original attributes of legislative control of the executive that are now, in part, directly exercised by civil society. The power of inquiry, to restrict myself to this example, has thus been largely captured by the media and associations. But one might say the same of impeachment: alongside legislative procedures, informal actions of impeachment are constantly brought. Here again, the "descent towards society" of such mechanisms as censure and veto has to be evoked. This transformation is probably impossible to understand except on condition of taking into account the fact that the key modern power has become the executive, while classical political theory always insisted on the *plurality* of powers, and ranked the legislative power first among them.

3. In certain ways, the forms of indirect democracy, moreover, lead beyond the opposition between liberalism and democracy. For they arise neither from Madisonian representative government nor from the alternative of direct democracy. In a way, they do lead to a growth of "liberalism," with all the limitations on power that the term implies. But this movement proceeds, remarkably, in the guise of democratic pressure rather than out of fear of the tyrannical potential of the majority. They make up, therefore, a new "economy of distrust" and of the balance of powers. It is in this sense that I propose to speak of the mixed regime of the moderns. Indirect democracy calls into being a wholly unprecedented division of powers, redesigning at the same time the network of checks and balances. Its innovations also suggest that the two great liberal mechanisms of the rule of law and the balance of power are reaching the point of fusing. Further still, it is possible to see beyond the distinction between input and output democracy.

4. Finally, it is worth adding the striking fact that indirect democracy has brought back to the modern world numerous political characteristics of the predemocratic universe. One might

suggest as much by exploring a series of privileged indicators. It seems to return, for example, to the ancient definition of the judge as overseer and guardian, just as it revivifies the substantive and moral understanding of power and the common good of medieval doctrine (along with its relative indifference to procedural concerns). And it also reanimates the premodern vision of consent as noninterference with power. The hypothesis of the reintegration of the old in the new, in which the old is of course reinterpreted to suit the new, would logically have to be accompanied by a reevaluation of the putative rupture between the two moments. It might even lead to a new interpretation of the totality of the history of democracy. The idea would be to understand how the modern democratic regimes were led, in their first phase, to a certain institutional and conceptual *polarization* of political forms, with the development of indirect democracy progressively departing from this original requirement.

The examination of these four different characteristics of indirect democracy might then lead to a further inquiry in which its "principles" would have to be formulated. But this theoretical vision, grounded in the study of a number of historical cases, would also allow for understanding the indeterminacies and contradictions that structure democracy's indirect form. And it would also provide the basis for interpreting its pathologies. Populism, to briefly turn to that example, might well be possible to reinterpret as a perverted form of indirect democracy, in the same sense that totalitarianism has been analyzed as a perversion of incarnated democracy.

This dynamic fashion of telling the history of indirect democracy, on the whole, would complement the conceptual history of electoral and institutional democracy that I have proposed in my prior works and of which this volume provides an overview. But this new research, since I plan to conduct it in a global and comparative framework, will in all probability lead to more synthetic results than those obtained in the prior studies of the French laboratory alone (even if I always understood my tril-

ogy as a point of entry into the general problematic of democracy
rather than as a treatment of a nation as an end in itself).

An Unpolitical Democracy

But does indirect democracy deserve the name? One can hardly
doubt it. There are certainly "democratic effects" caused by these
diverse and growing forms of the oversight and supervision of
leaders. So it certainly is a model of democratic social power,
more and more developed each day, even if it is a one that works
indirectly. The extent of its corrective effects to the insufficiencies or abuses of the representative system could, of course, be
extensively debated; but the global significance of the phenomenon is unmistakable.

And yet the *unpolitical character* of this kind of democracy
is both obvious and troubling. It is apparent in a double sense.
The diverse mechanisms or behaviors at issue have first of all the
effect of dissolving the expressions of a *generality*. In essence
negative and reactive, they cannot serve to structure or to bear a
collective project. Some have, in any case, argued of these independent authorities that it is a matter of creating a "politics without politicking." But it is actually a matter, very simply, of unpolitics. It is in fact more of "regulation" that one should speak
in trying to describe the nature of the exercised activity. To put it
briefly, this indirect and unpolitical democracy is characterized
by blending democratic *effects* and unpolitical *activity*. And it is
for this reason, too, that it is an original form escaping the traditional oppositions between liberalism and democracy and between representative government and direct democracy.

The spreading forms of indirect democracy tend, as a second
consequence, to diminish visibility and blur legibility. But these
have been two constitutive characteristics of the very essence of
the political. There is no politics, indeed, if actions cannot be
gathered together in a single narrative and represented on a single stage before the public. The development of indirect democ-

racy thus has indissociably complex and problematic implications. They are complex because the growth of social power occurs alongside populist and reactive tendencies. They are problematic, too, because the evolution toward a "civil democracy" in the offing promotes forms of fragmentation and differentiation where a coherent order and the imperative of totality have to be sought.

The unpolitical character of indirect democracy explains the contradictory fears that it inspires. Citizens cherish independent authorities for their action at the same time that they deplore the fact that they are unelected. It is from this tension, it seems to me, that the disenchantment marking contemporary democracy is flowing in its depths. It is not caused by a disappointment possible simply to overcome (by improving the procedures organizing the representative system, for example), but is instead structured by the aporia formed by the combination of the democratic with the unpolitical.

It is important to stress that this aporia is strengthened by the trend toward the *functionalization of participatory democracy* likewise underway. This phenomenon has shown itself in two ways. There is first the development of what one might call a "managerial democracy," by which I mean the fact that the opinions of actors of all kinds must henceforth be integrated more and more into the function of complex systems in order for them to run correctly. Even the appeal to an expressive democracy has, indeed, become a constitutive element of "good" management. In businesses as in government, the same call has sounded (in the French case, a whole series of legislative texts have organized the inclusion of associations in public programs in domains like health or the environment). But one must add, in the second place, that as different and decentralized organizations (both NGOs and domestic associations) have assumed regulatory functions, forms of "civil democracy" have also multiplied.

This presentation suggests that the enormous literature produced in recent years on the problem of governance has dealt with only a very small part of the problem I have been sketching. If it has taken up the new faces of "managerial democracy" or "civil democracy," it has nevertheless left unexplored the vast continent of indirect democracy. Similarly, the large literature critical of neoliberalism, attacking the invasion of the forces of the market in the diverse areas of social life and deploring the decline of political will, sees only a particular type of evidence of "unpolitics" today. The understanding of the sources and forms of indirect democracy, therefore, can secure powerful new arms for the critique of society, renewing and regrounding it at the same time.

Repoliticizing Democracy

The sketch I have offered of indirect democracy suggests, in the very terms of its exposition, what might be the next steps in this unprecedented stage of the progress of democracy. Far from conceiving of democracy as already realized, an already saved up capital now simply there to conserve, my approach forces the stress to fall on the paradox that the growth of social power, in essentially negative modes, has come linked to forms of the hollowing of the political. The response to undertake, on the basis of the foregoing understanding, has two components: the institutionalization and rationalization of the forms of indirect democracy on the one hand and its politicization on the other.

The first is easiest to grasp. It would involve the more methodical organization of the diverse kinds of oversight or rejection that exist today essentially in the form of informal social powers. To give only one possible example, citizen rating agencies could regularly evaluate the actions of certain public organisms. Indeed, there are many projects to imagine in this sphere. The second component of democratic progress to put in action, the politicization of indirect democracy, is the most important and the most difficult. For the challenge is to create what one might call *democratic projects*, to conceive political activity as the continuous action of society on itself and not simply as a series of episodic interventions.

In this framework, there is a whole range of practical works of resymbolization, of the production of generality, of translation, and of the interpretation of reality that has to be undertaken. Against exceptionalist conceptions of the political, the return of the political would have to be understood as proceeding from an ensemble of actions and discourses for producing commonality and making the system of social interactions both more legible and more visible. Giving meaning back to politics, then, cannot take place in the first instance through the elaboration of a doctrine or overall project. It is above all a matter of publicly reconstituting and exposing, in order to pave the way for their evaluation and modification, the effective modes by which the social system is produced. There is a work to be shouldered of writing and publication that in this regard amounts to the very foundation of the political. It would aim to give a vocabulary to social experience and to outline for it the framework in which it takes on meaning—and thus allow for it to reform itself. The enterprise of the politicization of indirect democracy thus calls for an authentic rediscovery of ordinary politics, conceived in terms that are at once simple, radical, and profound.

These perspectives, which can barely be glimpsed in this presentation of a work to be carried out, could allow for the political horizon of the left to be restored in three ways. First, they would give new tasks to the democratic ideal, saving them from the flat and restorationist nostalgia of a golden age of civic life. The point would be not so much to denounce the accretions on a system believed to be workable in itself or to wish to be free of its ponderous complexity (and therefore simply to call for the erection of stronger, more participatory, or more deliberative institutions). Rather, the hope would be to find practical engagements in a democracy conceived as a social activity. Democracy, to put it in the terms of some of the Greeks reread by Michel

Foucault at the end of his life, is more a matter of a permanent dietetic care than of anatomic and orthopedic curiosity. This approach might lead, in the second place, to a communion of the ideals of democracy with those of socialism. Historically, the first have above all been defined in procedural terms, while the second have been thought about in a substantive fashion. If politics is conceived, however, as the work of society on itself, then the experimentation with differences that makes it up is also its heart. Substance and procedure blend, in the end, to make democratic progress connect with the deepening of the exigency for social justice.

The perspective of a repoliticization of democratic life allows, third and finally, for the relations between national democracy and cosmopolitan democratic forms to be imagined in a new and different way. The usual understanding of this relationship consists in thinking in terms of a transfer, that is to say of a reproduction at a higher level of forms of regulation first achieved in the national forum. The notion of indirect democracy, however, suggests a mode of political regulation that is neither that of institutional government, nor that of the governance associated with the function of the market and the extension of the rule of law. It is in terms of the constitution of an indirect democracy at the international level that one might therefore define a final operational program. It is an indirect democracy still taking its first steps, and that has to be both developed as a collection of social powers (through the action of NGOs and diverse international organizations) and institutionalized in order that powers of oversight, control, or rejection might see the light of day. The objective will have to be, in this spirit, to develop "democratic projects" of the community of nations to keep ever present the force of justice and law.

In sum, the goal is to pursue simultaneously, on different scales, democratic progress and the construction of a cosmopolitan order. But while such convergence has often been conceived in the weak sense of a generalized dissemination of power, of a multiplication of forms of governance without government (whether in the dreamlike manner of a globalization of good feeling or in the more exalted mode of an epiphany of revolt), the task is to discover how to pursue it as the expression of an exigency that is strong and realist at once.

Notes

Introduction

1. Paul Berman, *Terror and Liberalism* (New York, 2002). For the prominent recent defense of "antitotalitarian liberalism" as the necessary response to the reelection of George W. Bush in 2004, see Peter Beinart, "A Fighting Faith: An Argument for a New Liberalism," *The New Republic*, December 13, 2004, notably the last section, "Toward an Anti-totalitarian Liberalism."

2. Scholarly databases suggest that the specific term "antitotalitarian" percolated occasionally in academic discussion in English throughout the postwar period, but with nothing like its current energy, while the coinage "antitotalitarianism" dates from the importation of the French discussion of the 1970s and 1980s. See Stanley Hoffmann, "Gaullism by Any Other Name," *Foreign Policy* 57 (Winter 1984): 52. Thanks to Nils Gilman for this information and comments on my text.

3. The emblem of this school is, of course, Michael Hardt and Antonio Negri, *Empire* (Cambridge, Mass., 2001), and more recently by the same authors, *Multitude: War and Democracy in the Age of Empire* (New York, 2004).

4. For a survey of *gauchisme* in the early 1970s, see Jean-Pierre Le Goff, *Mai 68, l'héritage impossible* (Paris, 1998), part II.

5. Pierre Rosanvallon, *L'âge de l'autogestion, ou la politique au poste de commandement* (Paris, 1976). On the CFDT, see Hervé Hamon and Patrick Rotman, *La deuxième gauche: Histoire intellectuelle et politique de la Confédération française démocratique du travail* (Paris, 1982).

6. The speech is to be found in Michel Rocard, *Parler vrai: Textes politiques* (Paris, 1979). Cf. the longer theoretical defense of the position authored by Rosanvallon, together with Patrick Viveret,

Pour une nouvelle culture politique (Paris, 1977). The periodical *Faire* was the basic organ of their position in the period.

7. I am preparing a historical study of Lefort's political theory and its legacy in the thought of several intellectuals working today, Rosanvallon included. Lefort's texts in English include *The Political Forms of Modern Society: Bureaucracy, Democracy, Totalitarianism*, ed. John B. Thompson (Cambridge, Mass., 1986) and *Democracy and Political Theory*, trans. David Macey (Minneapolis, 1988). See also now Bernard Flynn, *The Political Philosophy of Claude Lefort* (Evanston, 2005).

8. Lefort, *Éléments d'une critique de la bureaucratie*, 2nd ed. (Paris, 1979), 28.

9. François Furet, *Penser la Révolution française* (Paris, 1978), in English as *Interpreting the French Revolution*, trans. Elborg Forster (Cambridge, 1981). On the antitotalitarian moment, the pioneering work is Michael Scott Christofferson, *French Intellectuals Against the Left: The Anti-totalitarian Moment of the 1970s* (New York, 2004). But it is potentially misleading to wholly reduce all antitotalitarian theory to intraparty polemics and to deny the potential relevance of its theoretical work beyond that dispute. All theories, generally applicable or not, lasting or not, have conditions of origin that that are local and temporary.

10. Cf. Mark Lilla, "Introduction: The Legitimacy of the Liberal Age," in Lilla, ed., *New French Thought: Political Philosophy* (Princeton, 1994), and Martin Jay, "Lafayette's Children: The Reception of French Liberalism in America," in Jay, *Refractions of Violence* (New York, 2003). Rosanvallon's work, and "new French thought" generally, have often been received in the United States in too close a spirit to antitotalitarian liberalism, which mistakes the diversity and indeed the central thrust of the turn to politics in French intellectual life since the 1970s.

11. The essay is now available in Quentin Skinner, *Visions of Politics*, vol. 1, *Regarding Method* (Cambridge, 2002), as ch. 4. Since that time Skinner has offered the nuance that the "thinking for oneself" that antiquarianism demands can involve consideration of "roads not taken" or "lost theories" that it is the historian's task to recall to his contemporaries. But the normativity and engagement of the historian are still confronted with extreme anxiety. Skinner "wished, or was obliged," Rosanvallon concludes, "to limit his role to that of a Cambridge professor," foreclosing the prospect that the historian's work can enjoy a communion with present quandaries and even contribute to their solution. Rosanvallon cited in Jeremy Jennings, "'Le retour des émigrés'?: The Study of the History of

Political Ideas in Contemporary France," in Dario Castiglione and Iain Hampsher-Monk, eds., *The History of Political Thought in National Context* (Cambridge, 2002), 226–27.

12. See Rosanvallon, *Le Modèle politique français: La société civile contre le jacobinisme de 1789 à nos jours* (Paris, 2004), translated by Arthur Goldhammer as *The French Political Model: Civil Society against Jacobinism since 1789* (Cambridge, Mass., 2006).

13. It bears comparison, for example, with Alexander Keyssar, *The Right to Vote: The Contested History of Democracy in the United States* (New York, 2001).

14. See also Rosanvallon's entry on "Physiocrats" in Furet and Mona Ozouf, eds., *Critical Dictionary of the French Revolution*, trans. Arthur Goldhammer (Cambridge, Mass., 1989).

15. Indeed, to add to the flood of literature on contemporary French anti-Americanism, there is a book to be written on pro-Americanism, a fashion of the past few decades that often reposed on a startling ignorance of the history and realities of the United States, as if reading Tocqueville could serve as a proxy for such necessary learning.

16. On voluntarism against rationalism, it suffices to refer to the classic paper by Paul Kahn, "Reason and Will in the Origins of American Constitutionalism," *Yale Law Journal* 98 (January 1989): 449–517, reprint in Kahn, *Legitimacy and History: Self-Government in American Constitutional History* (New Haven, 1992). Few practice the kind of conceptual history Rosanvallon recommends on American materials, but much more could be said on both voluntarism and rationalism in American history, for example the role of voluntarism in American populism or the power of rationalism in the history of American legal thought, including such recent chapters of its unfolding as the legal process in school and law and economics. Cf. Richard Posner, *Law, Pragmatism, and Democracy* (Cambridge, Mass., 2003).

17. He argued, for example, that negative campaigning in the American presidential elections implies "a more general movement of modern democracies. . . . It appears that now an era of mistrust in all democracies has insidiously arrived, with the minimization of irritation and the moderation of expectation becoming the new horizons of politics. The most important political question of the twenty-first century will be to know how this disenchantment can be surmounted without a simple return to past illusions. America is now the distorting mirror in which everyone must recognize the shape of his or her own weighty problems and subterranean developments." Rosanvallon, "Les États-Unis et la démocratie néga-

tive," *Le Monde*, September 30, 2004. See also Rosanvallon, "L'Amérique, entre renouveau militant et démocratie de marché," *Le Monde*, October 14, 2004.

18. Rosanvallon, *Le Modèle politique français*, 434.

19. Cf. Perry Anderson. "Dégringolade," *London Review of Books*, September 2, 2004, and "L'Union Sucrée," *London Review of Books*, September 23, 2004, which have recently appeared in French as *La pensée tiède: Un regard critique sur la culture française* (Paris, 2005), with Pierre Nora's critical response.

20. One may compare, on this point, the important scholarship about civil society offered by Stefan-Ludwig Hoffmann, "Democracy and Associations in the Long Nineteenth Century: Towards a Transnational View," *Journal of Modern History* 75, no. 2 (June 2003): 269–99. The main conclusion is that Tocqueville's pessimism about the vibrancy of civil society in Europe is contradicted by the facts. Indeed, Hoffmann goes so far as to argue that civil society flowered in so many rival directions—including illiberal ones—that the contemporary penchant of drawing a natural or necessary connection between associational vitality and democratic health is likewise seriously flawed.

21. This is the central theme of my own essay, written together with Andrew Jainchill, on Rosanvallon's work considered as an attempt to revise Furet's antitotalitarian classic. See Andrew Jainchill and Samuel Moyn, "French Democracy Between Totalitarianism and Solidarity: Pierre Rosanvallon and Revisionist Historiography," *Journal of Modern History* 76, no. 1 (March 2004): 107–54.

22. "Like the fascists and totalitarians before them, these terrorists . . . try to impose their radical views through threats and violence," George W. Bush began noting shortly after the events. Speech, November 6, 2001. It is to accept, rather than resist, the extension of such rhetoric to say that Bush's own regime is an "inverted totalitarianism." See Sheldon Wolin, "Inverted Totalitarianism," *The Nation*, May 19, 2003.

23. Rosanvallon, "Europe in Perplexity," http://www.opendemocracy.net (posted July 14, 2004). He explained: "Terrorism represents neither an innovative political and social form nor a new type of state regime. Terrorist action blends non-political behavior (nihilist destruction) and a culture of resentment; it 'connects' with the other in an insanely violent way, and is not bound to the formulation of any utopia or any project of self-construction." On terror as a political form, see Arendt, *The Origins of Totalitarianism* (New York, 1951), part III and Lefort, *Un homme en trop: Réflexions sur "L'Archipel du Goulag"* (Paris, 1976), chap. 2.

24. Most prominently, see Mark Tushnet, *Taking the Constitution Away from the Courts* (Princeton, 1999) and Larry D. Kramer, *The People Themselves: Popular Constitutionalism and Judicial Review* (New York, 2004). On judicial empowerment as a global movement, see Ran Hirschl, *Towards Juristocracy: The Origins and Consequences of the New Constitutionalism* (Cambridge, Mass., 2004).

25. Laurence Tribe, "The People's Court" (review of Kramer, *The People Themselves*), *New York Times Book Review*, October 24, 2004, and their debate in *New York Times Book Review*, November 21, 2004.

26. Cf. Jed Rubenfeld, *Freedom and Time: A Theory of Constitutional Self-Government* (New Haven, 2001).

27. See Lefort, "Le Contr'Un," in Étienne de La Boétie, *Discours de la servitude volontaire*, ed. Miguel Abensour (Paris, 1976). The phrase "Le Contr'Un" figured as the subtitle of La Boétie's sixteenth-century discourse, and Lefort used it to describe the fusion of the people in totalitarian ideology. It appears in Rosanvallon's texts basically as a description as the desire for voluntaristic fusion in the French Revolution and in the tradition it bequeathed to modern history.

1. Inaugural Lecture

1. Roland Barthes, *Chaire de sémiologie littéraire: Leçon inaugurale faite le vendredi 7 janvier 1977* (Paris, 1977), 6.

2. [This work, dating from 1913 and republished many times, exists in English as *France, a Study in Nationality* (New Haven, 1930). Siegfried (1875–1959) also wrote a number of studies on American and British politics.]

3. Edgar Quinet, *Critique de la Révolution* (1867), reprint in *La Révolution*, 5th ed., 2 vols. (Paris, 1868), 1:11. [Cf. Rosanvallon, "'Il faut refaire le bagage d'idées de la démocratie française,'" *Le Monde*, November 21, 2002.]

4. [The distinction is, in French, between *le* and *la politique*, masculine and feminine forms of the same noun, rendered here as "the political" and "politics" respectively.]

5. Marc Bloch, *Apologie pour l'histoire ou métier d'historien* (Paris, 1974), 47. [The translation is from *The Historian's Craft*, trans. Peter Putnam (New York, 1964), 43.]

6. It is for precisely this reason that the historians of the *Annales* school were not interested in politics. It is also worth noting that it is on the same ground that Émile Durkheim did not believe that politics *stricto sensu* constituted a real object for sociology. "Wars,

treaties, the intrigues of courts and assemblies, the actions of statesmen," he wrote, "are *combinations of events which always lack any resemblance to one another.* They can only be narrated and, willy nilly, appear to flow from no definite law." Durkheim, with Paul Fauconnet, "Sociologie et sciences sociales" (1903), in Durkheim, *Textes*, 3 vols. (Paris, 1975), 1:147, emphasis added. [The translation is from Durkheim, "Sociology and the Social Sciences," in *The Rules of Sociological Method*, ed. Steven Lukes, trans. W.D. Halls (New York, 1982), 196].

7. [The references are to Roberto Michels, *Political Parties: A Sociological Study of the Oligarchical Tendencies in Modern Democracies* (1911), trans. Eden Paul and Cedar Paul (Glencoe, Ill., 1958), and Moisei Ostrogorski, *Democracy and the Organization of Political Parties*, trans. Frederick Clarke (New York, 1902), both in many subsequent editions. One large part of Ostrogorski's work is devoted to American electoral politics.]

8. [He refers precisely to Michels and Ostrogorski. Early in his career, he published on both. See Rosanvallon, "Avancer avec Michels," *Faire* 17 (March 1977): 31–34, and his reedition of Ostrogorski's book listed in the bibliography this volume.]

9. Anne Fagot-Largeault, *Leçon inaugurale faite le jeudi 1er mars 2001* (Paris, 2001), 29. The chair is in the philosophy of the biological and medical sciences.

10. Michel de Certeau, *L'Invention du quotidien*, vol. 1, *Arts de faire*, new ed. (Paris: Gallimard, 1990), 185. [The translation is from *The Practice of Everyday Life*, trans. Steven Rendall (Berkeley, 1984), 126.]

11. Ibid., 183 [in the English, 125].

12. Thomas Paine, *The Rights of Man*, in Michael Foot and Isaac Kramnick, eds., *The Thomas Paine Reader* (New York, 1987), 203–4.

13. Karl Marx, *The 18th Brumaire of Louis Napoleon*, in Robert C. Tucker, ed., *The Marx-Engels Reader*, 2nd ed. (New York, 1978), 595.

14. Marquis de Condorcet, "Sur le sens du mot révolutionnaire," *Journal d'instruction sociale* 1 (June 1, 1793): 10.

15. He added: "After having spread disturbance, incertitude, and ignorance everywhere, they added to the language a crowd of new words, with which they denominated those men whom they singled out, according to their whim, for the love or hatred of a misled people." Edme Petit, speech of 28 Fructidor An II (September 14, 1794), *Archives parlementaires*, 1st series, 97:175.

16. Cf. Jacques-Pierre Brissot, "De quelques erreurs dans les idées et dans les mots relatifs à la Révolution française," *La Chronique du mois ou les Cahiers patriotiques* 5 (March 1793).

17. Camille Desmoulins, *Le Vieux Cordelier*, no. 7, in *Le Vieux Cordelier*, ed. Pierre Pachet (Paris, 1987), 123.

18. ["L'histoire nous mord la nuque," a Trotskyist phrase revived in the post-1968 period, suggesting that history had accelerated.]

19. Marcel Mauss, *Œuvres*, 3 vols. (Paris, 1969), 3:579.

20. Jules Michelet, *Cours au Collège de France*, vol. 1, *1838–1844* (Paris, 1995), 20.

2. Toward a Philosophical History of the Political

1. This contribution clarifies and develops the thoughts set out in Pierre Rosanvallon, "Pour une histoire conceptuelle du politique (note de travail)," *Revue de synthèse*, 107, 1–2 (1986): 93–105.

2. Rosanvallon, *L'État en France de 1789 à nos jours* (Paris, 1990); Rosanvallon, *Le Sacre du citoyen: Histoire du suffrage universel en France* (Paris, 1992).

3. Claude Lefort, *Essais sur le politique (XIXe-XXe siècles)* (Paris, 1986), 8. [In English, *Democracy and Political Theory*, trans. David Macey (Minneapolis, 1988), 2.]

4. Aristotle, *Politics*, bk. 3, 1282b18–22. [In English, *The Basic Works of Aristotle*, ed. Richard McKeon (New York, 1941), 1192–93.]

5. Hannah Arendt, *Qu'est-ce que la politique?* (Paris, 1995), 31. [This text is available in English in Arendt, *The Promise of Politics*, ed. Jerome Kohn (New York, 2005).]

6. In the Middle Ages, "every private sphere has a political character or is a political sphere too." [Robert C. Tucker, ed., *The Marx-Engels Reader*, 2nd ed. (New York, 1978), 22; cf. Rosanvallon's discussion of this claim below, in chap. 8, this volume.]

7. The term "political history" is preferred to "intellectual history" because the latter continues to have a very narrow sense in the Anglo-Saxon world, treating intellectual output and intellectual circles as distinguishable from other aspects of politics and society.

8. Jacques Julliard, *Autonomie ouvrière: Études sur le syndicalisme d'action directe* (Paris, 1988).

9. Pierre Nora, *Les lieux de mémoire* (Paris, 1984–6), cf. especially volume l, "La République" and volume II, book II, "La nation," where politics occupies a very sizeable place. [Some of this material is in English as Nora, ed., *Realms of Memory: Rethinking the French Past*, trans. Arthur Goldhammer, 3 vols. (New York,

1996–98) and *Rethinking France: Les lieux de mémoire*, trans.
David P. Jordan et al. (Chicago, 2001–).]

10. André Burguière and Jacques Revel, eds., *L'histoire de France*
    (Paris, 1989–93).

11. Arendt, "Preface," in *Between Past and Future: Eight Exercises in
    Political Thought* (New York, 1968), 14.

12. On this point I am following the excellent comments in the article
    by Philippe Raynaud in Raynaud and Stéphane Rials, eds., *Dic-
    tionnaire de philosophie politique* (Paris, 1996, 2003), s.v. "Philoso-
    phie politique" (here p. 561).

13. Alphonse Aulard, *Histoire politique de la Révolution française:
    Origines et développement de la démocratie et de la république*
    (Paris, 1901). The subtitle of Aulard's book—"origins and develop-
    ment of democracy and the republic"—is in itself an illustration of
    this point of view.

14. Roger Chartier, "L'histoire aujourd'hui: des certitudes aux défis,"
    Raison présente 108 (1993): 45–56.

15. Michel Foucault, *Histoire de la folie à l'âge classique* (Paris, 1961);
    Foucault, *Les Mots et les choses* (Paris, 1966). [In English,
    *Madness and Civilization: A History of Insanity in the Age of
    Reason* (New York, 1965) and *The Order of Things: An Archaeol-
    ogy of the Human Sciences* (New York, 1970).]

16. Quentin Skinner, *The Foundations of Modern Political Thought*, 2
    vols. (Cambridge, 1978).

17. Cf. in particular, as representatives of the text school, Leo Strauss
    and Joseph Cropsey, who sum up their point of view well in their
    History of Political Philosophy (Chicago, 1963).

18. Cf. John Austin, *How to Do Things with Words* (Oxford, 1962).
    For Austin, one recalls, language is an activity that accomplishes
    something; it is not just a passive operator of meaning.

19. There is a huge bibliography on the Anglo-American debate
    around Skinner that has not produced much in the way of a
    French echo. To appreciate it, two fundamental articles were J.G.A.
    Pocock, "The History of Political Thought: A Methodological En-
    quiry," in Peter Laslett, ed., *Philosophy, Politics and Society*, 2nd
    series (Oxford, 1962), 183-202 and Peter L. Janssen, "Political
    Thought as Traditionary Action: The Critical Response to Skinner
    and Pocock," *History and Theory* 24, no. 2 (May 1985): 115-46. Of
    course, there are many other works.

3. Revolutionary Democracy

1. On the imagery of the people as Hercules, see the illuminating
   essay by James A. Leith, "Allégorie et symbole dans la Révolution

française," in Claudette Hould, ed., *L'Image de la Révolution française* (Quebec, 1989), 101–6. See too Lynn Hunt, *Politics, Culture, and Class in the French Revolution* (Berkeley, 1984), chap. 3, "The Imagery of Radicalism."

2. There are a number of interesting studies of these topics in Michel Vovelle, ed., *Les Images de la Révolution française* (Paris, 1988).

3. Cf., for example, Bibliothèque nationale de France, Estampes, De Vinck Collection, No. 3623.

4. On this project, see Antoine de Baecque, "The Allegorical Image of France, 1750–1800: A Political Crisis of Representation," in *Representations* 47 (Summer 1994): 114–43 and Judith Schlanger, "Le peuple au front gravé (1793)," in Jean Ehrard and Paul Viallaneix, eds., *Les Fêtes de la Révolution: Colloque de Clermont-Ferrand (Juin 1974)* (Paris, 1977), 387–96. I am grateful to Antoine de Baecque who guided me in my search for information on David's project.

5. Speech by David at the Convention, 17 Brumaire, Year II, recorded in *Réimpression de l'ancien Moniteur*, 32 vols. (Paris, 1850–1860), 18: 371.

6. See Charles Mazouer, "Le peuple dans les tragédies de Marie-Joseph Chénier," *Revue française d'histoire du livre* 68–69 (1990).

7. Circular of 30 Pluviôse, Year VII, in *Réimpression de l'ancien Moniteur*, 29: 612–13. See also the order of 28 Pluviôse, Year VI, instituting the festival in ibid., 157–58.

8. See esp. Lamartine's magazine *Le Conseiller du peuple*, *1848–1850*, 3 vols. (Paris, 1850) as well as its supplement *Le Passé, le Présent, l'Avenir de la République*. Lamartine defines the democratic republic as "the unity of the people instead of the privileged separation of classes."

9. Victor Hugo, *Choses vues*, ed. Herbert Juin, vol. 1, *1847–1848* (Paris, 1972), *passim*.

10. The idea of the people, Alain Pessin remarks, interests sociology, but in a particular sense, "not in order to search for a subject in the people, or to stage a dynamic of history born from its specification as a subject, but rather to see in it a sociability itself independent of all division and in spite of it, in order to see in it the social at the moment of its birth, the simple bonds of men, and the very nature of the collective life." Pessin, *Le Mythe du peuple et la société française du XIXe siècle* (Paris, 1992), 114.

11. "The sovereign people is the universality of French citizens," the Constitution of 1793 (Article 7) notes.

12. [The allusion is to Ernst Kantorowicz, *The King's Two Bodies: A Study in Mediaeval Political Theology* (Princeton, 1957).]

13. The *Dictionnaire de l'Académie française*, in its edition of 1786, likewise emphasized the polysemy of the term.
14. Speech of June 16, 1789, in *Réimpression de l'ancien Moniteur*, 1: 81.
15. Cited by Elisabeth Guibert-Sledziewski, "Le Peuple représenté," *Les Cahiers de Fontenay* 24–5 (December 1981): 11–20.
16. On this point, see the numerous references in Louis Chevalier, *Classes labourieuses et classes dangereuses à Paris pendant la première moitié du XIXe siècle* (Paris, 1958), and Pierre Michel, *Un mythe romantique, les barbares (1785–1848)* (Lyon, 1981). [The former work is available in English as *Laboring Classes and Dangerous Classes in Paris during the First Half of the Nineteenth Century*, trans. Frank Jellinek (New York, 1973).]
17. Charles de Rémusat, "Des mœurs et du temps," *Le Globe*, August 26, 1826; François Guizot, "De la démocratie dans les sociétés modernes," *Revue française*, November 1837.
18. Hugo, *Les Misérables*, in *Œuvres romanesques complètes* (Paris, 1962), 733. [In English, *Les Misérables*, trans. Norman MacAfee (New York, 1987), 1051: "Sometimes the people counterfeits fidelity to itself. The mob is traitor to the people."]
19. Jean-François Kervégan notes quite justifiably that political philosophy does not really know what to do with the notion of the people, "always tempted to demonize it or to idolize it." See his entry in Philippe Raynaud and Stéphane Rials, eds., *Dictionnaire de philosophie politique* (Paris, 1996, 2003), s.v. "Peuple" (here p. 544).
20. Hugo, *Les Misérables*, 623 [in English, 719]. "The social observer," he concludes, "should enter these shadows. They are part of his laboratory." Ibid., 802 [in English, 1262].
21. Abbé Sieyès, *Sur la question du veto royal* (Paris, 1789), 15.
22. The expression is used at the Constituent Assembly on August 27, 1789, by Jean-Xavier Bureaux de Pauzy, during a discussion of the declaration of rights. M. Mavidal and É. Laurent, eds., *Archives parlementaires de 1787 à 1860: Recueil complet des débats législatifs et politiques des Chambres françaises*, first series, 82 vols. (Paris, n.d.), 8: 492.
23. Joseph-Antoine Cérutti in 1791, cited in de Baecque, *Le corps de l'histoire, métaphore et politique (1770–1800)* (Paris, 1993), 123. [This book is available in English as *The Body Politic: Corporeal Metaphor in Revolutionary France, 1770–1800*, trans. Charlotte Mandel (Stanford, 1997).]
24. Toussaint Guiraudet, *Qu'est-ce que la nation? et qu'est-ce que la France?* (Paris, 1789), 104. "The French nation," he sums up, "is a society of about 25 million individuals. . . . The law only recog-

nizes the great association, numbers heads and not classes, counting rather than weighing." Ibid., 9–11. In a wonderful formula, Hugo noted, "Since '89, the entire people has been expanding in the sublimated individual." Hugo, *Les Misérables*, 714 [in English, 997].

25. Cited in Georges Bourgin, ed., *Le Partage des biens communaux: Documents sur la préparation de la loi du 10 juin 1793* (Paris, 1908), 103.

26. I follow the distinction offered in de Baecque, *Le corps de l'histoire*.

27. On the problem of the division of territory, see Mona Ozouf, "La Révolution française et la perception de l'espace national: Fédération, fédéralisme, et stéréotypes régionaux," in *L'École de la France* (Paris, 1984), 23–42 and Marie-Vic Ozouf-Marignier, *La Formation des départements: La représentation du territoire français à la fin du XVIIIe siècle* (Paris, 1989).

28. Sieyès, *Observations sur le rapport du comité de constitution, concernant la nouvelle organisation de la France* (Versailles, 1789), 2.

29. The notion of arithmetic of proportionality of the time also implies a purely mechanical relationship of individuals to the national territory.

30. Adrien Duquesnoy, speech of November 4, 1789, *Archives parlementaires*, 9: 671.

31. Sieyès wrote in this regard: "The natural consequence of this proposition is that the right to be represented belongs to citizens only in respect to what they have in common and not to what serves to differentiate them. Those assets and advantages that serve to differentiate citizens among themselves fall beyond the quality and character of citizenship." Sieyès, *Qu'est-ce que le Tiers état?* (Paris, 1982), 88. [In English as *What Is the Third Estate?*, in Sieyès, *Political Writings*, trans. Michael Sonenscher (Indianapolis: Hackett, 2003), 155.]

32. Sieyès papers, Archives nationales, 284 A.P. 5, folder 1 (sleeve 2).

33. Hence the difficulty of simply opposing "formal equality" and "real equality" as if the first were simply an incomplete version of the second. For on the contrary, there is an undeniable radicalism in the notion of formal equality in the sense that it affirms an essential equivalence among individuals. In a sense, it has a strong anthropological dimension, whereas the perspective of real equality is paradoxically much more limited and of a narrowly economic or social order.

34. On this point, see Mona Ozouf, *L'Homme régénéré: Essais sur la Révolution française* (Paris, 1989) and Bronislaw Baczko, *Lumières de l'utopie* (Paris, 1978).

35. *Révolutions de France et de Brabant* 1, reprint in *Œuvres de Camille Desmoulins*, 2 vols. (Paris, 1874), 1: 218–19.
36. Archives nationales, 284 A.P. 5, folder 1(2).
37. Sieyès, "Sur le projet de décret pour l'établissement de l'instruction nationale," *Journal d'instruction sociale* 5 (July 6, 1793, reprint Paris, 1981): 146.
38. Cited in Jacques Bouveresse, "De la société ouverte à la société concrète," *Pouvoirs locaux* 25 (June 1995): 99.
39. Jacques Rancière rightly notes: "Politics exists as soon as a separate sphere of appearance for a popular subject comes into being, a subject whose essence is to be different from itself." Rancière, *La Mésentente* (Paris, 1995), 125. [This work is in English as Rancière, *Disagreement: Politics and Philosophy*, trans. Julie Rose (Minneapolis, 1998).]
40. To this extent, one might say, representation is grounded in a *necessary fiction*. The fiction is in effect a condition for the possibility of integrating the whole diversity of the social in the unity of the political body.
41. Article 35 of the Declaration of June 1793 reads: "When the government violates the rights of the people, insurrection becomes, for the people and each of its parts, the most sacred and indispensable of duties."
42. On this point, see Albert Soboul, *Les Sans-culottes parisiens en l'an II* (Paris, 1958), 542–47. [This work is available in English as *The Sans-Culottes: The Popular Movement and Revolutionary Government, 1793–1794*, trans. Rémy Inglis Hall (Garden City, 1972).] In his *Histoire de la langue française*, Ferdinand Brunot signaled this elision too. Brunot, *Histoire de la langue française des origines à 1900*, 13 vols. (Paris, 1905–32), 9:855.
43. Speech of October 10, 1793 (19 Vendémiaire, Year II). Already on August 28, Claude Basire noted, "The simple execution of constitutional laws, made for times of peace, would be powerless in the middle of the conspiracies that menace us." *Archives parlementaires*, 73: 128. See on this point Olivier Jouanjan's illuminating article, "La suspension de la Constitution de 1793," *Droits* 17 (1993): 125–38.
44. D.A.F. Sade, *La Philosophie dans le boudoir*, in *Œuvres complètes du Marquis de Sade*, 15 vols. (Paris, 1986), 3: 510. On this point, see the interesting commentary of Claude Lefort, "Sade: Le boudoir et la cité," in *Écrire: À l'épreuve du politique* (Paris, 1992). [In English, "Sade: The Boudoir and the City," in *Writing: The Political Test*, trans. David Ames Curtis (Raleigh, 2000), from which the Sade citation is also taken (80).]

45. The formula is due to Marc-Antoine Jullien, cited in Raymonde Monnier, *L'Espace public démocratique: Essai sur l'opinion publique à Paris de la Révolution au Directoire* (Paris, 1994), 235.

46. Cited in Lucien Jaume, *Échec au libéralisme: Les Jacobins et l'État* (Paris, 1990). On this notion of representation as incarnation in Jacobin thought, one will also find a number of excellent analyses in Jaume, *Le Discours jacobin et la démocratie* (Paris, 1989).

47. Jacques Necker offered a very lively reproach of the "mysticism" of the Mountain in a text written in spring 1793: "They are always you, these representatives," he wrote, "and you with a perfect exactitude. Their interest and their will are yours. . . . And it is always the word *representative* that allows such a blind confidence! The word promotes the idea of another self." Necker, "Réflexions philosophiques sur l'égalité," *Œuvres complètes de M. Necker*, 15 vols. (Paris, 1820–21), 10: 435.

48. François Furet, *Penser la Révolution française* (Paris, 1978), 86. [In English, *Interpreting the French Revolution*, trans. Elborg Forster (Cambridge, 1981), 60, translation modified.] After Thermidor, one of the reproaches directed against Robespierre and his friends is precisely to have confounded their own representation of the people with the people themselves.

49. Cited in Patrice Gueniffey, "Les assemblées et la représentation," in Colin Lucas, ed., *The French Revolution and the Creation of Modern Political Culture*, vol. 2, *The Political Culture of the French Revolution* (Oxford, 1988), chap. 13.

50. Session of June 15, 1793, *Archives parlementaires*, 66: 542.

51. Saint-Just, *Discours sur la constitution de la France*, reprint in Saint-Just, *Œuvres complètes* (Paris, 1984), 423. [A long section of Rosanvallon's *La démocratie inachevée* chronicles Condorcet's attempt during the revolution to attain workable notions of representation and sovereignty.]

52. Speech of May 18, 1791, on whether deputies were eligible for reelection in *Archives parlementaires*, 26: 204.

53. It is a leitmotif of his interventions in 1793 and 1794. See, for instance, in his speech of May 10, 1793: "Begin with this incontestable maxim: that the people is good, and that its delegates are corruptible; that it is in the virtue and sovereignty of the people that one must search a safeguard against the vice and despotism of government. *Archives parlementaires*, 64: 430. On 8 Thermidor, Year II, the day before he fell, he spoke of the "representatives whose hearts are pure."

54. See, again, the classic works of Ozouf and Baczko.

55. Report to the National Convention on the theory of democratic government, session of 1 Floréal, Year II, *Archives parlementaires*, 89: 95. Gueniffey notes very suggestively that one may speak in regards to the Convention "of the representation of a people that does not yet exist, against the people that does exist." Gueniffey, "Les assemblées et la représentation," 252.
56. Billaud-Varenne, in *Archives parlementaires*, 89:99.
57. Werner Hofmann rightly emphasizes that Delacroix succeeds in this painting in offering "a harmonious imbrication of icon and narration," with "a singular composite of realism and the ideal." Hofmann, *Une époque en rupture, 1750–1850* (Paris, 1995), 605. The vision of the people in 1830 that emerges from it constrasts singularly with that of the people, a menacing and undifferentiated mob given to revolutionary riots, that Delacroix staged in his 1831 painting, *Boissy d'Anglas (les émeutes du 20 mai 1795)*. For an interesting commentary that compares these two works, see Michel Le Bris, *Journal du romantisme* (Geneva, 1981), 147–49.
58. Hugo, *Les Misérables*, 657 [in English, 821–22].
59. Victor Lefranc, "Le suffrage universel en action," *Almanach de la République française pour 1849* (Paris, 1849), 183.

4. The Republic of Universal Suffrage

1. Cited by William H. Sewell, Jr., *Work and Revolution: The Language of Labor from the Old Regime to 1848* (Cambridge, 1980), 198.
2. Cited by Iouda Tchernoff, *Le Parti républicain sous la monarchie de juillet: Formation et évolution de la doctrine républicaine* (Paris, 1901), 203.
3. Achille Roche, *Manuel du prolétaire* (Moulins, 1833), 3.
4. Cited from a report on a democratic banquet, *Journal du peuple*, July 5, 1840.
5. This includes the important study of Sieyès by Chapuys-Montlaville.
6. Albert Laponneraye, *Lettre aux prolétaires* (Saint-Pélagie Prison, February 1, 1833), 2. Cormenin used the same language: "Universal suffrage," he wrote, "therein lies the entirety of the republic. There will no longer be plurality, sinecures, civil lists, fat salaries, nor pensions . . . the budget of expenditures will be reduced to the strictly necessary." Cormenin, *Les trois dialogues de maître Pierre* (Paris: Aide-toi, le ciel t'aidera, 1833), 15.
7. Martin Bernard, "Sur les moyens de faire descendre la République dans l'atelier," *Revue républicaine* 3 (1834): 296 and 5 (1835): 62, 65

8. See the highly representative pamphlet by Constantin Pecqueur, *Réforme électorale: Appel au peuple à propos du rejet de la petition des 240 mille* (Paris, 1840).

9. 8th ed. (Paris, 1846). Cf. his *Avis au contribuable* of 1842.

10. Speech of November 30, 1847, in Alexandre Ledru-Rollin, *Discours politiques et écrits divers*, 2 vols. (Paris, 1879), 1:342.

11. *Journal du peuple*, July 11, 1841.

12. Stendhal, *Mémories d'un touriste* (Bordeaux, 1837). For his part, Lamartine said that one might poison a glass of water, but not a river.

13. Laponneraye, *Lettre aux prolétaires*, 4: "Under the monarchy," he writes, "there are enormous salaries, and still greater expenditures; there is a dilapidation of the state's funds. Under the republic, salaries are proportionate to the absolute necessities of officials, expenditures are limited, public funds are wisely allocated, because the nation itself overseas the allocation."

14. Cf. their speeches of February 24, 1878, reproduced in Ledru-Rollin, *Discours politiques et écrits divers*, 2:577-602.

15. Cf. on this point the information provided by Paul Bastid, *Un juriste pamphlétaire, Cormenin précurseur et constituant de 1848* (Paris, 1948), and the account by Garnier-Pagès in his *Histoire de la Révolution de 1848*, illustrated edition, 10 vols. (Paris, n.d.), 2: 2–4. See also the recent analysis by Alain Garrigou, "Le brouillon du suffrage universel: Archéologie du décret du 5 mars 1848," *Genèses* 6 (December 1991): 161–78.

16. On April 3, 1848, the Academy of Sciences received a report by Augustin Cauchy on the means, proposed by authors of various memoirs, of solving the difficulties presented by counting and registering votes under the new electoral system. Having stressed the technical difficulties, the report noted laconically: "Must we conclude that it is impossible to provide the electoral procedure with the mathematical certainty that is important to all important operations? . . . We think not." *Comptes-rendus hebdomadaires des séances de l'Académie des sciences* 26 (1848): 400.

17. There are many echoes of the reception of universal suffrage in the local monographs devoted to 1848. Among the mass of such monographs consulted on this question, the following stand out: Maurice Agulhon, *La République au village*, 2nd ed. (Paris, 1979); Albert Charles, *La Révolution de 1848 et la Seconde République à Bordeaux et dans le département de la Gironde* (Bordeaux, 1945); J. Dagnan, *Le Gers sous la Second République: La Réaction conservatrice*, 2 vols. (Auch, 1928–29); François Dutacq, *Histoire politique de Lyon pendant la Révolution de 1848 (25 février-15 juillet)*

(Paris, 1910); Jacques Godechot et al., *La Révolution de 1848 à Toulouse et dans la Haute-Garonne* (Toulouse, 1948); René Lacour, *La Révolution de 1848 dans le Beaujolais et la campagne lyonnaise*, 3 vols. (Lyon, 1954–55); G. Rocal, *1848 en Dordogne*, 2 vols. (Paris, 1934); F. Rude et al., eds., *La Révolution de 1848 dans le département de l'Isère* (Grenoble, 1949); Philippe Vigier, *La Seconde République dans la région alpine, étude politique et sociale*, 2 vols. (Paris, 1963), and *La Vie quotidienne en province et à Paris pendant les journèes de 1848* (Paris 1982).

18. *Bulletin de la République* 4 (March 19, 1848). For his part, Flaubert wrote in *L'Education sentimentale*: "First slavery had been abolished and now the proletariat! After the Age of Hatred, the Age of Love would begin!" (Paris, 1978), 331. [In English, Flaubert, *A Sentimental Education: The Story of a Young Man*, trans. Douglas Parmee (New York, 2000), 333.]

19. *Bulletin de la République* 9 (March 30, 1848).

20. With the exception of a brief synthesis: Gabriel Vauthier, "Cérémonies et fêtes nationales sous la Seconde République," *La Révolution de 1848* 18, 88 (June–August 1921): 51–63. [Mona Ozouf, *Festivals and the French Revolution*, trans. Alan Sheridan (Cambridge, Mass., 1988).]

21. Reported by Lacour, *La Révolution de 1848 dans le Beaujolais*, 2: 36.

22. Reported by Vigier, *La Seconde République dans la région alpine*, 1: 199

23. *Bulletin de la République* 19 (April 22, 1848).

24. Alphonse de Lamartine, *Histoire de la Révolution de 1848*, 2 vols. (Paris, 1849), 2: 346.

25. In addition to the monographs already cited, see also "Les Elections à la Constituante de 1848 dans le Loiret," *La Révolution de 1848* 2 (1905–6) and Philippe Vigier and G. Argenton, "Les Elections dans l'Isère sous la Seconde République," in Rude et al., *La Révolution de 1848 dans le département de l'Isère*.

26. Cf. for example the testimony assembled by Guillaume de Bertier de Sauvigny, *La Révolution parisienne de 1848 vue par les Américains* (Paris, 1984) and the memoirs of the marquis of Normandy, at the time ambassador of Great Britain, *Une année de révolution, d'aprés un journal tenu à Paris en 1848*, 2 vols. (Paris, 1858).

27. *Bulletin de la République* 20 (April 25, 1848).

28. 6,867,072 voters out of 8,220,664 registered.

29. Charles de Coux, "Du cens électoral dans l'intérêt des classes ouvrières," *L'Avenir*, April 6, 1831. De Coux was one of the founders of Christian political economy.

30. Published under the title *Réforme électorale, municipale, départe-mentale et communale* (Paris, 1840), 39.
31. Karl Marx, *The Class Struggles in France*, in *Marx-Engels Collected Works*, 49 vols. (New York, 1975–), 10:45–146, at 58. [Marx's quotation from Lamartine is from his speech before the Chamber of Deputies of February 24.]
32. Marx, "The Association for Administrative Reform," *Neue Oder Zeitung*, June 8, 1855, in ibid., 14: 243.
33. On the meaning of elections in such countries, see Guy Hermet, Alain Rouquié, and Juan Linz, *Des élections pas comme les autres* (Paris, 1978) and Roland Lomme, "Le Rôle des élections en Europe de l'Est," *Problèmes politiques et sociaux* 596 (1988).
34. After 1849, elections opposed two parties with very distinct programs.
35. On this critical point, see the synthesis of Pierre Pierrard, *1848 . . . Les pauvres, l'Évangile et la révolution* (Paris, 1977); also Edward Berenson, *Populist Religion and Left-Wing Politics in France, 1830–1852* (Princeton, 1984), and his article, "A New Religion of the Left: Christianity and Social Radicalism in France, 1815–1848," in François Furet and Mona Ozouf, eds., *The French Revolution and the Creation of Modern Political Culture*, vol. 3, *The Transformation of Political Culture, 1789–1848* (Oxford, 1989), chap. 29.

5. François Guizot and the Sovereignty of Reason

1. [The Ideologues were a philosophical and political school of the era of the turn of the nineteenth century, whose name gave rise to the generic concept of ideology.]
2. [So Guizot advised those who desired the vote under a regime of limited suffrage based on property and capacity. Rather than changing the legal hurdle, those who wanted the vote should, he said, simply surmount it.]
3. [The first line of the Communist Manifesto: "A specter is haunting Europe—the specter of Communism. All the powers of old Europe have entered into a holy alliance to exorcise this specter: Pope and Czar, Metternich and Guizot, French Radicals and German police-spies." Robert C. Tucker, ed., *The Marx-Engels Reader*, 2nd ed. (New York, 1978), 473).]
4. François Guizot, *Mémoires pour servir à l'histoire de mon temps*, 8 vols. (Paris, 1858), 1: 157–59. [There is an English translation of this work: *Memoirs to Illustrate the History of My Time*, 8 vols., trans. J.W. Cole (1858; reprint, New York, 1974).]

5. In *Le Globe*, November 25, 1826, introducing an article by Guizot, "On Sovereignty" [a portion of the longer study which Rosanvallon's remarks prefaced]. Cf. Maurice Barbé, *Étude historique des idées sur la souveraineté en France de 1815 à 1848* (Paris, 1904).

6. Guizot, *Du gouvernement de la France depuis la Restauration et du ministère actuel* (Paris, 1820), 201.

7. Cf. Benjamin Constant, *Principes de politique*, chap 1, in which he vigorously criticizes those whose "wrath has been directed against the holders of the power rather than against the power itself. Instead of destroying it, they have simply thought of replacing it." Constant, *Œuvres*, ed. Alfred Roulin (Paris, 1957, 1978), 1070. [In English in Constant, *Political Writings*, ed. Biancamaria Fontana (Cambridge, 1988), 176.] Cf. Marcel Gauchet's commentary in his edition: Gauchet, "Benjamin Constant, l'illusion lucide du libéralisme," in Constant, *De la liberté des modernes*, ed. Gauchet (Paris, 1980) [since reprinted as the introduction in Constant, *Écrits politiques*, ed. Gauchet (Paris, 1997)].

8. Cf. Constant: "Sovereignty has only a limited and relative existence. At the point where independence and individual existence begin, the jurisdiction of sovereignty ends. If society oversteps this line, it is as guilty as the despot who has, as his only title, his exterminating sword." Ibid., 1071. [In English, Constant, *Political Writings*, 177.]

9. Guizot, "Philosophie politique: De la souveraineté," chap. 18, in Guizot, *Histoire de la civilisation en Europe*, 363, 367.

10. Guizot, *Histoire des origines du gouvernement représentatif*, 2 vols. (Paris, 1851), 1: 120. [In English, Guizot, *The History of the Origins of Representative Government*, ed. Aurelian Craiutu, trans. Andrew R. Scoble (Indianapolis: Liberty Fund, 2001), 294–95.]

11. Guizot, "Élections" (1826), in *Discours académiques* (Paris, 1861), 406.

12. Guizot, *Histoire des origines du gouvernement représentatif*, 1: 98 [in English, 55].

13. Ibid., 2: 150 [in English, 295–96].

6. Political Rationalism and Democracy in France

1. Guilliame-François Le Trosne, *De l'ordre social* (Paris, 1777), 23.

2. "Maximes du Docteur Quesnay," in Eugène Daire, ed., *Physiocrates: Quesnay, Dupont de Nemours, Mercier de la Rivière, l'abbé Baudeau, le Trosne*, 2 vols. (Paris, 1946), 1:390.

3. Cf. Louis-Philippe May, *Le Mercier de la Rivière (1719–1801): Aux origines de la science économique* (Paris, 1975), and J. M. Cotteret,

"Essai critique sur les idées de Le Mercier de la Rivière" (law thesis, Paris, 1960).

4. P. P. F. J. H. Le Mercier de la Rivière, *De l'ordre naturel et essentiel des sociétés politiques* (1767; reprint, Paris, 1910), 82–85.

5. Ibid., 345.

6. On this point, see Akiteru Kubota, "Quesnay disciple de Malebranche," in *François Quesnay et la physiocratie*, 2 vols. (Paris, 1958), 1: 169–96. See also May, "Descartes et les physiocrates," *Revue de synthèse* 68 (July–December 1950): 7–38.

7. Le Mercier de la Rivière, *De l'ordre naturel,* 346. One must also bear in mind that Quesnay was the editor of the article on "Evidence" in the *Encyclopédie,* where he gave the following definition of the term: "The term evidence signifies a certitude so clear and manifest by itself that the mind cannot deny it."

8. "There are two kinds of certainty: Faith and evidence. Faith teaches us truths that cannot be known by the light of reason. Evidence is confined to natural knowledge." Ibid.

9. Letter to Damilaville, June 5, 1767, in Denis Diderot, *Correspondance,* ed. Georges Roth and Jean Varloot, 16 vols (Paris, 1955–70), 7: 75. "I do not believe," Diderot added, "that it ever occurred to anyone but him, that evidence was the sole force counterpoised against tyranny." Ibid., 76. Diderot did not hesitate to describe Mercier as a "new Solon."

10. On this point, see Philippe Raynaud's sound observations in "The Declaration of the Rights of Man," in Colin Lucas, ed., *The French Revolution and the Creation of Modern Political Culture,* vol. 2, *The Political Culture of the French Revolution* (Oxford, 1988), chap. 8.

11. Marquis de Voyer-Argenson, *Considérations sur le gouvernement ancien et présent de la France* (Amsterdam, 1764), 142.

12. Cf. Denis Richet, "Autour des origines idéologiques lointaines de la Révolution française: élites et despotisme," *Annales E.S.C.* 24, 1 (January–February 1969): 1–23.

13. Baron d'Holbach, *Politique naturelle au discours sur les vrais principes du gouvernement* (Paris, 1773), as cited in ibid., 20. On this point, see also the analyses of Edgar Faure, who correctly describes the "precarious contract" between a "mass without mandated representatives" (the French) and "a representation without mandate" (the parlements) in Faure, *La disgrâce de Turgot* (Paris, 1961).

14. Cf. Bernard Manin's entry in François Furet and Mona Ozouf, eds., *Dictionnaire critique de la Révolution française* (Paris, 1988), s.v. "Montesquieu" [in English as *Critical Dictionary of the French Revolution,* trans. Arthur Goldhammer (Cambridge, Mass., 1989)].

See also Marcel Dorigny, ed., *Montesquieu dans la Révolution française,* 4 vols. (Paris, 1990), an excellent collection of texts on Montesquieu from between 1785 and 1814.

15. Cf. Gabriel Bonno, *La Constitution britannique devant l'opinion française, de Montesquieu à Bonaparte* (Paris, 1932).

16. A.-R.-L. Turgot, *Œuvres de Turgot et documents le concernant,* ed. Gustave Schelle, 5 vols. (Paris, 1913–23), 5: 536. [An edition of Turgot's letter appeared in Richard Price, *Observations on the Importance of the American Revolution, and the Means of Making It a Benefit to the World: To which Is Added, a Letter from M. Turgot . . .* (London, 1785).]

17. See [John Stevens, often attributed to Richard Livingston, *Observations on the Government, including some Animadversions on Mr. Adams's Defence of the Constitutions of the Government of the United States of America; and of Mr. De Lolme's Constitution of England, by a Farmer of the United States* (1787),] a work translated by the Marquis de Condorcet and Dupont de Nemours as *Examen du gouvernement d'Angleterre, comparé aux Constitutions des États-Unis, où l'on réfute quelques assertions d'un ouvrage de M. Adams, intitulé "Apologie des Constitutions des États-Unis d'Amérique," et dans celui de M. de Lolme intitulé "De la Constitution de l'Angleterre," par un cultivateur de New Jersey* (London, 1789). In this pamphlet, Stevens/Livingston responded to Adams's work, itself a response to Turgot's letter challenging Price. Taken together, this set of texts constitutes the heart of the debate between French political rationalism and the Anglo-American vision. To be entirely thorough, Gabriel de Mably's *Observations sur le gouvernement et la loi des Etats-Unis d'Amérique* (Paris, 1791) should be added. A correspondence with Adams in which Mably denounces the mercantilist slide of the American republic, it is one of the first classic expressions of the critique of America.

18. *Examen du gouvernment d'Angleterre,* 76.

19. Ibid.

20. Ibid., 177.

21. Quesnay, *Œuvres économiques et philosophiques,* ed. Auguste Oncken (Frankfurt, 1888), 646; and Baudeau's interesting chapter "De l'Instruction économique et de son efficacité," in his *Première introduction à la philosophie économique* (1771, reprint, Paris, 1910), 136–63.

22. Le Mercier de la Rivière, *De l'instruction publique ou considérations morales sur la nécessité, la nature, et la source de cette instruction* (Stockholm, 1775), 13.

23. Ibid., 34.

24. Dominique-Joseph Garat, *Mémoires historiques sur la XVIIIe siècle et sur M. Suard*, 2nd ed., 2 vols. (Paris, 1929), 2: 94. Note that in the mid-twentieth century Action Française thought it worthwhile to "rehabilitate" the physiocratic critique of the theory of representative government. See the important work by Pierre Teyssendier de la Serve, *Mably et les physiocrates* (Paris, 1911).
25. Louis Sebastien Mercier, *L'an 2440, rêve s'il en fût jamais*, 3 vols. (Paris, 1787), 2: 61. [This work exists in English as *Memoirs of the Year Two Thousand Five Hundred* (1772; reprint, New York, 1974)].
26. Abbé Sieyès, *Essai sur les privilèges* in Sieyès, *Qu'est-ce que le Tiers État?* (Paris, 1982), 9. [In English in Sieyès, *Political Writings*, trans. Michael Sonenscher (Indianapolis: Hackett, 2003), 76].
27. Ibid., 89 [in English in Sieyès, *Political Writings*, 157].
28. On this point, see the classic work of Patrice Higonnet, *Class, Ideology, and the Rights of Nobles during the French Revolution* (Oxford, 1981), as well as Antoine de Baecque, "Le discours antinoble (1787–1792): Aux origines du slogan: le people contre le gros," *Revue d'histoire moderne et contemporaine* 36, 1 (January–March 1989): 3–28.
29. Jean-Baptiste Salaville, *L'organisation d'un État monarchique, ou Considérations sur les vices de la monarchie française* (1789), cited in Jean-Jacques Tatin-Gourier, *Le Contrat social en question: Échos et interprétations du "Contrat social" de 1762 à la Révolution* (Lille, 1989), 117.
30. *La Sentinelle du peuple* 1, cited in Tatin-Gourier, 119.
31. The formulation is from Sièyes, *Qu'est-ce que le Tiers État*, 88 [in the English, 155].
32. Ibid., 90 [in the English, 158].
33. It was the system of vote by assembly that would prevail during the French Revolution. See Patrice Gueniffey, *Le Nombre et la Raison: La Révolution française et les élections* (Paris, 1993).
34. On this point, I take the liberty of referring readers to my book *Le Moment Guizot* (Paris, 1985).

7. The Market, Liberalism, and Anti-liberalism

1. Milton and Rose Friedman, *Free to Choose: A Personal Statement* (New York, 1979), 13–14, as cited in J.-P. Dupuy, "La main invisible et l'indétermination de la totalisation sociale," *Cahiers du CREA* 1 (October 1982): 35
2. Hence all of the debates of the mid-1970s on the relationship of liberalism and *autogestion*; on this point, see my book *L'âge de l'autogestion* (Paris, 1976).

3. Pierre Manent, "Situations du libéralisme," in Manent, ed., *Les libéraux*, 2 vols. (Paris, 1986, 2001), 26.

4. Only the complex relation of Marxism to moral liberalism might qualify as an exception to this generalization (communist regimes, however, were rigorously anti-liberal, in general, in the moral domain).

5. This divergence follows from the fact that political divides are organized in the United States around questions of rights and morality, while in France the question of the market is more central. But it is striking to see how in France an issue like that of Pacte civile de solidarité (PACS), as in the debates of fall 1998, can make the critique of liberalism more complex and help shift its definition. [The PACS is a French civil union provision, available since 1999, accorded to both heterosexual and homosexual couples, and some attacks on it were analogous to opposition to similar proposals in the United States, especially after the Massachussetts Supreme Judicial Court decision of November 2003 allowing same-sex marriage.]

6. I disagree, therefore, with Mark Lilla, who in an otherwise quite stimulating article understands one of the contradictions I have just mentioned as a simple incoherence, calling upon economic liberals of the 1980s to accept the cultural revolution of the 1960s, and, conversely, demanding that defenders of the cultural turn of the 1960s adopt the Reagan revolution. The liberal revolution must, in his eyes, be unified. See Lilla, "A Tale of Two Reactions," *New York Review of Books*, May 14, 1998.

8. Marx and Civil Society

1. The latter is cited only once in *Capital* and then only to take relish at the fear that Smith inspired in the conventional public of his time, who accused him of spreading atheism.

2. [There are chapters on Hegel and Godwin, along with Thomas Paine, in the work of which this chapter forms a part. The general argument is that as theorists of civil society Godwin and Paine translated into political theory the dream of interest harmonization outside the state that Smith pioneered in economics.]

3. [Karl Marx's writings are cited parenthetically as "MER" from Robert C. Tucker, ed., *The Marx-Engels Reader*, 2nd ed. (New York, 1978) where possible, and as "CW" from *Marx-Engels Collected Works*, 49 vols. (New York, 1975–) where not.]

4. This analysis is better directed against a "clientelistic state" than against the modern state. On this question see the analysis of the

withering away of the state in my book, written together with
Patrick Viveret, *Pour une nouvelle culture politique* (Paris, 1977),
48–50.

5. It is well known that it was only thanks to this premise, already il-
luminated by Smith, that Marx could develop his whole theory of
surplus value.

6. [This section is undoubtedly a response to the Marxism, popular
in the 1970s when this work first appeared, of Louis Althusser,
who claimed to have discovered an "epistemological rupture" in
Marx's career between his early, humanist works and his later, scientific period.]

7. [See CW, 1:224–63.]

8. On this point, I have been strongly stimulated by Louis Dumont,
From Mandeville to Marx (Chicago, 1977), and Michel Henry,
Marx, vol. 2, *Une philosophie de l'économie* (Paris, 1976). [The
distinction between holism and individualism, for its part, is from
Dumont's earlier work *Homo Hierarchicus: The Caste System and
Its Implications* (1966), rev. ed., trans. Mark Sainsbury et al.
(Chicago, 1980).]

9. [The term refers to heroic acts of individual initiative, along the
lines of Daniel Defoe's *Robinson Crusoe*; Rosanvallon is referring
to the following passage in Marx's *Grundrisse*: "The individual
and isolated hunter and fisherman, with whom Smith and Ricardo
begin, belongs among the unimaginative conceits of eighteenth-
century Robinsonades (which were) the anticipation of bourgeois
society" (MER, 222).]

10. Agnes Heller, *The Theory of Need in Marx* (London, 1976).

11. See chap. 3 [of *Le capitalisme utopique*, on new forms of commerce and the reconceptualization of civil society as a market].

12. The fact that Marx uniformly uses the latter term makes translation difficult, since he sometimes means the "true" society and
sometimes bourgeois society. [In English, too, it is possible to
translate *bürgerliche Gesellschaft* both as civil society and bourgeois society; the English translations used here have sometimes
been altered to correspond to Rosanvallon's translation.]

13. In the "substantive" sense of the term, to use Karl Polanyi's distinction, i.e., the economy as the science of the production and distribution of wealth under conditions of scarcity. [Polanyi, *The
Great Transformation* (1944; Boston, 1957).]

14. [Rosanvallon is referring to his earlier treatment, in *Le capitalisme utopique*, chap. 5, of the political implication widely drawn in
the eighteenth century in light of the prospect of economic ordering, that the functions of the state would turn out to be simple.

The phrase "political arithmetic" is from Jean-François Melon and William Petty. Rosanvallon, *Le capitalisme utopique*, 128–36 at 131.]

15. List, secretary of an association of industrialists with the goal of abolishing internal tariffs, was one of the linchpins responsible for the erection of the *Zollverein* (German customs union).

16. Thinking of Marx as "Machiavelli's other," as Claude Lefort does, is therefore doubly justified and illuminating.

17. One should recall that for Helvétius the term "interest" is not economic. It is simply the general name for the power of human passions.

18. Adam Smith, *The Theory of Moral Sentiments* (Indianapolis, 1976), 56.

9. From the Past to the Future of Democracy

1. For Hegel, as Éric Weil notes, "politics is nothing other than the science of the will." Weil, *Hegel et l'État* (Paris, 1970), 32.

2. On this point, see the illuminating pages in Pierre Manent, *La Cité de l'homme* (Paris, 1994), chap. 4, "The Triumph of the Will." [This book is in English as The *City of Man*, trans. Marc A. LePain (Princeton, 1998).] See also Nicholas Tenzer's entry in Philippe Raynaud and Stéphane Rials, eds., *Dictionnaire de la philosophie politique* (Paris, 1996, 2003), s.v. "Volonté."

3. Cf. Rials, "La droite ou l'horreur de la volonté," *Le Débat* 33 (January 1985): 34–48.

4. On this question of the discovery of the unconscious and the dissolution of the image of man as master and possessor of himself, see the interesting work of Marcel Gauchet, *L'inconscient cérébral* (Paris, 1992). On the problems of and tensions in individual sovereignty in the contemporary world, see Alain Ehrenberg, *La Fatigue d'être soi: Dépression et société* (Paris, 1998).

5. It suffices to refer to Carl Schmitt, on the right, and Lenin, on the left, to recall specific examples. The fact that these authors have recently been celebrated in common would repay closer scrutiny.

6. Consider, for instance, the emblematic celebration of the figure of the worker by Ernst Jünger. "Technology," he writes, "is the means by which the worker mobilizes the world." Jünger, *Der Arbeiter*, as cited in Jean-François Kervégan, *Hegel, Carl Schmitt: Le politique entre spéculation et passivité* (Paris, 1992).

7. As an illustration, one can refer to all of the debates on the policies of employment of the decade 1980–1990. In the face of those

who deplored the absence of a "real political will" to lead the campaign against joblessness, the reminder to reflect on the meaning of the implicit and silent "preference" for unemployment that resulted from the actual behavior of economic and social actors was well taken.

8. One must also remember that civil society, in Albert Hirschman's terms, expresses itself frequently through "exit," as notably in the case of market allocation, while political society lives more in the universe of "voice." [Hirschman, *Exit, Voice, and Loyalty* (Cambridge, Mass., 1970).]

9. And see, recently, Benjamin Barber, *Strong Democracy: Participatory Politics for a New Age* (Berkeley, 1984).

10. See also on these points the work of Jean-Marie Donegani and Marc Sadoun, *La Ve République, naissance et mort* (Paris, 1998), as well as the discussion of their position, notably by Guy Carcassonne and Bernard Manin, in the forum dedicated to this work in *Le Débat* 106 (September–October 1999): 160–77.

11. Carl Schmitt, *Political Theology: Four Chapters on the Concept of Sovereignty*, trans. George Schwab (Cambridge, Mass., 1985), 36.

12. On this point, see the work of Patrick Riley, who has convincingly shown that Rousseau borrowed the idea of the general will from Malebranche, who restricted it to the description of God's intervention in history. Riley, *The General Will Before Rousseau: The Transformation of the Divine into the Civic* (Princeton, 1986).

13. This is the central theme of such works as *The Road to Serfdom* (Chicago, 1944) or *The Constitution of Liberty* (Chicago, 1960). This perspective presupposes, of course, the highly contestable belief that there is no difference between economic and political liberalism. On this point, see my article, "The Market, Liberalism, and Illiberalism," chap. 7 in this volume.

14. It bears emphasizing that numerous radical movements have dismissed the question of the political, in their own way, by situating themselves almost exclusively on the terrain of rights. See the illuminating remarks of Philippe Raynaud, "Les Nouvelles radicalités: De l'extrême gauche en philosophie," *Le Débat* 105 (May–August, 1999): 90–117.

15. If the problem were simply the need to find a strong will, the means would probably not be democratic: Carl Schmitt's lessons on this point are edifying enough to be worthy of reflection.

16. Multiple propositions on the latter score were put forward, for example, at the World Trade Organization in Seattle in December 1999.

17. [These enterprises are covered in an earlier section of the book from which this excerpt is taken, *La Démocratie inachevée,* 59–74.]

18. Adrien Lezay, *Qu'est-ce que la constitution de 1793?* (Paris, Year III), 10. The division of the individual powers is seen in this framework as the condition of a strengthened social power.

19. I prefer the term "social citizenship" to that of "civil citizenship" as used by Catherine Colliot-Thélène, "L'ignorance du peuple," in Gérard Duprat, ed., *L'ignorance du peuple: Essais sur la démocratie* (Paris, 1998), 17–40. Her term could lead one to think that it is not just as political as the form of citizenship involved in voting. But the basic idea is the same.

20. Cf. Dominique Turpin, "Les juges sont-ils représentatifs? Réponse: oui," *Commentaire* 58 (Summer 1992): 381–90. See also on this point the famous debates of the revolutionary period.

21. And one should add the possibility, which I cannot elaborate here, of representativity of a *moral kind* that certain actors possess thanks to their function of alerting the public to emergencies, of unnoticed examples of distress, etc.

22. Édouard Laboulaye, *Questions constitutionelles* (Paris, 1872), 373.

23. There is actually much to say on this subject, both on the actual decline in the use of the referendum and on the difficulties involved in its prospective extension as a solution to social problems. Lacking the space to develop this question here, I can refer for the time being and for a first approach to the following works: Gérard Conac and Didier Mauss, eds., *Le Référendum, quel avenir?* (Paris, 1990); Francis Hamon, "Actualité du référendum," *Le Débat* 96 (September–October 1997): 51–66; Laurence Morel, "Le référendum, état de recherches," *Revue française de science politique* 42, 5 (October 1992): 835–64; Rials, "L'avenir du référendum en France," *La Revue administrative* 32, 6 (November–December 1979): 647–58; Serge Sur, "Un bilan du référendum en France," *Revue du droit public* 101, 3 (May–June 1985): 591–602.

24. It should be noted that this always fiercely debated vision has been adopted without any difficulty, thanks to the new principle of right of appeal of verdicts from the Cours d'assises adopted in February 2000, in the notion of "democratic judgment" (by a popular jury judging "in the name of the French people"). One could also interpret the fact of cohabitation [of political parties in government] that results from contrasting expressions of the popular will according to this model of "prudential democracy."

25. Claude Émeri justly writes in this regard that "fear of judicial encroachment on governance also reflects a sacralization of the

election as the source of power." Émeri, "Gouvernement des juges ou veto des sages?," *Revue du droit public* (March–April 1990): 336.

26. One should, however, note Sismondi's contrasting reflections. From the fact that complete sovereignty can only be the attribute of a unanimous subject (with power and liberty perfectly reconciled in such a case), he saw the institutions of regulation and control as prudential systems linking the democratic principle of majority rule with the philosophical principles of unanimity. See J.C.L. Sismondi, *Recherches sur les constitutions des peuples libres* (reprint Geneva, 1965), chap. 2: "De la souveraineté du peuple." But most of the great liberal authors preferred to deconstruct the notion of sovereignty as such.

27. Ernest Renan, *La monarchie constitutionelle en France* (Paris, 1870), 127.

28. [Earlier parts of the work deal with direct democracy in French history.] The *indirect* character of representative government has its own positive function. It effectuates, at a minimum, a distinction between decision and deliberation, and therefore enlarges participation in deliberation (while direct democracy, enlarging participation in decision, reduces it in deliberation). On this point, see the profound remarks of George Kateb, *The Inner Ocean: Individualism and Democratic Culture* (Ithaca, 1992), chap. 1, "The Moral Distinctiveness of Representative Democracy," and of Robert Dahl, *Democracy and Its Critics* (New Haven, 1989), chap. 16, "Democracy, Polyarchy, and Participation."

29. This argument thus goes further than Iris Marion Young's concept of "deferred democracy," which consists only in the distinction of the various phases of proposition, deliberation, and decision, in a perspective actually quite close to Condorcet's. See Young, "Deferring Group Representation," in Will Kymlicka and Ian Shapiro, eds., *Ethnicity and Group Rights (Nomos 39)* (New York, 1996), chap. 12.

30. The bibliography on the question is considerable. The most important works are Christopher Aterton, *Teledemocracy: Can Technology Protect Democracy?* (Beverly Hills, 1987); Jeffrey Abramson, Christopher Aterton, and Garry Orren, *The Electronic Commonwealth: The Impact of Media Technologies on Democratic Politics* (New York, 1988); and Christal Darryl Slaton, *Televote: Expanding Citizen Participation in the Quantum Age* (New York, 1992).

31. Cf. "The Future of Democracy," *The Economist*, June 17, 1995 and "Happy 21st Century Voters: A Survey of Democracy," *The Economist*, December 21, 1996.

32. Cf. Francis Balle, "Mythes et réalités de la démocratie électro-
    nique," *Connaissance politique* 2 (May 1983): 106–12 and Michael
    Schudson, "The Limits of Teledemocracy," *The American Prospect*
    3, 11 (September 1992): 41–45.

33. A Charles Maurras could thus speak of "the immense and undi-
    vided moral and material heritage," noting: "The necessity of
    holding and saving the fruits of labor of our dead serves hence to
    define what we are allowed to order and interdict, to dispense with
    and to keep." He spoke on this ground of "the unjustified will of
    the sovereign voter." Maurras, "Discours préliminaire de l'enquête
    sur la monarchie," in *Dictionnaire politique et critique* (Paris,
    1932), 5: 405.

34. I prefer this expression to that of "continuous democracy," coined
    by Léo Hamon and taken up by Dominique Rousseau, though the
    two notions share commonalities. See Hamon, "Du référendum à
    la démocratie continue," *Revue française de science politique* 34,
    4–5 (August–October 1984): 1084–1101, and Rousseau, *La démoc-
    ratie continue* (Brussels, 1995).

35. On this decisive question, see the suggestive contribution of
    Stephen Holmes, "Precommitment and the Paradox of Democ-
    racy," in Jon Elster and Rune Slagstad, eds., *Constitutionalism and
    Democracy* (Cambridge, 1988), chap. 7.

36. Victor Hugo, *Choses vues*, ed. Hubert Juin, vol. 3, *1849–1869*
    (Paris, 1972), 352.

37. Cf. Fareed Zakaria, "The Rise of Illiberal Democracy," *Foreign Af-
    fairs* 76, 6 (November/December 1997): 22–43.

38. The atomistic perspective was never so much justified anthropo-
    logically as it was historically necessary, as a condition of the de-
    parture from a corporatist society. See on this question the salu-
    tary reflections of Alain Renaut, *L'ère de l'individu: Contribution
    à une histoire de la subjectivité* (Paris, 1989). [This book is in En-
    glish as *The Era of the Individual: Contributions to a History of
    Subjectivity*, trans. M. B. DeBevoise and Franklin Philip (Prince-
    ton, 1997)].

39. On this point, I permit myself to refer to two essays of mine on
    the subject: "Formation et désintégration de la galaxie 'auto'," in
    Paul Dumouchel and Jean-Pierre Dupuy, *L'auto-organisation, de
    la physique au politique* (Paris, 1983) and "Mais où est donc
    passée l'autogestion?," *Passé présent* 4 (1984): 186–95.

40. The change of tone since the approaches of the 1970s is evident in
    the report submitted by Jean Auroux, Minister of Labor at the
    time, in *Les Droits des travailleurs* (Paris, 1981). "Citizens of the
    political realm, workers have to be citizens too in their work," the

introduction reads (3). Economic democracy is therefore seen as a mandatory task. The report goes so far as to note that "there is no question of challenging the unity of direction and decisionmaking in private enterprise," and the word *autogestion* is not mentioned a single time.

41. Cf. the illuminating remarks of Jean Combacau, "Pas une puissance, une liberté: la souveraineté internationale de l'État," *Pouvoirs* 67 (1993): 47–58.

42. In a way, this change involves the rediscovery of the classic Aristotelian perspective. See Cornelius Castoriadis, *Les carrefours du labyrinthe* (Paris, 1978), and Manent, *La Cité de l'homme*. [Castoriadis's text is available in English as *Crossroads in the Labyrinth*, trans. Martin Ryle and Kate Soper (Cambridge, Mass., 1984)].

43. I use this expression [in English in the French text] by way of analogy with the notions of "market failures" or "state failures."

44. This essential distinction between regulation and institution would have to be invoked in any analysis of European integration or the notion of federalism, too.

45. On this point, cf. Daniel Cohen, *Richesse du monde et pauvreté des nations* (Paris, 1997); Allen Buchanan, *Secession: The Morality of Political Divorce* (Boulder, 1991); and Alberto Alesina and Enrico Spolaore, "On the Number and Size of Nations," *Quarterly Journal of Economics* 112, 4 (November 2000): 1027–56. [Cohen's book is available as *The Wealth of the World and the Poverty of Nations*, trans. Jacqueline Lindenfeld (Cambridge, Mass., 1998).]

10. The Transformation of Democracy and the Future of Europe

1. [The reference is to Benjamin Constant's nineteenth-century distinction, in a famous 1819 lecture, between the "ancient" freedom of belonging to a collective and living in public and the "modern" freedom of the individual pleasures of private life. In light of the danger that the hypertrophy of the latter under modern conditions could atomize and privatize the population to the point that self-government collapsed, Constant recommended a new synthesis of the two. See Constant, "The Liberty of the Ancients Compared with that of the Moderns," in *Political Writings*, ed. Biancamaria Fontana (Cambridge, 1988).]

2. [Albert Hirschman, *Exit, Voice, and Loyalty* (Cambridge, Mass., 1970).]

3. [The dualistic constitutional theory of Bruce Ackerman is the most prominent American description (and endorsement) of such a two-

track politics. See Ackerman, *We the People*, 2 vols. so far (Cambridge, Mass., 1991–).]

4. [Compare, for example, Jürgen Habermas, *The Postnational Constellation: Political Essays*, trans. Max Pensky (Cambridge, Mass., 2001) or David Held, *Democracy and the Global Order: From the Modern State to Cosmopolitan Governance* (Stanford, 1995).]

5. [Larry Siedentop, *Democracy in Europe* (New York, 2002), chap. 2.]

Postscript

1. Cited by Larry Kramer, *The People Themselves: Popular Constitutionalism and Judicial Review* (New York: Oxford University Press, 2004), p. 319.

Bibliography of
Pierre Rosanvallon's Principal Writings

Note: Aside from the first two items, this bibliography only records those items published since the beginning of Pierre Rosanvallon's scholarly career; it also omits newspaper and other similar public interventions since. The place of publication is Paris unless otherwise noted.

L'Âge de l'autogestion, ou la politique au poste de commandement (1976).
(with Patrick Viveret) *Pour une nouvelle culture politique* (1977).
"Marx et la société civile." *Commentaire* 4 (Winter 1978–1979): 468–77.
"Für eine Wirtschaft der Autonomie." In Joseph Hüber, ed., *Anders arbeiten—anders wirtschaften* (Frankfurt, 1979).
Le capitalisme utopique: Histoire de l'idéologie économique (1979). Reprinted as *Le libéralisme économique: Histoire de l'idée de marché* (1989) and *Le capitalisme utopique: Histoire de l'idée de marché* (1999).
(ed. and intro.) Moisei Ostrogorski. *La démocratie et les partis politiques* (1979).
"Oublier les modes." *Le Débat* 4 (September 1980): 80–83.
La Crise de l'État-providence (1981, 1992).
"L'idée de nationalisation dans la culture politique française." *Le Débat* 17 (Décembre 1981): 3–14.
"Boisguilbert et la genèse de l'État moderne." *Esprit* (January 1982): 32–52.
Misère de l'économie (1983).
"Formation et désintégration de la galaxie 'auto'." In Paul Dumouchel and Jean-Pierre Dupuy, eds., *L'Auto-organisation: De la physique au politique* (1983).

"Louis Dumont: le sacre de l'individu." *Libération,* 17 November 1983. Reprinted in *Cahiers Vilfredo Pareto* 22 (1984): 147–54.

"Mais où est donc passée l'autogestion?" *Passé Présent* 4 (1984): 186–95.

Le Moment Guizot (1985).

(ed. and intro.) François Guizot. *Histoire de la civilisation en Europe* (1985).

"Les conditions de l'émancipation de l'homme chez Marx." In Bernard Chavance, ed., *Marx en perspectives* (1985).

"Augustin Thierry." In André Burguière, *Dictionnaire des sciences historiques* (1986).

"Guizot, *Des moyens de gouvernement et d'opposition* (1821)." In François Châtelet et al., eds., *Dictionnaire des œuvres politiques* (1986).

"Pour une histoire conceptuelle du politique." *Revue de synthèse* 107, 1–2 (January–June 1986): 93–105.

"L'Autre et l'étranger dans l'État: Les figures de la citoyenneté pendant la Révolution française." *Cahiers de l'École des sciences philosophiques et religieuses* 1 (1987): 7–51.

"L'utilitarisme français et les ambiguïtés de la culture politique prérévolutionnaire." In Keith Michael Baker, ed., *The French Revolution and the Creation of Modern Political Culture,* vol. 1, *The Political Culture of the Old Regime* (Oxford, 1987).

"Histoire et politique en France à l'époque de la Restauration." Brochure published by the University of Bologna on its 900th anniversary (1987).

La Question syndicale: Histoire et avenir d'une forme sociale (1988, 1990, 1999).

(with François Furet and Jacques Julliard) *La République du centre ou la fin de l'exception française* (1988, 1989).

"Autogestion (Dictionnaire d'une époque)." *Le Débat* 50 (May–August 1988): 191–92.

"Guizot" and "Physiocrates." In François Furet et Mona Ozouf, eds., *Dictionnaire critique de la Révolution française* (1988). In English as "Guizot" and "Physiocrats." In Furet and Ozouf, eds., *Critical Dictionary of the French Revolution,* trans. Arthur Goldhammer (Cambridge, Mass., 1989).

"The Decline of Social Visibility." In John Keane, ed., *Civil Society and the State* (New York, 1988).

"Beyond the Welfare State." *Politics and Society* 16, 4 (December 1988): 533–44.

(with Jacques Le Goff et al.), *L'État et les pouvoirs* (1989).

"Les doctrinaires et la question du gouvernement représentatif." In François Furet et Mona Ozouf, eds., *The French Revolution and*

the Creation of Modern Political Culture, vol. 3, The Transformation of Political Culture 1789–1848 (Oxford, 1989).

"L'opinion et la représentation dans la démocratie moderne." Pouvoirs
locaux (Octobre 1989).

"Corporations et corps intermédiaires." Le Débat 57 (November–
December 1989): 190–94. Reprinted in Maurice Agulhon et al.,
1789: La commémoration (1999).

"The Development of Keynesianism in France." In Peter Hall, ed., The
Political Power of Economic Ideas (Princeton, 1989).

"Penser le libéralisme." In Rosanvallon, Le libéralisme économique:
Histoire de l'idée de marché (1989).

L'État en France de 1789 à nos jours (1990, 1993, 1998).

"De la Béatitude occidentale." Le Débat 60 (May–August 1990):
61–65.

"Le Déclin des passions." Autrement (May 1991): 94–105.

"Guizot et la Révolution française" and "Guizot et la question du suffrage universel au XIXᵉ siècle." In Martina Valensise, ed., François
Guizot et la culture politique de son temps (1991).

"La Représentation difficile, réflexion sur le cas français." In Daniel Pé-
caut and Bernardo Sorj, eds., Métamorphoses de la représentation
politique au Brésil et en Europe (1991).

Le Sacre du citoyen: Histoire du suffrage universel en France (1992,
2001).

"L'État au tournant." Revue française d'administration publique
(January–March 1992): 119–26.

"L'opacité française." Le Débat 70 (May–August 1992): 198–201.

(Preface) Jean-Marc Ferry and Paul Thibaud. Discussion sur l'Europe
(1992).

(Preface) Paolo Pombeni. Introduction à l'histoire des partis politiques
(1992).

"Histoire du mot démocratie à l'époque moderne." La Pensée Politique 1 (1993): 11–29. In English as "History of the Word 'Democracy' in France." Journal of Democracy 6 (October 1995):
140–54.

"La République du suffrage universel." In François Furet et Mona
Ozouf, eds., Le Siècle de l'avènement républicain (1993). In En-
glish as "The Republic of Universal Suffrage." Trans. Laura
Mason. In Biancamaria Fontana, ed., The Invention of Modern
Republic (Cambridge: Cambridge University Press, 1994).

"L'histoire du vote des femmes: Réflexion sur la spécificité française."
In Georges Duby et Michelle Perrot, eds., Femmes et Histoire: colloque, la Sorbonne, 13–14 novembre 1992 (1993).

La Monarchie impossible: Histoire des Chartes de 1814 et 1830
(1994).

"Rationalisme politique et démocratie en France (XVIIIe–XIXe siècles)." *Zinbun, Annals of the Institute of Research in Humanities* 29 (1994): 17–32. In English as "Political Rationalism and Democracy in France in the 18th and 19th Centuries." *Philosophy and Social Criticism* 28, no. 6 (November 2002): 687–702.

La nouvelle question sociale: Repenser l'État-providence (1995, 1998). In English as *The New Social Question: Rethinking the Welfare State*, trans. Barbara Harshav (Princeton, 2000).

"Esquisse d'une histoire de la déception démocratique." In Alexandru Dutu et Norbert Dodille, eds., *Culture et politique* (1995).

"Faire l'histoire du politique." *Esprit* (February 1995): 25–42.

"L'État-providence et les régulations sociales." *Cahiers français* 271 (May–June 1995): 35–44.

"Citoyenneté politique et citoyenneté sociale au XIXe siècle." *Le Mouvement social* (July–August 1995): 9–30.

"Témoignage." *Revue française d'histoire des idées politiques* 2 (1995): 361–76.

(with Jean-Paul Fitoussi) *Le nouvel âge des inégalités* (1996, 1998).

"Factions et partis." In Philippe Raynaud et Stéphane Rials, eds., *Dictionnaire de philosophie politique* (1996).

"État-providence et citoyenneté sociale." *Jean Monnet Chair Papers* (European University Institute) 37 (1996): 1–27.

"Le politique." In Jacques Revel and Nathan Wachtel, eds., *Une école pour les sciences sociales: De la VIe section à l'École des Hautes Études en Sciences Sociales* (1996).

(Preface) Christine Guionnet, *L'apprentissage de la politique moderne: Les élections municipales sous la monarchie de Juillet* (1997).

Le peuple introuvable: Histoire de la représentation démocratique en France (1998, 2002).

(with Daniel Cohen et al.) *France: Les révolutions invisibles* (1998).

"Culture politique libérale et réformisme." *Esprit* 251 (March 1999): 161–70. Reprinted as "Le marché et les trois utopies libérales." In Rosanvallon, *Le capitalisme utopique: Histoire de l'idée de marché* (1999).

"Les deux crises de la représentation politique." *Les Cahiers de la Villa Gillet* 8 (April 1999): 73–84.

(Preface) Dario Roldan, *Charles de Rémusat: Certitudes et impasses du libéralisme doctrinaire* (1999).

La démocratie inachevée: Histoire de la souveraineté du peuple en France (2000, 2003).

"L'Esprit de 1995." *Le Débat* 111 (September–October 2000): 118–20.

"Sur quelques chemins de traverse de la pensée du politique en France." *Raisons politiques* 1 (February–April 2001): 49–62.

Chaire d'histoire moderne et contemporaine du politique: Leçon inaugurale faite jeudi le 22 mars 2002 (2002). Reprinted as *Pour une histoire conceptuelle du politique* (2003).

"Fondements et problèmes de l'illibéralisme français." In Thierry de Montbrial, ed., *La France du nouveau siècle* (2002).

"Le déficit démocratique européen." *Esprit* 288 (October 2002): 87–100.

"Towards a Philosophical History of the Political." In Dario Castiglione and Iain Hampshire-Monk, eds., *The History of Political Thought in National Context* (Cambridge, 2002).

"L'Amérique, l'Europe, et nous." Preface to Thierry Chopin, *La République une et divisible: Les fondements de la fédération américaine* (2002).

"Les vertus d'un comparatisme dérangeant." In Marcel Détienne, ed., *Qui veut prendre la parole?* (2003).

(Preface) Alain Chatriot, *La Démocratie sociale à la française: L'expérience du Conseil national économique, 1920–1940* (2003).

Le Modèle politique français: La société civile contre le jacobinisme de 1789 à nos jours (2004), in English as *The French Political Model: Civil Society Against Jacobinism from 1789 to the Present*, trans. Arthur Goldhammer (Cambridge, Mass., 2006).

"Le miroir du Musée Social." Preface to Janet Horne, *Le Musée Social, aux origines de l'État-providence* (2004).

"Le laboratoire argentin." Preface to Geneviève Verdo, *L'Indépendance argentine entre cités et nation* (2005).

Index